SAN FRANCISCO BAY

SHORELINE

GUIDE

A STATE COASTAL CONSERVANCY BOOK

Rasa Gustaitis, project editor; Maureen Gaffney, 2nd edition revisions;
Jerry Emory, writing, research, text and maps; additional revisions and
updates by Laura Thompson and Lee Chien Huo.

UNIVERSITY OF CALIFORNIA PRESS
Berkeley | Los Angeles | London

SAN FRANCISCO BAY
SHORELINE
GUIDE

University of California Press, one of the most distinguished university presses
in the United States, enriches lives around the world by advancing scholarship in
the humanities, social sciences, and natural sciences. Its activities are supported
by the UC Press Foundation and by philanthropic contributions from individuals
and institutions. For more information, visit www.ucpress.edu.

University of California Press
Berkeley and Los Angeles, California

University of California Press, Ltd.
London, England

Although we have made every effort to be accurate, changes are inevitable in
some routes and places described. We would appreciate your comments to help
us keep this guide up-to-date. Contact us at www.baytrail.org

Library of Congress Cataloging-in-Publication Data

San Francisco Bay shoreline guide / Rasa Gustaitis, project editor . . . [et al.]. —
2nd ed.
     p.   cm.
   Includes bibliographical references and index.
   ISBN 978-0-520-27436-5 (pbk. : alk. paper)
   1. San Francisco Bay Area (Calif.)—Guidebooks. 2. Bay Trail (Calif.)—Guidebooks. 3. Shorelines—California—San Francisco—Guidebooks. I. Gustaitis,
Rasa. II. California State Coastal Conservancy.
   F868.S156S187 2012
   917.94'610444—dc23   2012010015

Manufactured in China

21   20   19   18   17   16   15   14   13   12
10   9   8   7   6   5   4   3   2   1

The paper used in this publication meets the minimum requirements of
ANSI/NISO Z39.48-1992 (R 1997) (Permanence of Paper).

Cover images: top, sailing lake, Mountain View (photo by Ron Horii);
middle, tyke on bike at Cesar Chavez Park, Berkeley (photo by Bay Trail Project);
bottom, San Fransisco waterfront (photo by Don Weden). Right, Caspian tern
(photo by Chet Clark).

Contents

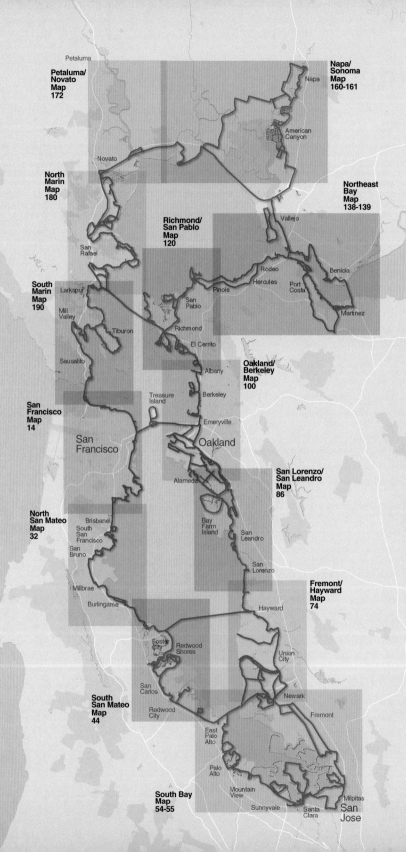

Petaluma

Petaluma/
Novato
Map
172

Napa/
Sonoma
Map
160-161

Napa

American
Canyon

North
Marin
Map
180

Novato

Northeast
Bay
Map
138-139

Richmond/
San Pablo
Map
120

Vallejo

San
Rafael

Rodeo

Benicia

Hercules

Port
Costa

South
Marin
Map
190

Larkspur

Pinole

Mill
Valley

San
Pablo

Martinez

Tiburon

Richmond

Sausalito

El Cerrito

Albany

Oakland/
Berkeley
Map
100

San
Francisco
Map
14

Treasure
Island

Berkeley

San
Francisco

Emeryville

Oakland

Alameda

San Lorenzo/
San Leandro
Map
86

North
San Mateo
Map
32

Brisbane

Bay
Farm
Island

South
San
Francisco

San
Leandro

San
Bruno

San
Lorenzo

Fremont/
Hayward
Map
74

Millbrae

Burlingame

Hayward

Foster
City

Redwood
Shores

Union
City

San
Carlos

Newark

South
San Mateo
Map
44

Redwood
City

Fremont

East
Palo
Alto

Palo
Alto

South Bay
Map
54-55

Mountain
View

Milpitas

Sunnyvale

Santa
Clara

San
Jose

ABOUT THIS GUIDE AND SAN FRANCISCO BAY

Welcome to the second edition of the *San Francisco Bay Shoreline Guide*. Since the book's first publication in 1995, over 150 miles have been added to the San Francisco Bay Trail. These new segments take you to the hustle of an industrial working waterfront at the Port of Oakland, bring you solitude near a restored wetland in Sonoma, or allow you a car-free commute on a Marin multi-use path. This book is your passport to San Francisco Bay and its shoreline. It was created to guide you to hundreds of beautiful places owned in common by the inhabitants of this region, the citizens of California, and the United States. Few people who live nearby—and even fewer of those who visit—know that more than 40 percent of the bay's shoreline is open to the public.

For most people, San Francisco Bay means a view. Its gleaming waters are typically seen from a distance, glimpsed as a sideways blur from a fast-moving car, briefly studied from a house or restaurant window, or momentarily admired from a hilltop. The bay is out there, before our eyes, but at the same time it's invisible. Few come to know it intimately. Few realize what this great 450-square-mile estuary offers.

You can walk or bicycle for miles on trails that meander along the bay shoreline, tasting winds fresh off the water that are spiced by the rich blend of salt and marsh grasses. You can watch thousands of migrating shorebirds, get lost in a flock of feeding terns, listen to the smacking and popping of a recently exposed mud flat, watch the water shimmer and change. You can get to know landscapes close to

"In the midst of all this activity, the bay remains a refuge of open space, in the heart of the fifth largest urban area in the United States, as essential for recreation and wildlife as it is for industry."

SAVING THE BAY

home that are unique, elemental, and accessible.

It's easy to get to the water's edge, once you know the way. Over 325 miles of shoreline are already open to the public by means of the Bay Trail, which will eventually extend for 500 miles and enable you to circle the entire bay without once getting into a car. Many more Bay Trail segments are in the works, linking local and regional trails that have been built for walking, hiking, bicycling, and other forms of non-motorized travel. The Bay Trail leads to places where you can fish off piers, windsurf, swim, drop a kayak or canoe into the water, picnic, or get into shape on a parcourse; and to shoreline towns and historic sites, museums, nature study centers, wildlife refuges, and scenic overlooks. It connects with other trails that will take you inland along creeks and streams, up into the hills, and to the edge of the Pacific Ocean, where you can pick up the Coastal Trail and move north or south. You will also be able to follow trail links to the 550-mile Bay Area Ridge Trail, which is forming a second, wider ring around the bay. As of 2012, over 330 miles of the Ridge Trail have been completed.

In this book we show you the route that will take you around the bay along the completed and proposed segments of the Bay Trail. There are still a few important gaps. To cross the Richmond–San

Rafael Bridge, and move between a few other trail segments, you still need to go by bus or car. Along stretches of the proposed route, where the trail is still only a set of dashed gray lines on a plan, you will have to use streets. Anyone ambitious enough to want to do the entire trail—and several have—will probably be undeterred. Others will find ample opportunities along the Bay Trail as it currently exists.

Anywhere you begin to explore the bay shoreline, using this book or just your eyes and ears, you are likely to be surprised and pleased at what you find. Stand a moment at the foot of Market Street in San Francisco and consider: at this spot, in 1850, you would have been half a mile out from shore. Below you now are the remains of hundreds of sailing ships, abandoned here during the Gold Rush.

Take the ferry to Oakland. Notice the waterfowl bobbing on the water or flying across the bay. As you glide under the Bay Bridge, look up. In the girders, under the fast-moving lanes of daily traffic, a pair of peregrine falcons nest in the spring. These raptors have returned from near extinction and adapted to urban life. They hunt for food above the city streets, diving on urban pigeons in midair. Under the Bay and Richmond bridges, double-crested cormorants raise their young. They used to nest on rocks and in

Handcycle on Tiburon Bay Trail

standing dead trees, but these are scarce around the bay, so they have adapted to our architecture.

We share the bay with an amazing diversity of wildlife. The great shallows of the South Bay are protected within the Don Edwards San Francisco Bay National Wildlife Refuge and are critical habitat for hundreds of thousands of migrating shorebirds that stop to feed and rest on their annual journey between the far north and Central America. Nearly 300 bird species visit or live here year-round. The tidal marshes, creeksides, and grassy uplands shelter many other creatures, including the endangered salt marsh harvest mouse, clapper rails, burrowing owls, and the animals that eat them: foxes, skunks, and raccoons.

Human and natural history is layered along the shore. The Oyster Bay Regional Shoreline in San Leandro is just one of the shoreline parks built atop former landfills. Take a picnic to this park's highest knoll and you won't see or smell any hint of its past. Visit Wildcat Marsh in Richmond, where birds and other creatures find sanctuary in a wetland that has been restored near a large oil refinery.

Along the Carquinez Strait, the sleepy town of Port Costa was once a major shipping port. Just offshore, 200-pound sturgeons still lumber along the murky bay bottom. Across the northern reaches of San Pablo Bay, thousands of canvasback ducks and scaups rest in winter months, more than anywhere else along the Pacific Coast. Go north to the Sonoma Baylands, where dredge material from the Port of Oakland helped to re-create a tidal marsh bustling with birds and wetland plant species. The many wonders of San Francisco Bay are obscured by buildings, freeways, roadside sound walls, billboards, utility poles—and by the intense speed and daily routines of most of us who move along its shores. You have to slow down, turn off, stop, and look. If you get to know a stretch of shoreline nearest to your home or job, you will probably want to explore further. You will find yourself experiencing the moods and seasons of the bay, and this will help you to comprehend its past and potential future, and your own place within this landscape.

HOW RIVERS, MOUNTAINS, AND THE OCEAN MADE THE BAY

The smooth shorelines and gentle hillsides around San Francisco Bay mask one of North America's most complicated and dynamic geologic puzzles. The Bay Area—and most of the Pacific Coast—rides above a break in the Earth's

White pelican flock

crust that divides the Pacific Plate from the North American Plate. Some 200 million years ago, the Pacific Plate began to scrape under the western edge of the North American Plate, moving in an easterly direction in a process called subduction. About 29 million years ago, the Pacific Plate changed course toward the northwest and began to slide past the North American Plate. It is sliding today at a rate of perhaps 2 inches a year. The two plates meet along the San Andreas Fault System, which extends through western California from the Mexican border to Point Arena in Mendocino County. In the Bay Area, the Crystal Springs Reservoir is on the San Andreas Fault, as are the Bolinas Lagoon, Tomales Bay, and Bodega Bay. If you stand on the western side of the fault, you are moving toward Alaska, leaving most of California behind you.

Enormous pressures at the boundaries of the two plates have fractured the surface of the Earth

into countless faults, all part of the San Andreas Fault System. Rocks have been compressed, twisted, and folded. Some 10,000 years ago, when vast glaciers capped the Sierra, the sea level was lower, and the coastal shoreline lay some 20 miles or more to the west, near the Farallon Islands. There was no San Francisco Bay as we now know it. What is now the North Bay was a valley cut by a steep canyon that had been carved by the rivers known today as the Sacramento and San Joaquin. Their powerful combined flow created a 350-foot-deep canyon at what is now known as the Golden Gate.

During this time, gentle rivers meandered through the landscape that became the South Bay and formed the valley now named Santa Clara. The tip of the peninsula on which San Francisco stands was once mostly a dunescape, covered with river-brought sand. Cypresses, firs, pines, and junipers dominated the uplands. Mammoths, horses, giant buf-

falo, and sloths roamed where deer, raccoons, and shorebirds live today. As the climate warmed and dried and glaciers melted, the ocean began to rise, drowning canyons and channels to create the bay. Rivers brought sediments that accumulated along the shoreline, forming broad and fertile marshes and uplands.

THE PEOPLE OF THE BAY AND THE YEARS OF DESTRUCTION

It was on the shores of this fertile embayment that the ancestors of today's Native Americans arrived from the north several thousand years ago. They lived here with grizzly bear, deer, elk, antelope, wolves, and countless birds. Offshore there were whales, dolphins, and otters, as well as enormous sturgeons and many other fish species. Salmon came upriver to spawn. Oysters and mussels covered the bay floor close to shore. Tens of thousands of people lived in villages around the bay before

the Europeans arrived, and they spoke some 12 different languages. Soon after Gaspar de Portol "discovered" the bay in 1769, a ship captain described this as a place of "inexpressible fertility."

Before long, however, newcomers felled the oaks and cut down the redwoods on nearby hills. They used oak bark to tan hides, oak wood for fuel, and redwood to build the bay cities. The people of this land were killed or enslaved, or they succumbed to diseases to which they had no resistance. The grizzlies were hunted to extinction, and the vast flocks of waterfowl and shorebirds were decimated. Marshes were filled and diked to make room for agriculture, industry, and cities. By the 1950s, 85 percent of the bay's wetlands had been destroyed—either buried under fill, diked off and dried out, or converted to salt ponds. Freshwater inflow that was essential to maintaining a healthy bay had been diverted to other uses.

Much of what you will find in these pages seemed destined for destruction four decades ago. The photograph on p. 6 and its caption, published in the *San Francisco News* on June 18, 1958, now symbolize what seemed to be an inexorable trend.

THE BAY IS REDISCOVERED

In 1962, three women changed the course of the bay's history. Catherine Kerr, Sylvia McLaughlin, and Esther Gulick, all wives of University of California officials, could see the bay, with garbage dumps burning on the shore, from their homes in the Berkeley hills. Shortly after an Army Corps of Engineers' map appeared depicting the Bay as little more than a river if current filling were to continue, they called a meeting of about a dozen people whom they expected to be as concerned as they were. The Save San Francisco Bay Association was born. In 1965, through the efforts of Senator J. Eugene McAteer and Assemblyman Nicholas Petris, a bill was passed establishing the San Francisco Bay Conservation and Development Commission (BCDC) and directing it to prepare a plan for the long-term use and protection of the bay and for regulating development in and around it.

The commission was given permanent regulatory authority in 1969 and directed to carry out the essential features of the San Francisco Bay Plan. Anyone seeking to alter the shoreline now must seek a permit from BCDC (see p. 8). If BCDC grants a permit, it requires that public access be provided whenever possible. What remains of the bay's marshland today is protected, and some of what was lost is being restored, as you will find in this book. The historic turnaround of the 1960s opened the way to new visions. Communities began to look at their shoreline as a potential public amenity. Many asked for help from the State Coastal Conservancy, which was able to craft solutions to the land use conflicts that inevitably arose and to undertake projects that realized the new visions.

The Save San Francisco Bay Association evolved into a citizens' stewardship organization known as Save the Bay. It is now working to assure that the bay is protected as the legislature has directed, and in 1999, Save the Bay also launched a restoration campaign to restore 100,000 acres of wetlands around the bay. About 44,000 acres of healthy tidal marsh exist today, and 32,000 acres of restorable shoreline areas have been acquired and are being planned for restoration, including the South Bay Salt Pond Project, Bair Island, Hamilton Field, and other areas (see p. 170, "Wetland Restoration Around the Bay"). Public agencies and a growing number of local and regional citizens' organizations are trying to restore degraded streams, to protect wetlands, wildlife habitat,

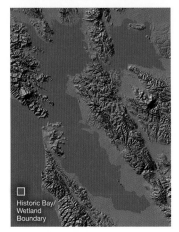

San Francisco Bay, 1849

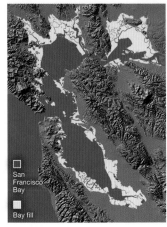

San Francisco Bay, 1969

and open spaces, and to find ways to help people live in closer harmony with the bay.

HOW THE BAY TRAIL BEGAN

A new dream was launched one autumn day in 1986, when Senator Bill Lockyer of Hayward was having lunch with a local editor in a waterfront restaurant. The end-of-session legislative frenzy was over, and Senator Lockyer was in a reflective mood. "Let me try this idea out on you," he said to his companion. "What if we tried to develop a pedestrian and bicycle path around the bay, with access to the shoreline?" His luncheon

Bay Filling

This house did go, along with the habitat for mud flat creatures, fish, and shorebirds, as the bay shoreline was extended with fill to build the access road to Candlestick Park, the Bayshore Freeway, and other construction and development projects.

Every bayshore community seemed to have plans to expand bayward. Hills near the shore were gouged and carved to provide bayfill. In 1961, the U.S. Army Corps of Engineers published a map that showed what the bay was likely to look like in the year 2020: not much more than a river winding between new developments on fill. About 4 square miles of bay were being filled each year. Gigantic plans were under way for replacing bird and fish habitat with roads and houses. San Mateo County planned a freeway, parallel to the Bayshore Freeway, on some 23 new square miles of land to be created by gouging into San Bruno Mountain. The Port of Oakland's plans included 2 square miles of fill from the Bay Bridge toll plaza almost to Treasure Island. San Rafael had filling plans for some 75 percent of its tidelands.

"Two weeks ago William Manuel could stand out on the end of his 'pier' and watch the water lapping underneath his house-on-stilts at Candlestick Cove. Today his beach and the waterfront he leases have become part of the road to the new Giants Stadium. And soon his house must go."

San Francisco Bay, projected fill by 2020

for the preparation of a Bay Trail Plan by July 1, 1989.

The Bay Trail Plan (see p. 9) shows a network of trails that meander and loop along the shore, connecting all nine surrounding counties and linking with the Ridge Trail. By mid-2012, over 60 percent of both trail systems were completed and in use. This book is evidence of what can be accomplished, and what more can be done.

Today you will not likely find any "pristine" shoreline. Almost every inch has been altered by riprap, fill, levees, dikes, and various structures. And yet, more than two centuries after European settlement began, the San Francisco Bay shoreline retains an allure, a history, a diversity of people and places—and a wildness—unequaled by other settled shores. Under those power poles, surrounding those levees, hidden among the riprap, on top of the former land-

partner applauded the idea and urged the senator to pursue it. The outcome was SB 100. Coauthored by all Bay Area legislators, the bill passed. It defined parameters of the planning process, designated the Association of Bay Area Governments (ABAG) as the lead agency, and provided $300,000

fills, and across thousands of acres of wildlife refuges and parks, amazing life abounds. It would be impossible to restore the bay's former character. But we can rejoice in getting to know what has been preserved. Consider this book as a claim check for priceless heirlooms that we almost lost but have now recovered. We offer it in hopes it will help us enjoy them and pass them on to future generations of humans and fellow creatures.

San Francisco Bay Area Water Trail

Another way to explore the bay is to paddle the open water and sloughs along the shoreline. Over 100 ramps, marinas, piers, and beaches allow for small-boat access to the bay. Kayaks, canoes, rowboats, dragon boats, and sailboards serve as vessels of adventure for boaters of all skill levels. The vision of the San Francisco Bay Area Water Trail is to formalize this network of launch and landing sites, or "trailheads," for human-powered small boats. Water Trail users will enjoy the historic, scenic, and environmental richness of San Francisco Bay through single- and multiple-day trips on the bay. The Water Trail will promote safe, responsible boating and increase appreciation and protection of the bay's environmental resources.

Boating in Alviso Slough

Association of Bay Area Governments (ABAG)

The Association of Bay Area Governments (ABAG) is the regional planning agency and council of governments for the nine counties and 101 cities and towns of the San Francisco Bay region, thus making it the perfect home for the San Francisco Bay Trail Project. ABAG is committed to leading the region through advocacy, collaboration, and excellence in planning, research, housing, and member services to advance the quality of life in the San Francisco Bay Area. ABAG's planning and service programs work to address regional economic, social, and environmental challenges.

State Coastal Conservancy

The State Coastal Conservancy plays a major role in the development of the Bay Trail, the Bay Area Ridge Trail, and the San Francisco Bay Area Water Trail and has been the principal funding source for all three trail systems. Established in 1976, the Conservancy is a state agency that uses entrepreneurial techniques to protect and improve coastal and Bay Area natural resources and to provide public access to the shore. The Conservancy works in partnership with local communities, other public agencies, nonprofit organizations, and private landowners. The Bay Trail Project and the Conservancy hope this guide will help you discover new and delightful shoreline jewels. Look at your maps, check the text, and be adventuresome.

Metropolitan Transportation Commission (MTC)

The Metropolitan Transportation Commission (MTC) is the transportation planning, coordinating, and financing agency for the nine-county San Francisco Bay Area. MTC is responsible for the Regional Transportation Plan, a comprehensive blueprint for the development of mass transit, highway, airport, seaport, railroad, bicycle, and pedestrian facilities. With its focus on providing alternative transportation options between neighborhoods, transit, work centers, and schools, the Bay Trail serves as the backbone of MTC's Regional Bicycle Plan. MTC provides funding for the administration of the San Francisco Bay Trail Project.

The San Francisco Bay Conservation and Development Commission (BCDC)

In 1965, the California legislature passed the McAteer-Petris Act, in response to urgent pleas from the Save San Francisco Bay Association, formed three years earlier by citizens who were alarmed at the rapid filling of the bay. Four square miles of bay were being lost every year. As mentioned earlier, the legislation established the San Francisco BCDC as a temporary state agency charged with preparing a plan for the long-term use and protection of the bay and with authority to regulate development in and around the bay.

The San Francisco Bay Plan, completed in 1969, includes policies on 22 issues critical to the wise use of the bay, including fill, ports, waterfront parks, public access, appearance and design, marsh protection, water-related recreation, and climate change. The state legislature adopted this plan in 1969 and gave BCDC permanent planning and regulatory authority over the bay. In 1977, the legislature expanded that authority to include the protection of the 85,000-acre Suisun Marsh, the largest remaining wetland in California.

BCDC also has the authority to use the federal Coastal Zone Management Act to carry out the provisions of the Bay Plan, the Suisun Marsh Protection Plan, and state laws. It has issued hundreds of permits for development and other projects, many with conditions requiring public access, wetland protection, and open space. Thanks in large part to the work of the commission, the State Coastal Conservancy, and local jurisdictions, as well as to the actions of vigilant citizens, public access to the bay continues to be expanded and thousands of acres of wetlands are now being restored.

Presidio Bay Trail before

Presidio Bay Trail after

San Thomas Aquino Trail before

San Thomas Aquino Trail after

"The Bay Trail is our gateway to the bay and all its complexity, beauty, and inspiration."

SAM SCHUCHAT, Executive Officer of the State Coastal Conservancy

THE BAY TRAIL IS A WORK IN PROGRESS

The San Francisco Bay Trail is a hiking and bicycling trail system around San Francisco Bay. It links communities, parks, piers, wildlife reserves, boat launches, and other areas open to the public along the shore. It connects with trails that lead inland; with the Ridge Trail, which is forming a second, wider ring around the bay; and with the Water Trail, forming a network of launch and landing sites for human-powered watercraft. Over 325 miles (65 percent) of the planned 500-mile Bay Trail is complete and work is under way on numerous other segments.

The route of the trail, as included in the Bay Trail Plan and as continuously modified by the Bay Trail Steering Committee, is shown in the maps of this guide. You will note that the trail is not simply "a string of pearls connecting gems," as had earlier been envisioned; it has tendrils and loops, inviting you to explore parks and open spaces and move inland, sometimes along creeks, toward the Pacific Ocean, or into inland park areas.

The Bay Trail Project, a non-profit organization housed within ABAG, coordinates work on the Bay Trail. It encourages and promotes diverse efforts to further this trail system's completion. Bay Trail policies and guidelines are intended to complement the adopted regulations of local management agencies. Trail segments are built by local, regional, state, and federal agencies, in partnership with citizens' organizations, business, and industry.

Numerous towns, cities, counties, and park districts are ultimately responsible for construction and maintenance of the Bay Trail. However, citizen groups, bicycle coalitions, and individual efforts have been key to its success. When Bay Area citizens attend public hearings, contact their elected representatives, vote for park bonds, take part in public events, or organize trail clean-up days, the Bay Trail moves ever forward. To find out how you can be involved, contact us through our website, www.baytrail.org.

HOW TO USE THIS BOOK

A few hints will help you to use this guide to full advantage and to enrich your experience of the shoreline as you follow the Bay Trail. You'll find that some of the sights listed are not directly on the Bay Trail, but are in close proximity. You may also find gems that *are* directly on the Bay Trail that we have not listed here—to be sure, there are too many special places around the Bay to possibly capture them all!

SEE WHERE YOU ARE

First, spend some time getting acquainted. Glance at the table of contents and the index. Look at the map of the entire bay. Locate yourself in relation to what's around you.

THE ORDER OF THINGS

Read the introduction. Note that chapters are organized counterclockwise around the bay, moving south from San Francisco and ending at the Golden Gate Bridge after Marin County. You, of course, will choose your own route of travel.

KEYS TO THE BAY TRAIL

While the overall map at the beginning of the guide provides the conceptual overview of what the nine-county regional trail system will look like upon completion, your actual guide maps for what's available today are located at the beginning of each section. Note that the solid red lines denote trails, not roads, and thus no vehicles are allowed. Many Bay Trail segments are paths through parks, preserves, and other open spaces that exclude motor vehicles, although other segments do run alongside streets, roads, or even highways, and some are merely sidewalks or road shoulders.

REACHING THE BAY TRAIL

The maps indicate roads, streets, and highway turnoffs, as well as major public transit routes that lead to places described in the guide. For detailed directions, see the text, especially the "Getting Around" sections. There are phone numbers in the chapters, as well as in "References/Resources," for finding out whatever else you need to know about the places described. Before heading out, look up the Shoreline Web Guide on the Bay Trail website. Here you will find information regarding parking, birdwatching, the best sites for photography, and much more.

THE BAY TRAIL IS A NETWORK

The Bay Trail is not a single trail but an interconnected trail system that links parks, open spaces, points of interest, and communities on or near the bay shoreline. It will take you all the way around the bay, but also will encourage you to loop inland toward nearby open spaces and preserves, to wander up streams, and, if you choose, to move on to the Ridge Trail, which, with the Bay Trail, forms the second of two concentric rings around the bay. In mid-2012, over 325 miles (about 65 percent) of the planned 500-mile Bay Trail had been completed.

RED, HOLLOW RED, ORANGE, HOLLOW ORANGE, DASHED GRAY, PURPLE, AND DASHED PURPLE . . . OH MY!

The solid red line on the maps indicates completed trail segments separated from roads. Hollow red indicates on-street bicycle lanes and sidewalks (in rural areas, sidewalks may be absent). Solid orange is unimproved, off-street Bay Trail—likely a narrow path and/or rough surface. Hollow orange indicates an unimproved, on-street alignment—essentially a "we're working on it" designation. Dashed gray is a future route that is not currently developed. Solid purple is an existing connector trail, and dashed purple is a planned connector trail.

——— **Bay Trail** (off street)
Shared-use paved or gravel paths

——— **Bay Trail** (on street)
Bike lanes and sidewalks

——— **Unimproved Bay Trail** (off street)
Narrow path and/or rough surface

——— **Unimproved Bay Trail** (on street)
No bike lanes and/or no sidewalks

- - - - - **Planned Bay Trail**
Future route – not developed

——— **Other Trails**
Paved or gravel paths connecting to Bay Trail

- - - - - **Planned Other Trail**
Future connection to Bay Trail – not developed

⚓ Boating/Marina

Ⓟ Parking

🐟 Fishing Pier

Some of these trail segments are yet to be adopted by the local jurisdictions they pass through; some lack amenities that will be added later; some are busy streets or roadways rather than trails. They are a way to go, however, if you want to move from one completed stretch of Bay Trail to another, staying as close as possible to the bay's edge. Inaccessible segments of the Bay Trail route appear in dashed gray. Some of these are private property. Please do not trespass. With this guide you should be able to circle the entire San Francisco Bay shoreline.

Consulting the Bay Trail map

Bay Trail signs in action

ICONS

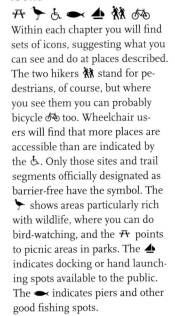

Within each chapter you will find sets of icons, suggesting what you can see and do at places described. The two hikers 🏃🏃 stand for pedestrians, of course, but where you see them you can probably bicycle 🚲 too. Wheelchair users will find that more places are accessible than are indicated by the ♿. Only those sites and trail segments officially designated as barrier-free have the symbol. The 🐦 shows areas particularly rich with wildlife, where you can do bird-watching, and the ⛶ points to picnic areas in parks. The ⛵ indicates docking or hand launching spots available to the public. The 🎣 indicates piers and other good fishing spots.

MORE COLORS

Green areas on the maps are public parks and wildlife reserves. Blue means water. Yellow indicates airports, military reservations, and some other public institutions. The maps also include major transit lines, such as BART and Caltrain, shown as labeled colored lines.

CHANGES TO COME

In the text we have indicated places where new trail segments are pending, or where road and highway projects are expected to change access routes to trails and other shoreline features within the next few years.

TAKE YOUR GUIDE TO THE SHORE

Once you have a sense of the book, take it along on a bayshore excursion. Get to know the stretch of shoreline closest to your home or workplace, and then explore outward. You may be surprised to discover that you are only a few minutes from a shoreline park, wildlife area, or historic site. Any point on the entire bay is within two hours' traveling distance from wherever you start on the shore. So why not venture from Petaluma to the San Francisco Bay Wildlife Refuge in the South Bay, or from Redwood City to the upper reaches of the Napa River? Bring your bike, your hiking shoes, and don't forget this book.

SIGNAGE

Not all access points for the Bay Trail and other shoreline features are clearly indicated by signs. While the Bay Trail Project staff undertook an effort in 2008 to sign all existing segments of trail, some small parks and trails still lack signage and you may get the impression these areas are not accessible. Don't get discouraged. Use the guide to find your way, and you'll likely be rewarded!

DOGS

Do respect regulations regarding dogs. Some parts of the Bay Trail are off-limits to dogs, and most sections require dogs to be on leash. Your pet needs exercise, but not in places where wild creatures will be disturbed. You may not see the harm in your dog's joyfully setting a flock of shorebirds to flight. But yours is probably one of many dogs to do this every day, disturbing these birds' feeding and resting patterns. Be especially careful near wildlife reserves and watch for signs indicating where dogs are required to be on leash or not allowed at all. The "References/Resources" section highlights major dog parks along the Bay Trail.

WATCHING WILDLIFE

Always consider yourself a guest in wildlife habitat, and do your best not to disturb the residents. If you see a wild creature, freeze. Listen.

Dogs on the Bay Trail

Fishers in Vallejo

Relax and look without moving. Don't try to sneak up on birds and animals, which will cause them to flee. They need their energy for feeding and other activities. Stay on trails to reduce human smells, sounds, and movements in the wild. Immerse yourself in na-ture. Leave no traces. Visit www .cawatchablewildlife.org for fur-ther tips on wildlife viewing.

FISHING

There are more than 40 public piers on the bay, and you don't need a license to fish from them or from along the shoreline. Those age 16 and over must be licensed for all other fishing in California. For more information, inquire at your local sports store, or contact the Department of Fish and Game at 831-649-2870 or www.dfg.ca.gov.

BIKES, TRANSIT, AND BRIDGES

More people in the Bay Area are choosing to include biking as part of their commute. BART, Caltrain, Valley Transportation Agency (VTA) light rail, and other transit agencies offer many options for cyclists to use bikes on transit, such as bike racks, free secure parking, and bike lockers. Be aware of rules and restricted schedules for bikes. Bikes are allowed on most BART trains, except those highlighted on the schedule during peak commute times, or at any time on crowded cars. Folding bikes are allowed at any time. On all transit lines, bicyclists must yield to other passengers and give up priority seating to seniors and persons with disabilities. Details can be found at www.511.org.

Bikes and Bridges

Four of the region's eight toll bridges have a bicycle and pedestrian pathway on the span, and a fifth, the eastern span of the Bay Bridge, is scheduled to open in 2013. Bridges with bike and pedestrian access, along with relevant info, are listed here:

511.org
Overall transit, bridge, bicycle, and pedestrian information, including bicycle route mapping

Golden Gate Bridge
24-hour bicycle access; restricted pedestrian access. www.goldengate.org

Dumbarton Bridge
24-hour pathway access. bata.mtc.ca.gov

Carquinez Bridge
24-hour pathway access. bata.mtc.ca.gov

Benicia-Martinez Bridge
24-hour pathway access. bata.mtc.ca.gov

San Francisco–Oakland Bay Bridge
No bicycle/pedestrian access. See www.dot.ca.gov for Caltrans bike shuttle info.

San Mateo Bridge
No bicycle/pedestrian access. See www.actransit.org for public bus info.

Richmond–San Rafael Bridge
No bicycle/pedestrian access. See www.goldengatetransit .org for schedules and maps of Golden Gate Transit Routes 40/42.

San Francisco

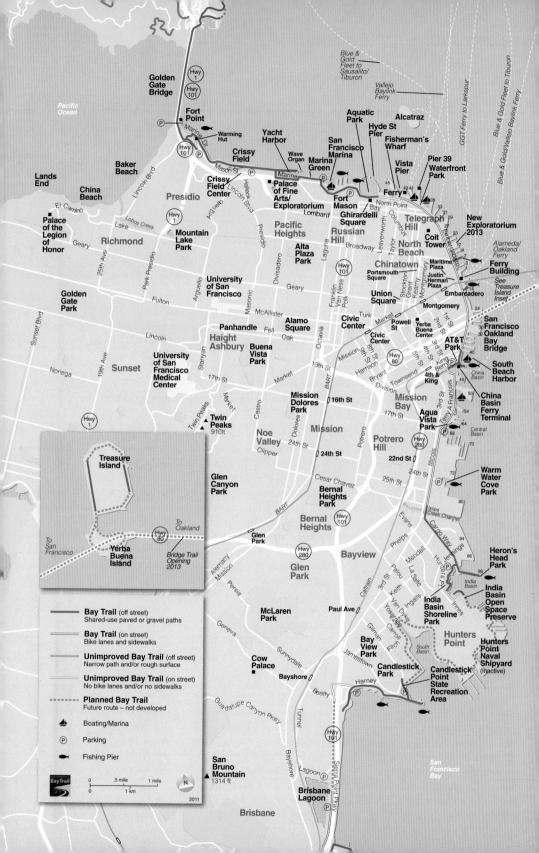

FORT POINT TO AQUATIC PARK

From Fort Point to Candlestick Point Recreation Area, almost the entire San Francisco bay-front is manmade. Beneath the streets, parks, and buildings lie abandoned ships, excavated hilltops, rotting piers, compacted 19th-century trash, and massive amounts of rubble dumped into the bay after the 1906 earth-quake and fire. Above all that,

Bay Trail at Aquatic Park

you will find one of the world's most inviting urban waterfronts. The northern bayfront, as well as the city's ocean shoreline, lies almost entirely within the Golden Gate National Recreation Area (GGNRA), the first urban national park in the United States. Walking or biking along the Golden Gate Promenade, you will pass historic forts and ships, windy beaches, a restored Army airfield, the historic San Fran-cisco Presidio, the unique nature center at Crissy Field, and much more. Eventually you will arrive at Aquatic Park, where hardy souls swim in chilly waters alongside the historic ships.

FORT POINT

On a promontory directly under the Golden Gate Bridge, Fort Point stands as an intact example of pre–Civil War American military ar-chitecture. Built in 1861 to protect San Francisco's harbor and deter foreign ventures along the coast, the fort replaced the 1794 Span-ish Castillo de San Joaquin, which stood some 80 feet upslope. No-body ever fired on Fort Point, and it was soon obsolete: its brick and granite walls could not have with-stood the rifled cannons designed in the late 1860s. Today rangers lead thousands of visitors past cannons and up spiral staircases to soldiers' and officers' quarters and jail cells. Lantern tours are available on winter nights.

Outside the compound, turn north and you will be directly beneath the bridge. Look up at the powerful girders and listen to the cars speeding across. Note

how the bridge's arches frame the fort. Below you, sea stars and numerous algae cling to rocks, where they can be seen at low tide or between waves. Don't climb down to them; the surging water is extremely dangerous. Before you, 1 mile across the Golden Gate, the Marin Headlands loom to the northwest, Fort Baker is tucked into the shore just east of the bridge, the town of Tiburon is to the northeast, and Angel Island stands offshore.

COASTAL TRAILS AND BEACHES

The Fort Point Trail winds under the bridge toward the toll area en route to the Coastal, Ridge, and San Juan Bautista de Anza Trails and leads south to Baker Beach, China Beach, Lands End, the Cliff House, Ocean Beach, and Fort Funston. At low tide, you can explore the tide pools at China

Beach. But please, don't collect or trample tide pool creatures. Be careful along coastal cliffs: they are unstable and dangerous. Keep to main trails. In San Francisco, only China Beach and Aquatic Beach (at Aquatic Park) are safe for swimming, and only when a lifeguard is present. Baker Beach has a strong riptide. Please note: At the time of publication in 2012, this trail was closed due to con-struction. It is expected to reopen in 2013.

GOLDEN GATE PROMENADE

East of Fort Point, Marine Drive leads to the Golden Gate Prom-enade, a 3.5-mile bayshore trail. The pier near the start of this trail is open sunrise to sunset. Take the Promenade past Crissy Field toward Marina Green, to Fort Ma-son, and on to Aquatic Park and the San Francisco Maritime Na-tional Historical Park. Watch the

Historic Fort Point

"Among American cities, San Francisco is that rarity, an exciting town to walk."

MARGOT PATTERSON DOSS,
SAN FRANCISCO AT YOUR FEET

Golden Gate Promenade at Crissy Field

Elegant, historic Presidio housing

birds, boats, and people. Stroll in the wind while scanning the bay and the skylines of San Francisco, Marin, and the East Bay.

PRESIDIO

The San Francisco Presidio's history dates back to 1776, when Spanish Captain Juan Bautista de Anza, Padre Pedro Font, and six soldiers camped near the lagoon and freshwater springs in what was then duneland. In 1822, Mexican independence ended Spanish rule, and in 1848, when Mexico ceded California to the United States, the U.S. Army took over. In response to soldiers' complaints about the harshness of conditions, more than 60,000 trees were planted in the 1880s.

Now the Presidio is a forested 1,400-acre reserve, one-third larger than Golden Gate Park, rich in history and natural resources. Among more than 800 buildings is the finest collection of military architecture in the West. At the Presidio Army Museum, artifacts and displays offer insights into the past. Abundant plant life includes 240 native species. Springs still supply water to the Presidio. San Francisco's last free-flowing stream, Lobos Creek, rises in the Presidio near 16th Avenue and empties into the ocean at Baker Beach. In 1994, the Presidio passed into the hands of the National Park Service. In 2002, the Presidio Trust was formed as a management and funding model unique among national parks, with the aims of preserving the Presidio's natural, scenic, cultural, and recreational resources and of making the park financially self-sufficient. The Trust manages the interior 80 percent of Presidio lands, including most buildings and infrastructure. The National Park Service manages coastal areas.

Presidio's Endangered Plants

In 1816, a Russian expedition set anchor near the Presidio. Adelbert Chamisso and Johann Eschscholtz, the ship's naturalist and surgeon, collected 82 species of plants. Many of California's native plants were first described from their collections: yerba buena, California poppy, wax myrtle, and coffeeberry. Today, some 240 California native species have been recorded within the Presidio's 1,400 acres. San Francisco lessingia, an herb related to the sunflower, is a federally listed endangered species, and the flowering pink herb San Francisco campion is listed as rare. However, the National Park Service has a policy that all rare plants are treated as though they have full protection of the Endangered Species Act.

San Francisco campion

View of Crissy Field

Marina Green

CRISSY FIELD

The Golden Gate Promenade passes between Crissy Field and a sandy beach with dunes and restored dune grasses. The field was built on fill as a racetrack for the 1915 Panama-Pacific International Exposition. It was converted to an airstrip soon thereafter and named after Major Dana Crissy, who was killed after taking off from this runway during a 1919 transcontinental air race. In 1920, dozens of biplanes arrived here to begin active duty as the 91st Aero Squadron. By 1936, the airstrip was no longer needed: the new Hamilton Field in Marin County (see p. 181) accommodated larger and faster aircraft, so Crissy Field was decommissioned.

The beach here is a popular viewing spot for air shows, such as the aerial displays of the Navy's Blue Angels during Fleet Week (October), and for Fourth of July fireworks. It also attracts kite flyers and skilled and daring windsurfers (winds and tides are extremely powerful here). Two sets of trails for two types of user exist at Crissy Field. The trail nearest the bay is a natural-surface path, good for slow-moving cyclists, pedestrians, bird- and people-watchers, and families. The paved trail nearest the street is best for the speedy set—commute cyclists dashing to and from the Golden Gate Bridge or inline skaters in need of a smooth, fast surface. The sand dunes and the whole of Crissy Field underwent a massive restoration effort beginning in 1999 (see Crissy Field Restoration below).

PALACE OF FINE ARTS

Hundreds of acres of bayshore in today's Marina District were filled with thousands of tons of sand and bay sediment for the 1915 Panama-Pacific International Exposition. The only building that remains is the Palace of Fine Arts. It was designed by Bernard Maybeck for a short life span but was

Tides at the Golden Gate

Tides manifest the gravitational pull of the sun and moon on the earth. This pull creates a "long-period wave," or bulge, which moves across the oceans, creating tides twice a day. At the Golden Gate, tides can fluctuate from 2 to 7 feet as an estimated average of 2.3 million cubic feet of salt- and freshwater surge in and out of the bay. Through time, this action, together with powerful river flows, has helped scour the bay floor down to nearly 350 feet deep where the water enters the open ocean. In contrast, South Bay waters are barely 10 feet deep. Every few years, the topic of wave energy arises, and with it, the notion of turbines on the sea floor below the Golden Gate. Time will tell if this form of alternative energy takes hold below the bay surface.

Crissy Field Restoration

In 1999, the Golden Gate National Parks Conservancy joined efforts with local philanthropists and thousands of volunteers to turn an abandoned airfield covered in asphalt and debris into today's immensely popular public open space, as well as one of the most well-used segments of Bay Trail in the nine-county region. Since restoration, herons, egrets, ducks, gulls, and other marsh-loving wildlife abound.

The Crissy Field Center strives to actively engage people with their environment by focusing on the convergence of urban and natural settings through multicultural perspectives. Since its opening in May 2001, the Center has served over 800,000 people through school field trips, public workshops, afterschool programs, summer camps, and more. The Warming Hut snack bar is made from reclaimed and recycled materials from top to bottom.

rebuilt in 1968 and housed the Exploratorium, a hands-on science museum founded by physicist Frank Oppenheimer. In 2013, the Exploratorium will move to a new waterfront location at Piers 15 and 17 along the Embarcadero.

MARINA GREEN

Want to jog, fly a kite, fish, relax, feed the gulls, contemplate the bay, or check out the latest in exercise apparel? This is the place. On the western end of the Marina Green, a wind-sheltered patch of grass invites sunbathing. Just off the promenade, next to the Saint Francis Yacht Club and the bay, is a comfortable wood and stone rest area perfect for boat watching. East on the jetty, past a small stone lighthouse and the Golden Gate Yacht Club, is the Wave Organ, a stone sound sculpture. The San Francisco Marina is on the eastern edge of the Marina Green.

The number and variety of kites flown here on weekends is staggering. Watch the show, then try to figure out what the Magnetic Silencing Range Building does (read the placard next to the fenced-in white building on the bayside of the Green), or slide a quarter into one of the pay telescopes at the eastern end of the Green and scope Alcatraz, Angel Island, and boats on the bay. On the riprap shore here, people go poke-poling after

San Francisco Ferry Boats

Historic Pacific Golden Gate Ferries

Before the bay had bridges, it had ferries. The first ferry service on the bay began in 1850. By 1929, more than 50 ferries plied bay waters. During 1930, they transported 6 million vehicles and about 60 million passengers from San Francisco's waterfront to Vallejo, Sausalito, Tiburon, Richmond, Oakland, Berkeley, Alameda, and even Sacramento. The ferry *Eureka,* moored at the Hyde Street Pier, was capable of carrying 2,300 people and 120 autos.

Motor vehicles and the construction of the Bay Bridge (1936) and the Golden Gate Bridge (1937), combined with policies favoring auto traffic, doomed the major ferry routes. To pay off the bonds for the Bay Bridge, local officials enacted policies that put ferries at a disadvantage. Bay Bridge tolls were set below the price of a ferry ride; the interurban electric railways stopped service to ferry terminals in 1939 and crossed the Bay Bridge instead. Finally, the Bridge Bond Act of 1944 made it illegal to operate a ferry across the bay within 10 miles of the Bay Bridge. Eventually almost all ferry crossings were replaced by bridges.

In the 1970s, ferry service was revived to Sausalito, Tiburon, Larkspur, Vallejo, and eventually to Oakland and Alameda. Tourist-oriented ferries navigate to Angel and Alcatraz islands. The 1989 earthquake proved the lasting value of ferries: they carried thousands of East Bay commuters across the water while the Bay Bridge was repaired. Today, new ferry terminals and services are being planned around the bay under direction of WETA, the Water Emergency

Transportation Authority. WETA will assimilate and streamline existing ferry services (except Golden Gate Transit) in an effort to triple ridership and to serve as the regions' transportation backbone during an emergency.

Red & White Fleet at Pier 43½

Foghorns

San Francisco Bay's first fog signal was a manually operated cannon ignited every half hour to guide ships through the fog. It was installed in 1857 at Point Bonita, north of the Golden Gate, but was soon replaced by a mechanized bell. By 1860, bells were added at Fort Point and Alcatraz. In 1875, a large whistle was installed at Yerba Buena Island, and eventually a boisterous mix of sirens, trumpets, bells, and whistles serenaded residents around the bay. The airhorns' soothing sound was as much a part of San Francisco as its fog until the U.S. Coast Guard replaced most of them with electronic signals, though four are still in use on the Golden Gate Bridge. The lobby of the Argonaut Hotel in Fisherman's Wharf houses the San Francisco Maritime National Historical Park's Visitors Center and Interactive Museum, where you'll find a Farallon lens, shipwrecked boat, and permanent and changing exhibits, among other nautical delights.

The Wave Organ—will it play for you?

Historic Fort Mason

monkey-faced eels that hide in the rocks. They use bamboo poles, short leaders, and hooks baited with shrimp.

WAVE ORGAN

Odd. Beautiful. Eerie. These are some of the adjectives you might hear visitors mutter at this "wave-activated acoustic sculpture" conceived by Peter Richards of the Exploratorium and built in 1986 by stone mason/artist George Gonzales on the jetty beyond the Saint Francis and Golden Gate yacht clubs. The walk-in sculpture is made of materials salvaged from old sidewalks, destroyed buildings, and even demolished mausoleums. Its fractured columns and granite amphitheater are arranged around a series of pipes that "play" the waves. With low moans and backwash gurglings, the Wave Organ interprets the moods of the bay for receptive audiences. If the

organ doesn't perform for you, the jetty affords a fantastic view of the Golden Gate Bridge, perhaps the best in the entire bay. It is also a peaceful spot to relax and observe the busy Marina Green. On a surprising little beach on the jetty's north side, shorebirds rest and feed at low tide.

FORT MASON

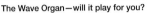

Fort Mason (formerly Black Point) has played a perennial role in regional and national history, serving first as the site of the Spanish fort Batería de San José, then as Mexico's Punta Medanos de Arena (Sand Dune Point), and then as a strategic U.S. military base. Upon California's entry into the Union, the U.S. Army claimed Fort Mason and then decommissioned it. It was later reactivated in preparation for Confederate attack during the Civil War. Expanded after the

1906 earthquake, Fort Mason saw some 1.5 million soldiers embark from its piers during World War II and the Korean War.

At nearby Pier 45, the World War II Liberty ship *Jeremiah O'Brien* is a quiet reminder of one of the greatest mass-production efforts in U.S. history: over 2,750 Liberty ships were constructed between 1941 and 1945 at several bayside facilities.

Today, the lower 13 acres of Fort Mason, with three covered piers and four three-story warehouses, house the Fort Mason Center, a self-supporting hub of San Francisco's cultural diversity. Over 20 nonprofit organizations occupy the former warehouses, while the piers are used for special events. The 50 acres of upper Fort Mason house the GGNRA and Golden Gate National Parks Conservancy headquarters, the Fisherman's Wharf Hostel, the San Francisco

Dune Restoration

Although dune-colonizing plants endure sand blast, poor soils, and intense exposure to the sun, they are nonetheless vulnerable to invasive species and to trampling. The dunes of Crissy Field may be remnants of a larger dune system: it's edged by salt marshes and lagoons that once covered much of today's Presidio and Marina District. The National Park Service has been revegetating the dunes with native species, including sand verbena, seaside daisy, yerba buena, and San Francisco silver lupine. Dunes at Baker Beach and Fort Funston have also been revegetated.

Dune restoration at Crissy Field

Aquatic Park from Municipal Pier

Conservation Corps, an exercise course, vast lawns, and the Black Point Battery. To move between the two areas, use the long stairway over the 90-foot retaining wall or go to the corner of Marina and Laguna and follow the path. Resting against the retaining wall is the stern of the *Galilee*, an 1850s clipper ship that once rode the winds between New York and San Francisco.

AQUATIC PARK

The Promenade winds east through Fort Mason, up and over Black Point (the site of a Civil War–era cannon installation), and then drops down toward Aquatic Park, with its small beach. The exposed shoreline face of Black Point is one of the few remnants of the city's original shoreline. In the sheltered bay off Aquatic Park, devoted swimmers brave the chilly waters (55°F average) year-round. Most belong to the Dolphin Swimming and Boating Club or the South End Rowing Club. Both clubs were established in the 1870s and have sponsored rowing and swimming races in the bay for generations.

The well-worn Municipal Pier arcs 1,850 feet into the bay from the western edge of the park and attracts fishermen and crabbers. From the end of the pier, the spectacular views of the Golden Gate Bridge, tankers, sailboats, and Aquatic Park are well worth the walk. The abandoned pier to the west once served Alcatraz Island. At the Hyde Street Pier, to the east, the National Park Service's San Francisco Maritime National Historical Park offers tours of seven vessels. Three other ships are moored nearby. This pier, built

for ferries in 1922, also houses the park's Maritime Store.

The Maritime Park's Museum is at the foot of Polk Street, in a three-story art deco building that resembles a ship, built by WPA crews during the Depression. The library and archives are at Fort Mason's Building E. Next to the museum, settle into the concrete bleachers and watch the scene: octogenarians adjusting swimming caps, enormous cargo ships entering the bay, children playing in the sand. In a quiet western corner of this park, serious games of bocce ball take place daily. On Sundays, drummers often gather for jam sessions on the bleachers. Plenty of shops and restaurants are in converted factories nearby.

GETTING AROUND

The Bay Trail follows the Golden Gate Promenade between Fort Point and Aquatic Park. At the Saint Francis Yacht Club, a path atop a jetty leads to the Wave Organ. Just past the Fort Mason gate, follow the path up and over the hill, where a paved but steep bayside trail leads down to Aquatic Park.

Baykeeper on patrol

Baykeeper

San Francisco Baykeeper was founded in 1989 to protect San Francisco Bay from pollution. Using advocacy, science, on-the-water patrols, and the law, Baykeeper compels polluters to stop illegal discharges and holds regulators accountable for safeguarding and restoring the waters of San Francisco Bay.

FISHERMAN'S WHARF TO MISSION BAY

Along these 3 miles of waterfront, working fishermen unload their catches in the early morning, next to the tourist magnet of Fisherman's Wharf. Ferries leave for various destinations, weaving among rafts of sea lions and boisterous gulls. Old and new piers reach into the bay, providing vistas, fishing spots, and commerce opportunities.

Docked fishing boats at Fisherman's Wharf

FISHERMAN'S WHARF
♿ 🚶 🚲

Tourists crowding the waterfront between Hyde Street Pier and Pier 45 experience the old and the new, the sublime and the garish. This is historic Fisherman's Wharf. Bay winds blend the aroma of warm sourdough bread, glistening fresh fish, steaming crab pots, crusty pier pilings, and boat diesel into a smell unique to the waterfront along Jefferson Street. Behind neon signs and lumbering tourist buses, tradition prevails.

The true fisherman's waterfront survives on Fish Alley (at the foot of Leavenworth), on Pier 47, and on Pier 45, where commercial boats unload their catches of herring, bass, and salmon under clouds of gulls. Most of the real work takes place between 3 a.m. and 9 a.m. Between November and June, some 1 million pounds of Dungeness crab arrive at Pier 45 from beyond the bay. Work your way around some of the narrow byways, and you'll catch a glimpse (and a whiff) of history: many of these fishermen and fisherwomen are grandchildren and great-grandchildren of San Francisco's fishing pioneers.

San Francisco's fishing industry began during the Gold Rush. Italians, and some Dalmatians and Greeks, realized their "pot of gold" was more attainable on the waters than in the gold mines. A variety of seafood was soon for sale at the expanding Fisherman's Wharf: salmon from the Sacramento River, bay herring, shrimp (collected almost exclusively by Chinese immigrants), oysters, mussels, and sardines (from 1920 until the late 1940s). True to the history of this city and this industry, many recent immigrants continue to join San Francisco's fishing fleet. A World War II submarine, the USS *Pampanito*, can be toured at Pier 45 for a fee.

PIER 43 TO PIER 39
♿ 🐟 🚶 🚲

Just east of Fisherman's Wharf, by Pier 43, you can rest on a bench and observe waterfront activities from Vista Pier and the public pier between Piers 41 and 39. The derelict Pier 43 once serviced railroad ferries that carried freight to Richmond and Tiburon. It was recently rebuilt for public access.

Pier 39 is the largest shopping complex on the waterfront, with about 20 restaurants, numerous specialty stores, and an aquarium. The exhibits at the Aquarium of the Bay focus on the bay's diverse aquatic animals and distinctive

Pacific sardine

A busy day at Pier 39

Sailboats at the Golden Gate

Alcatraz Island, aka "The Rock"

ecosystems. Sharks, octopus, jellies, bat rays, and skates are just a few of the aquatic animals that can be seen here in 300-foot crystal-clear acrylic tunnels that hold over 700,000 gallons of filtered bay water.

The pier's biggest attraction, however, may be its uninvited itinerant population of California sea lions. Hundreds of sea lions invaded Pier 39's "K-Dock" in 1990. What at first was seen as a problem soon became a tourist bonanza. Management surrendered the dock to the sea lions. Some 600 rambunctious, mostly male pinnipeds loll about on floating docks in midwinter. Most of them migrate south in May to breed at the Channel Islands and along Mexico's Pacific shore. While the sea lions took a brief and rather abrupt vacation from Pier 39 in the winter

of 2009, they have since reappeared.

The Marine Mammal Center has an informational kiosk adjacent to the sea lions at K-Dock, and most weekends a volunteer is available mid-day to answer questions. More sea lion information and interactive exhibits are available on Level 2 at the Marine Mammal Center's Interpretive Center and gift store. For a one-hour or more in-depth experience, book a "Sea Lions in the City" tour with the Marine Mammal Center by calling or visiting the center's website. The sea lions

Pier 39's most famous residents

can also be observed from Pier 41. Between Piers 41 and 43, the Blue & Gold Fleet and the Red & White Fleet offer boat tours of the bay.

ALCATRAZ—THE ROCK

Originally, the name Alcatraz (Spanish for "pelican") had been given to what is now Yerba Buena Island, but in 1826, on a map, Captain Frederick Beechy mistakenly transferred the name to this rocky island with steep cliffs that were perfect for nesting seabirds. The mistake stuck. In the early 1850s, the U.S. Army took command and placed artillery on the island. In 1854, the first lighthouse on the West Coast was built here. The Alcatraz Citadel was completed in 1859 and was used mostly as a military prison until 1933, when it was converted to a maximum-security federal penitentiary. Among famous inmates on "The Rock," as Alcatraz is unofficially called, were Al "Scarface" Capone, "Machine Gun" Kelly, and the "Birdman of Alcatraz," Robert

Stroud. The prison was shut down in 1963.

In 1964, a small group of Sioux arrived on the island to claim it on the grounds that an 1868 treaty promised Native Americans home-steading rights on surplus government lands. They were quickly removed by federal marshals. In November 1969, 90 Native Americans from more than 20 tribes occupied Alcatraz in the name of Indians of All Tribes. They held it until June 1971. Each year, Native Americans and friends return for "Un-Thanksgiving Day." Since 1973, Alcatraz has been part of the GGNRA. More than 1 million people visit annually.

THE EMBARCADERO PROMENADE
♿ 🐟 🚶 🚲

The Embarcadero ("boarding place" in Spanish) is a stretch of water-front about 2 miles long, edged with both active and neglected piers and restaurants. The entire Embarcadero is built on fill and the abandoned hulls of 19th-cen-tury sailing ships. In 1959, further construction of the elevated Em-barcadero Freeway ended due to citizen protest. The freeway had been scheduled to connect the Bay and Golden Gate bridges, but it was stopped after reaching the foot of Market Street in front of the Ferry Building. It carried traf-

fic between the Bay Bridge and North Beach until 1989, when an earthquake damaged it. In 1992, it was demolished, spurring a reha-bilitation of the Ferry Building and a waterfront renaissance of sorts.

Immediately east of Pier 39, the Embarcadero Promenade begins at East Waterfront Park with a gar-den and observation deck. From Pier 33, you can take dining and dancing cruises on the bay. Across from Pier 23—the Foreign Trade Zone—is another small park with a nice lawn. Crossing the Embar-cadero from near the Explorato-rium at Piers 15, 17, and 9 (look for the working tugs docked here) is the Waterfront Histori-

1850s Shoreline

From Fort Point to Candlestick Point, the shoreline was once fringed with marshes, creeks, and coves that supported abundant shellfish, wild-life, and Ohlone villages. By the 1950s, San Francisco's 12.5 miles of bay waterfront were dominated by 42 piers with more than 18 miles of ship-berthing space. The piers, roads, and small parks along today's waterfront were all built on landfill. Take a walk along the 1850s shore-line—North Beach to Mission Bay—and consider the previous landscape. From Fisherman's Wharf, walk up to

Columbus and Taylor (six blocks from Pier 45), and imagine a 1,600-foot pier shooting north into the bay from that corner. In 1850, you would have been standing on the shoreline, at the foot of Meiggs Pier. The pier was eventually enclosed by a sea wall that now forms the foundation of Fisher-man's Wharf. The shoreline curved down to the corner of present-day Bay and Taylor streets and then moved south, up from Embarcadero to Broadway. From there it bowed in-land and formed Yerba Buena Cove, San Francisco's most important 19th-century anchorage. The plaque

Pre-1850s shoreline, and today's

in the sidewalk at First and Mar-ket marks the approximate historic shoreline. Imagine standing on this spot in the early 1850s, looking to-ward Yerba Buena Island, and count-ing more than 800 sailing vessels. Hundreds of boats arrived at Yerba Buena Cove during the Gold Rush, only to have their entire crews jump ship and head toward the Sierra. Some 770 ships were abandoned and subsequently used for storage or housing, or were scrapped. Over the decades, the shoreline was filled and moved bayward toward today's Fire-boat Dock, and then continued south to Townsend, where it turned inland to form Mission Bay.

1882 view from Telegraph Hill with Meiggs Pier

A colorful opening of new public access at Pier 14

Pier 7 illuminated

cal District. Looming across the Embarcadero is the sheer face of Telegraph Hill. During the mid-19th century, portions of the hill were excavated and used as ballast for ships and to fill Yerba Buena Cove, the first six blocks of today's Market Street.

Pier 7, built in 1990, is a public-access pier, open for strolling and fishing. It offers views of the Bay Bridge; Treasure, Yerba Buena, and Angel islands; and the East Bay. Looking inland, you see Coit Tower and the Financial District. Between Piers 5 and 3, notice the Santa Rosa Ferry, built in 1927. It once carried 65 vehicles and 1,200 passengers daily, but is now used for offices, conferences, and parties. The public is welcome aboard Monday through Saturday.

Pier Mathematics

Before the turn of the century, San Francisco's piers were numbered and named for the streets at which they began. That changed when the Embarcadero was built. Now piers between the Ferry Building and Fisherman's Wharf have odd numbers, and those between the Ferry Building and the northern edge of Hunters Point have even numbers. (Fort Mason's piers are separately numbered.)

Southeast of Pier 1, the 1896 Ferry Building served over 100,000 commuters daily during the 1920s. While far fewer ferry riders pass through today, the renovated Ferry Building, with its high-end food-themed bou-

Pier 7, April 1914

tiques, eateries, and thrice-weekly farmers' market, has become the pride of the city. This regional hub serves the Golden Gate Ferry to Sausalito and Larkspur, the Red & White Fleet's ferries for bay cruises, WETA ferries to Alameda and Oakland, and the Blue & Gold Fleet's ferries from Alameda and Oakland. Ferry Plaza East, with fishing spots and benches, wraps around the Ferry Building. Beneath it, BART crosses the bay. Between the Ferry Building and the Fireboat Dock (next to Pier 24, below the Bay Bridge) are concrete benches where Financial District workers eat bag lunches and gaze at the bay. Across the Embarcadero is Maritime Plaza and Justin Herman Plaza, where various special events occur.

After pausing under the Bay

San Francisco Ferry Building

Bridge to listen to the click-clack of cars passing overhead, check out Red's Java House, a historic working person's lunch spot.

Bay Bridge

In 1955, the American Society of Civil Engineers honored the San Francisco–Oakland Bay Bridge as one of the seven "Modern Civil Engineering Wonders" of the world. Opened in November 1936, it spans more than 4 miles of water and is actually two distinct types of bridges joined at Yerba Buena Island. At first the bridge carried autos on its top deck, and trucks, buses, and two tracks for the key system rail service on the lower deck. In 1958, the rails were removed and both levels were assigned to motor vehicles.

During the 1989 Loma Prieta earthquake, a segment of the east span of the bridge collapsed. Although it was repaired relatively quickly, long-term seismic safety required replacing the span altogether. After a long design selection process, the iconic single anchor suspension (SAS) tower was chosen, and as of the publication of this guide, the new span was scheduled to open to traffic in 2013 (see p. 108). Through concerted efforts of the bike coalitions, the Bay Trail Project, key stakeholders, and the public, a 15.5-foot multi-use path on the south side of the span will link Oakland to Treasure Island for bicyclists and pedestrians. Efforts are currently under way to incorporate a multi-use path on the west span. Though many years away, such a facility would finally complete the Bay Trail on the Bay Bridge.

The San Francisco–Oakland Bay Bridge

Cupid's Span in Rincon Park is one of the larger public art installations along the Bay Trail. The foot of Pier 14, a public-access pier atop breakwater, sports a changing array of statuary and eclectic artworks. Also notice the art tiles depicting historic vs. modern ships that grace the railings as you make your way to the end of the pier. The observant will discover old sea shanties near the end. In need of a rest? George Jetson–like stainless steel swivel chairs invite you to sit a spell.

SOUTH BEACH HARBOR

South Beach Harbor, next to Pier 40, is a municipal marina. To the south of the harbor lies the San Francisco Giants baseball stadium—AT&T Park. On game days, boats of all sizes slowly circle McCovey Cove, hoping to recover a "splash ball"—an out-of-the-park homer shot into the bay. As you move south, the Third Street Bridge (aka "Lefty O'Doul" Bridge) crosses Mission Creek. It is a drawbridge, as are the Fourth Street and Islais Creek bridges. In the early days of European settlements, Mission Creek was navigable all the way to Mission Dolores. Mission Rock Terminal (Pier 50) is built atop Mission Rock, a well-known nearshore feature in the 1850s. The schooner *C. A. Thayer* (now docked at the Hyde Street Pier) unloaded lumber from the north at the thriving shipyards here in the 1890s, while several blocks to the south thousands of whalebones and tanks of whale oil cluttered the shore at the Pacific Steam Whaling Company.

MISSION BAY

Terry Francois Boulevard, just after the Third Street Bridge, brings you to the area of Mission Bay. Before it was filled, Mission Bay was a sheltered embayment edged by rich tidal marshland backed by

Pier Piling Biology

San Francisco's fertile bay waters support many kinds of fish and shellfish. On countless pier pilings, barnacles, mussels, sea stars, and anemones grip these columns of artificial habitat as crabs and fish circle about, feeding among them and on them.

dunes, and the site of commerce during the Gold Rush. Mission Creek emptied into the bay where King Street now meets Division Street. What we now call Mission Creek is a tidal inlet in the approximate location of the historic mouth of the creek. A houseboat community has survived here for many years. The creek itself is culverted. Today this no-nonsense urban waterfront is occupied by heavy industry and enormous dry docks, though the ever-expanding UCSF Medical Center at Mission Bay is bringing changes to this

Yerba Buena and Treasure Islands

Yerba Buena Island Naval Barracks, ca. 1900

Yerba Buena Island was known as Alcatraz in the early 1800s (see p. 23) and then as Goat Island in the mid-1800s, when many goats were grazed here. In 1931, it was officially renamed after a sweet-smelling native plant, which the Spanish called *yerba buena*. In the late 1930s, a 400-acre island was constructed with bay dredgings to the north of

Yerba Buena Island and was attached to it. The new island, named Treasure Island, was the site for the 1939–40 Golden Gate International Exposition. Some 4,000 trees and 2 million flowering plants were planted for the occasion. Many of the palms and varieties of eucalyptus are still alive.

Treasure Island International Exposition, 1939

The Navy took possession of the man-made island after the fair. Future plans include transferring control to the city of San Francisco and building 8,000 new residential units, three hotels, a 400-slip marina, restaurants, retail shops, and entertainment venues—plus nearly 300 acres of parks and open space. With this project, a new segment of the Bay Trail will encircle the island and connect to the Bay Bridge pathway.

Anchored Tankers

Just south of the Bay Bridge, enormous tankers often anchor mid-bay. They wait here for high tides, so they can move into port, or for open berths to unload crude oil or take on petroleum products. Tankers are among the largest craft that enter the bay. They often have deep drafts requiring that they be "lightered"—i.e., have their cargo offloaded onto barges so the tankers can ride higher in the water and reach port.

area. There is a small public boat launch at Pier 52, near the Bayview Boat Club (see p. 7 for information about the Water Trail). From Terry Francois Boulevard, glimpse tankers and military ships hauled out on dry docks at Piers 68 and 70, their huge propellers riding high and dry. Agua Vista Park, an open patch of waterfront just north of Mission Rock Resort, has a public pier.

Yerba Buena

Yerba buena (*Satureja douglasii*) is a mint common to the Pacific Coast of North America. Between April and September, it produces small flowers whose color ranges from white to lavender. When the Spanish arrived, they learned that the local Ohlone people placed great faith in the medicinal qualities of this plant. Accordingly, the Spanish named it *yerba buena*, the "good herb." Ohlones, Spaniards, Mexicans, and early Californians brewed an aromatic tea from its dried leaves as a remedy for fevers and stomach ailments. Its medicinal qualities are still appreciated today. The name Yerba Buena appears frequently throughout San Francisco's history. The settlement that became San Francisco was known first as Yerba Buena, a community that began to form in 1835 on the shore of the anchorage the Spaniards had called Yerba Buena Cove. In 1847, the city was officially renamed after Saint Francis.

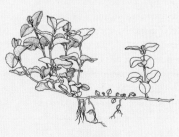

Yerba buena

GETTING AROUND 🚶🏃

From Aquatic Park, the Bay Trail follows Jefferson Street to the Embarcadero, continues along the Embarcadero to South Beach Harbor, and then turns south on Third Street and east on Terry Francois Boulevard. On the south side of AT&T Park, fans can watch Giants baseball for free at the public viewing area.

CHINA BASIN TO CANDLESTICK POINT

The waterfront winding for some 7 miles between China Basin and Candlestick Point is unknown territory for most tourists, and even for many San Franciscans. In the 1890s, this stretch of the Port of San Francisco was noisy with shipbuilding and other water-related industry. The Arctic Oil Wharf was at today's Pier 64, the Union Iron Works at Pier 68. Bethlehem Steel's shipyard and handsome brick buildings (still standing) extended behind Pier 70 at today's 22nd Street. The Pacific Rolling Mills and

AT&T Park: home of Giants baseball

California Sugar Refinery were at Pier 72. Now port activity is less intense, resulting in many derelict structures and piers. Anyone interested in the city's waterfront history or industrial architecture will find it here. Some colorful eateries and several small parks and fishing piers provide views of rusty cranes and other structures that now appeal as found art.

WARM WATER COVE PARK

This small park at the foot of 24th Street is a planted patch of bayfill near the Army Street Terminal (Pier 80). The park was named for the warm water that was released into the bay by the Potrero Power Plant as part of its cooling process before it was closed in 2011. Look north toward Pier 70 at the historic dry-dock buildings, and south, toward Pier 80, at tankers docked and anchored. Oakland is across the bay. To the west, the foot of Potrero Hill marks the original bay shoreline. This park is isolated and not recommended for solitary exploration.

ISLAIS CREEK

Like Mission Creek, Islais Creek was once an embayment. The creek itself flowed from Twin Peaks, meandering through marshes toward the bay. Today, it's underground, trickling into a channeled tidal inlet at the Highway 280 overpass and mixing with saltwater as it flows bayward under the Third Street drawbridge. The word "Islais" derives from the Salinan Indian word for "wild cherry." Upstream from the drawbridge, see the old copra (coconut oil) docks of the Cargill

Company. Downstream are petroleum docks, a huge container facility, a wharf where tallow is shipped to Asia, and the port's abandoned grain terminal. Fishermen use two small parks on the east side of the bridge.

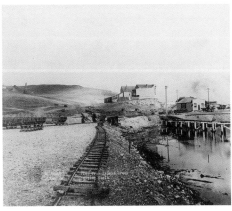

Islais Creek, ca. 1905

Islais Creek today

Bay Trail at India Basin

INDIA BASIN AND HERON'S HEAD PARK

Heron's Head Park is a landfill jetty created for the Southern Crossing Bridge, which was never built. Its name derives from the aerial view of the park—a "heron's head," to be sure. It is now an open space and intertidal marsh area for migrating birds, developed by local residents and managed by the Port of San Francisco. The group

Double-Crested Cormorant

Three species of cormorants can be found along the Pacific Coast, but the double-crested is the one you're most likely to see on bay waters. Cormorants live almost entirely on fish that they catch under water, sometimes at great depths. They are often seen standing atop rocks, posts, or pier pilings, drying their outspread wings. Some have nested in the understructure of the Bay Bridge.

Double-crested cormorant

Literacy for Environmental Justice opened the EcoCenter at Heron's Head Park in 2010. It is the first environmental justice education facility in the Bay Area and San Francisco's first 100 percent "off-grid" building, modeling solar power and alternative wastewater technologies.

Many forms of algae and other life forms cling to rocks here. You can see fine views of birds on the water from the end of the spit, as well as views of Hunters Point, the Bay Bridge, and Oakland. On the southern edge of the jetty is a small marsh. Great blue herons, egrets, and gulls feed among pickleweed, cordgrass, and eelgrass. Offshore rafts of cormorants and scoters troll the waters seasonally. From the base of the spit, a developed dirt trail wraps around the back of the former PG&E Hunters Point Power Plant to a cove where mud flats are busy with a variety of birds at low tide. This path connects to the paved Bay Trail at India Basin Shoreline Park.

Across India Basin, to the south, a cove with boats at anchor served as a Chinese shrimp camp until the 1940s. To get to Heron's Head Park, turn east off Third Street near Islais Creek channel

onto Cargo Way. The park is at the end of Cargo Way.

HUNTERS POINT

In 1849, entrepreneur Robert E. Hunter tried to found a new city on this point, which the Spanish had named Punta de Concha ("Shell Point"). But what took hold instead was shipbuilding. An enormous stone dry dock was built here in 1868, and through the turn of the 20th century, the area was known for its construction and repair of West Coast ships. During World War I, the Bethlehem Steel Company produced large cargo ships at Hunters Point, and during World War II the Navy expanded the point into the bay on fill to make room for urgent war production. Large machine shops and warehouses were built around the dry docks. A

World War II shipyards, Hunters Point

Hunters Point today

workforce, mostly African Americans, was hired and housed just upslope from the shipyards, in an arrangement similar to that at the Marinship yards and Marin City, and in Richmond.

Today the city of San Francisco is in the process of redeveloping this former naval shipyard. Visions for the future include a mix of housing, retail, office, open space, and an inviting 4.4-mile segment of shoreline Bay Trail. Nearly 300 artist studios thrive at Hunters Point Shipyard today and are well worth a visit during Open Studios or by appointment.

CANDLESTICK POINT STATE RECREATION AREA

Candlestick Point State Recreation Area is a refreshing surprise for those who thought Candlestick

was only for ball games and traffic jams. A reclaimed landfill that wraps around the stadium has been turned into a park with ample lawns and exercise stations. At low tide, mud flats are exposed and shorebirds arrive to feed. Fishermen try for perch, shark, jacksmelt, and flounder off two piers here. Hunters Point Shipyards lies to the north. Jets from San Francisco Airport gain altitude overhead. To the west is Candlestick Stadium and Bay View Park atop the hill that was carved away and terraced to fill the bayshore. Between Candlestick Point and Hunters Point is Yosemite Slough, which is slated to be restored. To the southwest is San Bruno Mountain and the explanation for wind in

Candlestick State Recreation Area

this area: Alemany Gap, which acts as a funnel. If the San Francisco 49ers are playing, expect heavy traffic. Windsurfers favor this site.

GETTING AROUND

The Bay Trail route moves from Terry Francois Boulevard to Illinois Street, onto Cargo Way and to Heron's Head Park, where a dirt path leads to developed Bay Trail at India Basin Shoreline Park. From here south to Candlestick State Recreation Area, the Bay Trail is a planned alignment that runs through the currently shuttered Hunters Point Naval Shipyard. Until the trail is fully developed here, use the city's bike network to get to Candlestick. Take Cargo Way back to Third Street and head south. Then pick up Phelps, Palou, Keith, Carroll, Fitch and then Gilman to the state park entrance. Exercise normal caution in isolated industrial areas.

INFORMATION

Public Transit
Call 511 or visit 511.org.

Transit & Trails
www.transitandtrails.org

Blue & Gold Fleet
www.blueandgoldfleet.com
415-705-8200

Golden Gate Ferry
www.goldengateferry.org
415-455-2000

Red & White Fleet
www.redandwhite.com
415-673-2900

San Francisco Municipal Transportation Agency (MUNI) www.sfmta.com
415-701-2311

Aquarium of the Bay
www.aquariumofthe
bay.org
415-623-5300

Argonaut Hotel/SF Maritime National Historical Park Visitors Center and Interactive Museum
www.argonauthotel.com
415-563-0800

BayKeeper
www.baykeeper.org
415-856-0444

Candlestick Point State Recreation Area
www.parks.ca.gov
415-671-0145

Dolphin Swimming & Boating Club
www.dolphinclub.org
415-441-9329

Exploratorium
www.exploratorium.edu
415-561-0360

Fort Mason Center
www.fortmason.org
415-345-7500

Fort Point
www.nps.gov
415-556-1693

General Golden Gate National Recreation Area
www.nps.gov/goga
/index.htm
415-561-4700

Golden Gate National Parks Conservancy
www.parksconservancy
.org
415-776-0693

Marina Yacht Harbor
www.sfrecpark.org/
MarinaYachtHarbor
415-831-6322

Marine Mammal Center
www.MarineMammal
Center.org
415-289-7330

National Maritime Museum
www.maritime.org
415-561-6662

Pier 39 Information
www.pier39.com
415-981-7437

The Point (for information about Open Studios)
www.thepointart.com
415-822-9675

South End Rowing Club
www.south-end.org
415-776-7372

U.S. Park Police
www.nps.gov/uspp
415-561-5505

USS Pampanito
www.maritime.org
415-561-6662

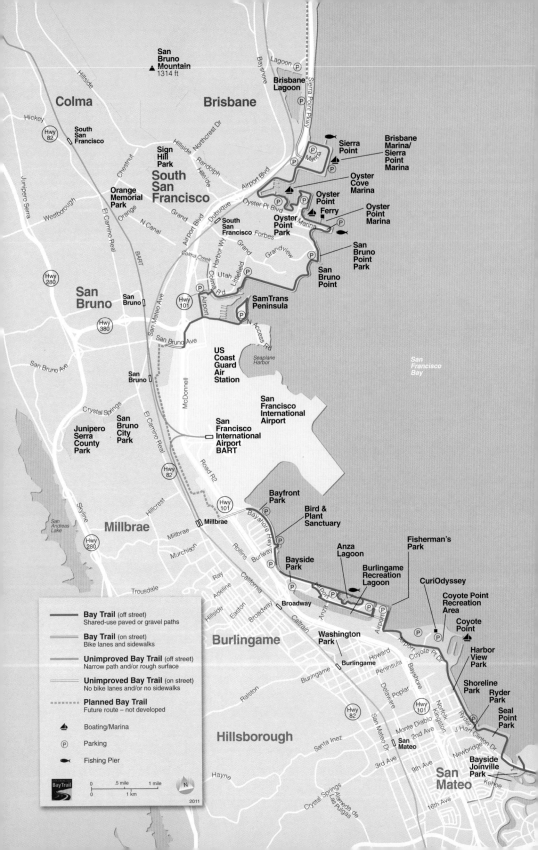

SIERRA POINT PARKWAY TO SAMTRANS PENINSULA

South of Candlestick Point, bay waters once met land farther west. The shoreline skirted the eastern foot of San Bruno Mountain, then meandered south into marshes. Almost all these wetlands have been filled and put to industrial and commercial uses. Yet there is much to discover along this stretch of bayshore: diverse opportunities for recreation, as well as remnants of history and natural landscape.

View of San Francisco Bay from San Bruno Mountain

BRISBANE LAGOON AND SIERRA POINT

South of Candlestick Point and inland from Highway 101 is Brisbane Lagoon, which was a cove until the highway cut it off from the bay. Culverts under the highway still admit the tide, allowing bay fish to survive here. To reach the lagoon's northern shore, turn on Lagoon Way, or pull into the parking lot off Sierra Point Parkway. This small turnout has a dozen parking spaces and spots for fishing. It's also a good place for watching waterbirds.

Sierra Point was built on fill and is now an office park. A public shoreline trail loops around the point, passing the wooden Brisbane Fishing Pier. A typical catch here might include brown smoothhound sharks, staghorn sculpin, and various perch species. Along the point's eastern edge are the Brisbane and Sierra Parkway marinas.

SAN BRUNO MOUNTAIN

San Bruno Mountain looms out of the peninsula's urban jumble like a giant stranded whale attempting to return to the bay. Its two parallel ridges undulate for 5 miles and rise to 1,314 feet, sheltering a valley that was once a salt marsh. One of the Spaniards who first saw this marsh in 1774 described it as "teeming with geese, ducks, cranes, and herons." The marsh is gone, replaced by an industrial

Brisbane Fishing Pier

Bayshore Freeway under construction southeast of Candlestick Point, 1955

San Bruno Mountain

park and quarry, but the mountain survives as a unique island in time, offering a glimpse of the land as it was before the Europeans' arrival.

Natural scientists who know the mountain call it a botanical treasure. Its slopes and ravines support four native plant communities: grassland, coastal scrub, foothill woodland, and salt marsh. In spring, the grassy slopes come alive with wildflowers. The inner ravines are lined with live oak, California bay, holly leaf cherry, and California buckeye. On outcroppings of the greenish-gray sandstone, called Franciscan graywacke, the endangered San Bruno manzanita (found nowhere else in the world) grows, along with other rare and unique plants. The endangered Mission blue butterfly feeds on lupine here. The endangered San Bruno elfin butterfly

survives here and in only a few other spots on the peninsula. Look for it in shady canyons where you see moss and lichen. Today, 2,400 acres of the mountain are preserved in parks and open space, but only after intense citizen efforts against decades of development schemes, including one serious proposal to level the mountain and use it to create thousands of acres of bay fill.

From the western ridge peak—the highest point on the northern San Francisco peninsula—you can see the entire region spread

San Bruno elfin butterfly

out before you: ocean, bay, and the distant peaks of Tamalpais, Diablo, and Hamilton. To the immediate north, San Francisco's downtown thrusts upward. To the south, the soft lines of the coastal mountains offer rest for the eyes. If you come here when the Pacific fog is gently pushing up into the canyons (part of the area's natural air conditioning), you might see the great "hand of God" phenomenon, as giant white fingers of fog probe the ground. To reach the mountain from the Bayshore Freeway, take Bayshore Boulevard toward Brisbane and Daly City. Go west on Guadalupe Canyon Parkway and turn left on Radio Road.

OYSTER POINT

Oyster Point did not exist until after 1900, when filling slowly began. In the 1870s, the area immediately

Some Native Plants

The best season for exploring San Bruno Mountain is spring, when the wildflowers bloom. But don't hesitate to come in other seasons. Walk some of the trails and see the native plant communities that survive here almost undisturbed. Below are a few of the native plants you may find.

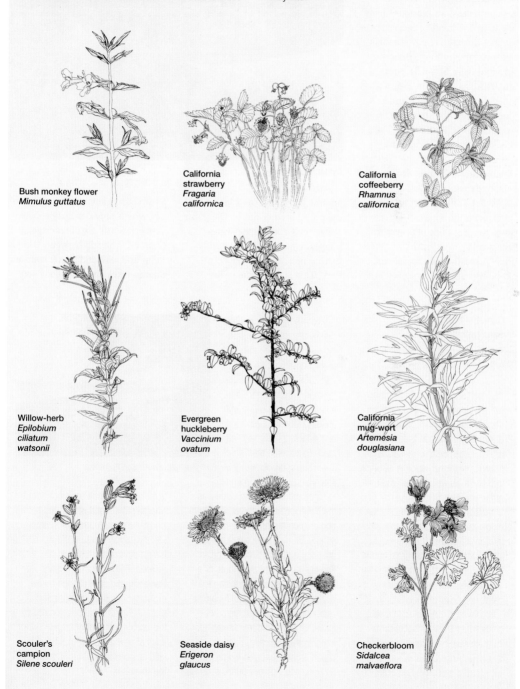

Bush monkey flower
Mimulus guttatus

California
strawberry
*Fragaria
californica*

California
coffeeberry
*Rhamnus
californica*

Willow-herb
*Epilobium
ciliatum
watsonii*

Evergreen
huckleberry
*Vaccinium
ovatum*

California
mug-wort
*Artemesia
douglasiana*

Scouler's
campion
Silene scouleri

Seaside daisy
*Erigeron
glaucus*

Checkerbloom
*Sidalcea
malvaeflora*

north of today's Oyster Point—Oyster Cove—encompassed a calm inlet and the site of Samuel Purseglove's Corville and Company oyster beds. Oysters were raised here for almost 40 years until bay pollution and health concerns over the consumption of bay shellfish destroyed the industry. Between 1912 and 1983, Shaw-Batcher Shipbuilding, Western Pipe and Steel, American Bridge, and U.S. Steel occupied the shores of the cove. Ships for World Wars I and II were built here, and piping was manufactured for the Hetch Hetchy, Grand Coulee, Shasta, and Folsom dams.

Oyster Point Marina

The Bay Trail runs from Sierra Point along the edge of Oyster Cove, passing a few old piers that bear witness to a century of enterprise. A small fringe marsh and old pilings line Oyster Cove and approach Oyster Cove Marina on the point. Farther out on the point are various businesses, warehouses, a yacht club, the park's fishing pier, and Oyster Point Park. This is the home of the South San Francisco Ferry Terminal, which provides ferry access between South San Francisco and Oakland. The trip between Oyster Point and Oakland's Jack London Square takes approximately 30

Climate Change and San Francisco Bay

The nine-county San Francisco Bay Area is home to approximately 7 million people, making the bay one of the world's most urbanized estuaries. Development has changed the shoreline in a number of ways, populating it with houses, industrial facilities, large commercial structures, schools, highways, landfills, airports, and parks, as well as over 300 miles of the Bay Trail. But despite this urbanization, the bay continues to be a magnificent body of water that helps sustain the economy of the western United States, provides great opportunities for recreation, nourishes fish and wildlife, affords scenic enjoyment, and helps to enrich our lives.

In coming years, though, climate change has the potential to drastically alter the bay shoreline and life in the Bay Area. Global warming is expected to cause the San Francisco Bay to rise by 16 inches (40 cm) by mid-century and 55 inches (139 cm) by the end of the century.

In 2009, the Bay Conservation and Development Commission released *Living with a Rising Bay: Vulnerability and Adaptations in San Francisco Bay and on the Shoreline*. This report outlines the steps necessary to respond to these projections and discusses the development of shoreline protection projects that can address widespread flooding from storm activity and sea level rise. Shoreline protection can be structural, natural, or a combination of both. Choosing the appropriate form of shoreline protection—one that both protects public safety and minimizes ecosystem impacts—is critically important. The report urges the region to engage in an open and vigorous public dialogue

High tide in South San Francisco

to make the difficult decisions about what to protect and where, what kind of new development is appropriate in vulnerable areas, and where further development should be avoided. The location of existing Bay Trail segments may change as the region tackles these difficult decisions. The trail could be relocated to the top of flood control levees, to the edge of new marshes, or further inland as development retreats from the shoreline.

South San Francisco Bay Trail

minutes. The numerous biotech firms with offices along the shoreline area of South San Francisco benefit from this transportation connection.

SAN BRUNO POINT

Beneath the fill-extended shore of San Bruno Point are remnants of a smaller peninsula that became known as China Point in the 1870s. After the completion of the transcontinental railroad in 1869 released thousands of Chinese workers, this peninsula became the site of one of the largest Chinese fishing camps that formed on the bay. Another big camp was on today's Hunters Point. Many of the railroad workers had been fishermen in their native Guangdong Province, and they sent home for their equipment or built it anew. Some junks (flat-bottomed ships with high poops and battened sails) would haul in about 7,000 pounds of bay shrimp daily.

Today, nothing remains of these Chinese camps. (See p. 184 for the sole exception, preserved in Marin County.) If you come here by car, park in the lots north of San Bruno Point Park (crowded during weekdays), and then venture south along a half mile of trail to the tip of the point and imagine a fleet of junks, in full sail, returning with tons of bay shrimp.

South of San Bruno Point (across two bicycle/pedestrian bridges and north of the airport) is a service area for SamTrans buses (just off North Access Road). This was a marsh at the end of Colma Creek before it was filled. Stop in the parking lot and explore the half-mile perimeter trail and parcourse. On its western side, a vibrant marsh grows between abandoned World War II shipbuilding piers next to the South San Francisco/San Bruno Water

Chinese shrimp camp

San Francisco International Airport

San Francisco International Airport began in 1927 as Mills Field Municipal Airport. Although it's in San Mateo County, it's owned by the city and county of San Francisco. More than 30 million travelers and over 300,000 airplanes passed through the airport in 2010. The airport's 5,200 acres are mostly bay fill; about half are developed, and for now the rest are open space and tidelands, albeit a bit noisy.

Quality Control Plant. At low tide, marsh islands are exposed in the inlet, and shorebirds and ducks feed calmly despite the proximity of Highway 101, overhead jet traffic, and revving SamTrans buses. The sewage treatment plant discharges treated wastewater a mile off San Bruno Point.

GETTING AROUND

The Bay Trail ends at Candlestick Point State Recreation Area, but surface streets connect to the bike lanes on Sierra Point Parkway in Brisbane. To visit San Bruno

Oysters

For the local Ohlone people, shellfish was a staple food, as evidenced by the mounds of oyster and other mollusk shells that once ringed the bay and its creeks. Many European immigrants and newcomers from the East Coast loved oysters too, but found that San Francisco Bay's native oyster, with its dark meat, strong flavor, and small size (about 2 inches across), was a poor substitute for the ones they remembered.

After 1851, when it was discovered that oysters from Shoalwater Bay in Washington State (today's Willapa Bay) were similar to Eastern oysters, several Bay Area oyster companies began importing them. Some 125,000 bushels were shipped to San Francisco annually and either sold or stored in bay waters off Sausalito's shoreline to grow more.

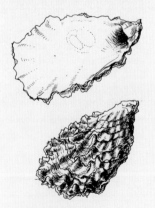

Eastern Oyster
Crassostrea virginica

In the 1860s and 1870s, however, hydraulic mining in the Sierra Nevada added thousands of tons of sediment to the normal silt load carried into the bay by the Sacramento and San Joaquin rivers. By 1862, the Sausalito storage area was covered with silt, and that year's entire crop perished. Oyster beds in the North Bay were soon abandoned for the shallow, calmer, and relatively silt-free waters of the South Bay, mostly along the western bayshore of San Mateo County. In 1869, when the transcontinental railroad was completed, Eastern oysters began to be shipped west in iced railcars to the bay's oyster beds. They quickly dominated the industry.

Between 1895 and 1904, well over 10 million pounds of oyster meat were harvested off San Mateo County's shoreline. The Morgan Oyster Company was the largest producer and eventually bought out all other oystermen on the bay. By 1923, Morgan owned 16,580 acres of tidal lands in San Mateo County (where most production took place), 13,550 acres in Alameda County, and 1,700 acres in Santa Clara County.

Oysters are filter feeders, pumping up to 6 gallons of water across their

Oyster harvesting, ca. 1880

gills every hour while feeding. They consume minute organisms and organic material at the base of the bay's food chain, and they process everything in the water, including the bacteria in human and animal waste, chemicals, and surface-runoff pollutants. These substances accumulate and concentrate in their fatty tissues.

As early as the 1870s, the outpouring of raw sewage from the city of San Francisco and other nascent cities, as well as heavy ferry and steamer traffic, began to pollute the bay and affect the oysters. In the South Bay, the diversion of freshwater streams for agricultural irrigation diminished the seasonal flushing action of winter rains. By 1905, oyster seed could no longer survive in the bay. Outbreaks of typhoid fever were blamed on contaminated oysters. By 1940, commercial oyster growing in the bay ceased, and a once-vital Bay Area industry disappeared.

Mountain, go west on Guadalupe Canyon Parkway (off Bayshore Boulevard) to Radio Road. Beginning at Sierra Point, 8.5 miles of continuous Bay Trail extend through the Brisbane and Sierra Parkway marinas, Oyster Point Marina, and the South San Francisco shoreline to Airport Boulevard. The trail continues along the shore of the SamTrans Peninsula off North Access Road and under the highway to San Bruno Avenue. To reach Bayfront Park, on the south side of San Francisco International Airport, use streets.

BAYFRONT PARK TO SHORELINE PARK

Children who aspire to be pilots, want to learn more about nature, or simply like to watch birds on the water will find this section of shoreline fascinating: it has the best park for airplane watching, one of the Bay Area's premier natural history museums, good fishing spots, an elegant bicycle/pedestrian bridge, and even a sandy beach. Plenty of adults will also find things to do and enjoy here.

View of San Francisco International Airport from Bayfront Park

Great egret

BAYFRONT PARK

 🚶 🚲

Airplanes come in low over bay waters from the south and lift off to the east at San Francisco International Airport. You can watch these landings and takeoffs from benches along a walkway in this park, between a manicured lawn and a marsh popular with shorebirds. The noise is tolerable since you are several hundred yards from the closest runway.

PLANT AND BIRD SANCTUARY

South of Bayfront Park on Bay-shore between Mahler and Burl-way roads is a small plant and bird sanctuary maintained by the city of Burlingame.

BAYSIDE PARK

Eucalyptus tower at the edges of this park, which includes lighted fields for soccer and baseball, a playground, a dog park, and

Bayside Park

lawns. Across the street on the bay is a small public fishing shore. A wastewater treatment plant abuts the park to the south.

ANZA LAGOON AND BURLINGAME RECREATION LAGOON

On the northern peninsula of Anza Lagoon, a unique half-circle pier arcs out over the water. The entire area surrounding Anza and Burlingame lagoons (both tidal) rests on bay fill and is now covered with office buildings, restaurants, and hotels. On the eastern tip of this area, Fishermen's Park offers angling, parking, and an unimpeded view of Coyote Point.

Anza Lagoon

Half-circle pier in Burlingame

COYOTE POINT

In 1824, Russian Captain Otto von Kotzebue sailed into the South Bay to resupply at Mission Santa Clara (Mission Dolores was low on provisions). En route, he and his men rested on what the captain described as a "pleasant little island" with grassland and oak trees. He

Coyote Point Recreation Area

Magic Mountain Playground at Coyote Point

thought he was the first human to set foot on the island, but large shell mounds indicate otherwise. In the later 19th century, this island was "The Coyote," separated from the peninsula by the Samphire Marsh. After the marsh was filled and the island linked to the shore, it became Coyote Point. Hundreds of eucalyptus trees have replaced the oaks, and lawns have replaced native grasses. Today, the 670-acre Coyote Point Recreation Area is the site of the nationally recognized science center and museum CuriOdyssey (formerly known as Coyote Point Museum).

CuriOdyssey Museum at Coyote Point

Inside the museum, kids of all ages can explore exciting hands-on science exhibits and learn how nature's complex systems work together to create our environment. Outside, visitors will find wildlife habitats that house some 50 live native, non-releasable animals. Guests may attend daily animal programs to meet and learn about the animals

living at the museum. CuriOdyssey is accredited by the Association of Zoos and Aquariums (AZA). Fewer than 10% of zoos and aquariums nationwide are accredited by AZA.

The western edge of the county park features a large beach area (in front of the Peninsula Humane Society), which is popular with windsurfers in spring, summer, and fall. At the eastern end of the beach, a ramp built for wheelchairs provides safe and easy access into the water. Picnic areas, the Magic Mountain Playground, several restaurants, and a firing range are also within the park.

On the eastern side of the point, where the park wraps around the county-operated golf course, are the Coyote Point Marina and Yacht Club. East beyond the marina, some natural and artificial islands and sand bars make for good birding and offer views of the East Bay and the San Mateo Bridge.

SHORELINE PARK AND MORE

Shoreline Park extends south from Coyote Point for 2 miles atop a large levee and beneath numerous electrical towers looming along the bayshore. The landscape is stark yet beautiful—it's just you and

Shoreline Park

Seal Point Park

the bay. In 2005, Shoreline Park was transformed with new park areas and trails, a 105-foot bicycle/pedestrian bridge over San Mateo Creek, a tidal water feature, new playgrounds, a kayak and windsurf launch area, and restored wetlands.

Shoreline Park is comprised of two parts: Ryder Park and Seal Point Park. Ryder Park boasts an interactive tidal water feature, playgrounds, and picnic shelters, making it a popular place on a hot summer day. Across an elegantly designed bicycle/pedestrian bridge is Seal Point Park, the former San Mateo landfill and now a destination for expansive views and shoreline access. The parks can be reached from the levee or along J. Hart Clinton Drive. South of Shoreline Park near the outlet of

Bay marshes

Marina Lagoon is the Bay Marshes boardwalk, extending above restored wetlands for a view of the mud flats and Seal Point Park.

GETTING AROUND

From Millbrae to San Mateo, over 9 miles of Bay Trail traverse the edge of the bay shoreline.

Shoreline Park tidal water feature

Between Bayfront Park and Bayside Park, the paved Bay Trail route, at times narrow, passes in front of a series of hotels and restaurants. A few trail gaps in this area require bicyclists and pedestrians to use Bayshore Highway to get around them. The trail follows the shore around Anza Lagoon, while another branch of the trail moves across Airport Boulevard to Burlingame Lagoon. On the eastern end of Burlingame Lagoon, the trail crosses a small bridge en route to Coyote Point. Numerous pathways and trails crisscross Coyote Point. The Bay Trail route is paved, with an adjacent gravel jogging path through Coyote Point Park and Ryder Park, across the bridge, and along the shoreline of Seal Point Park.

INFORMATION

Public Transit
Call 511 or visit 511.org.

Transit & Trails
www.transitandtrails.org

Burlingame Parks & Recreation Department
www.burlingame.org
650-558-7300

California Department of Fish and Game
www.dfg.ca.gov/marine
831-649-2870
"Ask Marine"

City of San Mateo Parks and Recreation Department
www.cityofsanmateo.org
650-522-7400

Coyote Point Recreation Area
www.co.sanmateo.ca.us
650-363-4020

CuriOdyssey at Coyote Point
www.curiodyssey.org
650-342-7755

Millbrae Recreation Department
www.ci.millbrae.ca.us
650-259-2360

Oyster Point Marina/ Park
www.smharbor.com
/oysterpoint
650-952-0808

San Bruno Mountain State and County Park
www.parks.ca.gov
650-363-4020

South San Francisco Parks & Recreation Department
www.ssf.net
650-829-3800

FOSTER CITY TO BAIR ISLAND

Along this stretch of bayshore, the sights and sounds of San Francisco Bay are close by. Paved trails, parcourses, parks, and restored wetlands border planned communities, and the marshes of the Don Edwards San Francisco Bay National Wildlife Refuge extend to the south.

FOSTER CITY

Developer T. Jack Foster had a vision for a new city on the shores of San Francisco Bay. It was to

T. Jack Foster

be completely planned before the first load of concrete was poured and to be built partly on bay fill, with every home having access to water. In 1958, he bought Brewer's Island, with 4 square miles of bayshore. In the next six years, he had 14 million cubic yards of sand pumped from the bay to shape islands, peninsulas, and a sinuous 200-acre lagoon. In the process, hundreds of acres of tidal wetlands were destroyed. Many of them had been covered by lush marsh vegetation and were home to many bird species. Today, Foster City has 21 parks, over 13,000 residential units, and about 30,000 residents.

The Bay Conservation and Development Commission, as well as state and federal laws, protects remnant marshes on the bay as vital wildlife habitat. Foster City represents the 1950s version of the

Central San Mateo County shoreline

Foster City shoreline

Foster City today

dream of a planned community that had earlier inspired Venice in Los Angeles as well as diverse other development projects in this country and abroad. Along the bayside of Foster City, off Beach Park Boulevard, small marshes and mud flats exposed at low tide

are good spots for birding. Windsurfers use several nearby access ramps into the bay. A wider marsh and a parcourse border Belmont Slough. Respect the marsh as a sensitive wildlife area; keep dogs on leash.

San Mateo Bridge

Island Park

SAN MATEO BRIDGE

The 7-mile San Mateo Bridge, with its 2-mile-long, six-lane span, arches 135 feet over the bay's navigation channel, then leads east to southern Alameda County just above bay waters. In 2003, the bridge underwent a seismic retrofit to protect against earthquake damage, and the eastern span was widened to six lanes. It carries some 92,000 cars daily. This bridge was opened in 1967, replacing a two-lane bridge built in 1929. You can walk underneath the bridge, which is only a few feet above your head here. The sound and vibrations are impressive. Part of the old bridge was converted to the San Mateo County Fishing Pier—the longest pier on the bay. Unfortunately, the pier has fallen into disrepair and is now closed. From the Bay Trail, you can observe bay currents swirling around the bridge's massive footings, watch workers cleaning and painting the bridge, and in spring marvel at the swarms of barn swallows buzzing their mud nests on the bridge's underside. To the south, ducks bob on the surface while cormorants rest on the electrical towers marching across the bay.

ISLAND PARK

Island Park is a great place to relax between Foster City and Redwood Shores. Although it's next to Highway 101, the park has large lawns that are close enough to Belmont Slough to attract resting shorebirds and gulls. A parcourse starts here and swings around Oracle Parkway toward the Redwood Shores complex. A bicycle and pedestrian bridge over Highway 101 near Ralston Avenue connects downtown Belmont to the Belmont Sports Complex and the Bay Trail.

REDWOOD SHORES

This planned community, built partly on former salt ponds, is a newer and much smaller version of neighboring Foster City. It is bordered by marshes and features an industrial park, seven small parks, and a variety of single-family homes and apartment complexes. Before relocating to Vallejo, Marine World amusement park operated on this small peninsula from 1968 until 1986.

A paved trail stretches along Belmont Slough, passing by office parks and a branch of the Redwood City Library, which features inter-

Redwood Shores

active exhibits about the bay and shoreline habitat. At the tip of the peninsula, you'll find overlook platforms for views across the wetlands to the bay. Along Steinberger Slough, a gravel trail atop a levee stretches from the South Bayside System Authority Wastewater Treatment Plant, which services most of southern San Mateo County, to San Carlos Airport. This trail offers excellent views of the southeast bay and the Coast Range. Before sunset, ducks and egrets gather at a pond between the trail and the wastewater plant. At low tide, the slough transforms into a mud flat busy with feeding shorebirds.

The wildlife refuge extends to the south and offers a glimpse of what much of the South Bay once looked like. Power poles run south, providing roosts for cormorants and various birds of prey. The lone concrete building

Bridge over Belmont Slough

at the end of Radio Road was built by the General Electric Company to house a shortwave radio station during World War II. Messages sent from here reached troops throughout the Pacific.

White-Tailed Kite

This striking white-and-black marsh inhabitant (formerly known as the black-shouldered kite) hovers like a hawk and soars like a gull. It eats small rodents and insects in marshes and grasslands bordering the bay. Although this kite's population plummeted throughout its range in recent decades because of pesticide contamination and habitat loss, it appears to be making a comeback. The white-tailed kite lives mostly in California west of the Sierra, in southern Texas, and throughout Latin America.

White-tailed kite

BAIR ISLAND

Just south of Redwood Shores near the San Carlos Airport is a wetland area known as Bair Island, which is actually three islands: Inner, Middle, and Outer. The 3,000-acre wetland complex is part of the Don Edwards San Francisco Bay National Wildlife Refuge and is managed by the U.S. Fish & Wildlife Service, which is restoring over 1,400 acres at Inner Bair Island to return the area to its natural condi-

Northern Harrier

The northern harrier (marsh hawk) is common throughout the bay. It glides over marshes with wings in an open "V" as it searches for rodents. The white rump patch is distinctive in both sexes. Adult males are gray and white with a barred tail. Females are a dark brown.

Northern harrier

tion of tidal wetlands. Part of the restoration involves raising the level of the island so that when tidal action is reintroduced, the area will quickly become a more natural vegetated marsh. To fill the area for habitat restoration, builders are using clean dredge materials from the bay, with some material coming from the Port of Redwood City's channel. This "beneficial reuse" of dredge materials supports the continuing maritime commerce that is an important element of Redwood City's and the region's economy. A portion of the Bay Trail (including a bicycle and pedestrian bridge to Inner Bair Island, observation platforms, and shoreline paths) will be constructed as part of the restoration.

GETTING AROUND

The Bay Trail is paved from the mouth of Marina Lagoon to the San Mateo Bridge, then all the way around Foster City. Cross the bridge near Oracle to continue into Redwood Shores along a paved trail adjacent to Belmont

Western Meadowlark

Most might associate the flowing, melodious song of the meadowlark with grasslands. On warm days, these small birds with striking yellow breasts, black collars, and cheering songs perch atop fence posts or marsh grasses along the entire bay.

Western meadowlark

Slough. Follow the paved trail near the tip of the peninsula through a residential area with observation platforms. From the sewage treatment plant (at end of Radio Road), a gravel trail continues along Steinberger Slough to the San Car-los Airport, where the trail ends. For a shorter route, a pathway by-passes Redwood Shores and goes directly from Marine Parkway to Redwood Shores Parkway via Twin Dolphin Drive. Use streets to access the pathway adjacent to Highway 101 from the terminus of Skyway Road. Bair Island remains closed to the public as the restoration and trail construction work continues.

Mud Flat Viewing

If you work your way toward the bayshore during low tide, moving past brass buttons, pickleweed, and finally cordgrass, you'll find yourself at the edge of a glistening mud flat. What at first might appear as an odoriferous wasteland is actually one of the richest and most ecologically important habitats in the bay. In 1 cubic inch of tideland mud, more than 40,000 organisms can live—from minute phytoplankton, diatoms, bacteria, and zooplankton to more visible worms, snails, shrimp, mussels, clams, and crabs. Countless shorebird species probe and peck for food at low tide in the mud flats. When the tide moves back in, so do rays, flounder, young bass, crabs, diving ducks, and cormorants, also coming to feed. In summer, an abundance of sea lettuce (a common algae) and, occasionally, eelgrass gives the mud flats a bright green sheen. Most mud flat species are burrowers, so inspect the surface. In summer and fall, you may notice large jelly masses, which protect the eggs of lugworms. These worms make the small coils of sand you may see atop the mud. The darker sand mounds, which look like miniature volcanoes, are entrances to the burrows of pink ghost shrimp. As the shrimp strain mud for bacteria and other food, they deposit filtered sand on the surface.

NOTE: Never walk out onto a mud flat. This will harm mud flat organisms and get you stuck! Keep to the trails.

Ghost shrimp
Callianassa californiensis

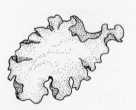

Sea lettuce
Ulva spp.

Boring clam (shell)
Zirfaea pilsbryi

Native oyster
Ostrea lurida

Mud shrimp
Upogebia pugettensis

Mud flat crab
Hemigrapsus oregonensis

PORT OF REDWOOD CITY TO DON EDWARDS SAN FRANCISCO BAY NATIONAL WILDLIFE REFUGE

Lessons in history, salt production, wetland restoration, and the reclamation of former landfill sites are available between the Port of Redwood City and Ravenswood Open Space Preserve as the nearshore explorer takes in the vast marshland of the Don Edwards San Francisco Bay National Wildlife Refuge.

Redwood City as a lumber port in 1850s

Port of Redwood City

Pacific Shores Center

PORT OF REDWOOD CITY

🚻 ♿ 🐟 ⛵ 👫 🚴

Redwood City grew up around a lumber port. In the 1850s, the shores of Redwood Creek (near today's modern port) were lined with docks stacked with wood products destined for San Francisco and the Sacramento region. By the mid-1860s, a typical week saw 50,000 board feet of lumber, some 2 million shingles, 100,000 fence posts, and hundreds of cords of firewood loaded onto ships here. Also nearby, the

McLeod Company was busy building oceangoing schooners averaging 100 feet in length with masts 85 feet high.

The Port of Redwood City, along the only deep-water channel in southern San Francisco Bay, is located between Redwood Creek and Seaport Boulevard and is used for bulk maritime shipping, recreational boating, and commercial operations. This is a pleasant area to rest and watch boat traffic along a section of the Bay Trail. At the tip of Seaport Boulevard adjacent

to Westpoint Slough, the Pacific Shores Center office complex includes a 3-mile extension of the Bay Trail and restored wetlands. The new Westpoint Marina is located adjacent to the office park. The former marsh area between the Pacific Shores Center and Highway 101 to the south was used by Cargill to manufacture salt and is under consideration for development, yet efforts are under way to save the remaining salt ponds from development and restore them to wetlands.

BEDWELL BAYFRONT PARK

🚻 🦆 ♿ 👫 🚴

This former landfill is now a neatly contoured park with a 2-mile loop trail. The entrance is at the bayward end of Marsh Road near Haven Avenue and Bayfront Ex-

Bedwell Bayfront Park's Great Spirit Path

pressway. Crisscrossing the park is the Great Spirit Path, a series of rock clusters inspired by Native American pictographs (look for a free guide brochure in the parking area). Marsh hawks and meadowlarks work the grasslands here and perch atop the 5-foot white pipes used for checking methane gas leaks. From the park's top knoll, a 360-degree view awaits willing hikers. To the north and south are former salt ponds. Bayward, Greco Island's marshes are part of the refuge. Between Bayfront Park and Greco Island are a decommissioned sewage treatment plant and the City of Menlo Park Methane Recovery Plant. Methane is extracted from the former dump through an underground network of pipes and used to generate elec-

tricity that is then sold to Pacific Gas and Electric Company.

DON EDWARDS SAN FRANCISCO BAY NATIONAL WILDLIFE REFUGE

The Don Edwards San Francisco Bay National Wildlife Refuge was the first urban national wildlife refuge established in the United States. It encompasses over 30,000 acres of bay sloughs, salt ponds, marshes, mud flats, vernal pools, open water, and uplands circling the South Bay from Redwood City's Bair Island to Coyote Hills in Fremont. The refuge is managed by the U.S. Fish & Wildlife Service. In southern San Mateo County, the refuge includes Greco Island, the Ravenswood Unit, and Bair Island.

On the north side of Dumbarton Bridge is the Ravenswood Unit of the refuge (no dogs). A levee trail extends beneath high-voltage transmission towers into a barren landscape of earthen banks and muddy holes. A little farther out, however, you'll come upon more pleasant scenery as the trail loops around a salt pond flanked by open bay and marsh. The Ravenswood Unit and Ponds A5–A8 in Santa Clara County are accessible to waterfowl hunters by foot. All other waterfowl hunting areas require the use of boats. During the hunting season, trails here are closed to all visitors except hunters and their hunting dogs. The hunting season is always in the fall and early winter, but it can vary by a few weeks from year to year.

Bair Island is actually composed of three islands

Caspian tern

Check with the refuge for exact dates of closure.

On the south side of the Dumbarton Bridge is the Ravenswood Open Space Preserve. This 1.4-mile out-and-back trail includes wayside exhibits, observation decks, benches, and restroom facilities. The trail offers prime views of the San Francisco Bay and a first-hand look at habitat restoration of a former salt pond. Several islands have been created for birds to nest or to loaf, making this preserve an ideal location for viewing waterbirds.

Waterfowl Hunting in the Refuge

Waterfowl hunting is generally from mid-October to the end of January. Limits and seasons are determined by the California Department of Fish and Game. Ducks typically harvested are shovelers, mallards, gadwalls, scaup, and pintails. There are only two trails in the refuge that are closed during the hunting season—the Ravenswood Unit, north of the Dumbarton Bridge, and a portion of the Mallard Slough Trail near the Environmental Education Center in Alviso. In other locations,

Trains

In the 1850s, several companies were organized, and reorganized, to connect San Francisco by railway with San Jose, which was then the state capital. Construction of a peninsula railroad line began in May 1861, and two years later the first train steamed south from San Francisco via Daly City to Mayfield (today's Palo Alto). From Mayfield, passengers rode stagecoaches to San Jose. The rail line reached San Jose in 1864. In 1907, the Bayshore Cutoff was completed near Point San Bruno, shortening travel time by allowing trains to bypass Daly City and many curves.

such as the Moffett Field Trail, hunters are required to hunt inside blinds. All hunting areas near trails are signed, alerting trail users of this activity.

GETTING AROUND

From Redwood Shores, use the pathway at the terminus of Skyway Road and surface streets to reach Seaport Boulevard and the Port of Redwood City. The Bay Trail is not

51

complete around the San Carlos Airport, and Bair Island remains closed to the public as the restoration and trail construction work continues. Between the port and Bayfront Park, the use of streets is required. A dirt trail circles Bayfront Park, while the Bay Trail between the Dumbarton Bridge and Ravenswood Pier is paved and well-signed. A 1.4-mile out-and-back gravel section of the Bay Trail continues south from the bridge into the Ravenswood Open Space Preserve. The Bay Trail crosses the Dumbarton Bridge on a walking and biking path separate from traffic all the way to Newark.

INFORMATION

Public Transit
Call 511 or visit 511.org.

Transit & Trails
www.transitandtrails.org

Bedwell Bayfront Park
www.menlopark.org
650-330-2223

Don Edwards San Francisco Bay National Wildlife Refuge
www.fws.gov/desfbay
510-792-0222

Foster City Parks & Recreation Department
www.fostercity.org
650-286-3380

Port of Redwood City
www.redwoodcityport.com
650-306-4150

Redwood City Parks & Recreation Department
www.redwoodcity.org/parks
650-780-7250

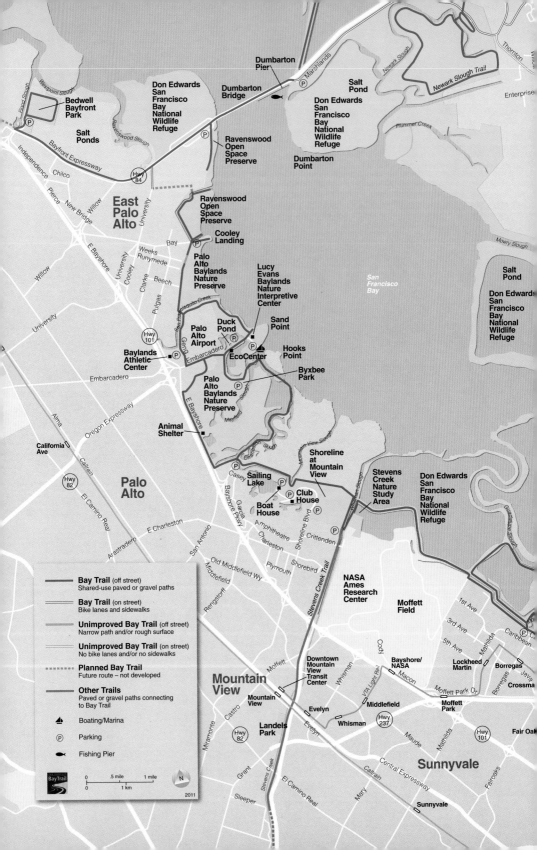

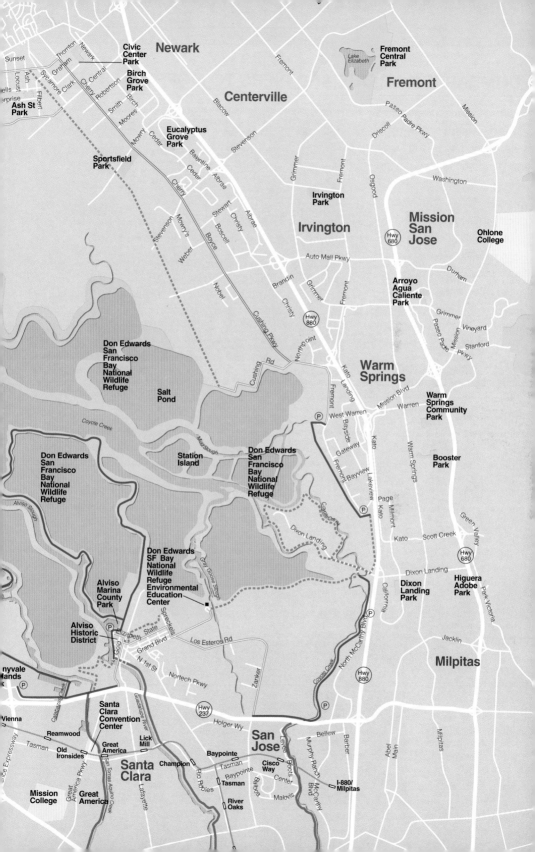

DUMBARTON BRIDGE AND PIERS TO MOFFETT FIELD

At the Dumbarton Bridge, between Ravenswood Point on the western shore and Dumbarton Point to the east, the bay constricts to a width of approximately 1 mile before widening again to the south. Along this portion of the bay's western shoreline, six creeks and four sloughs enrich the marshes and mud flats, all vital habitat for resident and migratory wildlife. Here you can hike, fish from piers, or watch the birds. You can also play golf, sail, and attend open-air concerts.

Looking northeast toward Dumbarton Bridge with Cooley Landing and the Ravenswood Open Space Preserve in the foreground

DUMBARTON BRIDGE AND PIERS

The original Dumbarton Bridge, built in 1927, was the first automobile bridge to span the bay. Today's bridge was built alongside the original bridge in 1982, with a bicycle/pedestrian path on the south side. In 1985, the original bridge was demolished and its approaches were converted to fishing piers: Ravenswood Pier on the west shore, Dumbarton Pier on the east shore. Ravenswood Pier, closed for many years due to safety concerns, was removed as part of a more recent seismic upgrade to the bridge. The Dumbarton Fishing Pier is only open when the gates to the Don Edwards San Francisco Bay National Wildlife Refuge are open.

Hours are: March–Sept, 7 a.m. to 8 p.m.; Oct.–Feb., 7 a.m. to 6 p.m. Cross the bridge to Newark, and then turn right onto Marshlands Road. From the end of Dumbarton Pier, you can see most of the South Bay and get a fine view of the Cargill Salt ponds at Newark. But if you're moving south on the west shore of the bay, you can continue from here to the Ravenswood Open Space Preserve and Palo Alto Baylands.

DUMBARTON CUTOFF

Just south of the Dumbarton Bridge, remnants of Southern Pacific's Dumbarton Cutoff train bridge span the bay. The cutoff was built between 1908 and 1909, the first bridge across the bay. It opened for service in 1910. The structure you see is the original, but the western section was set on fire by vandals after it closed. This bridge carried six to eight freight trains daily until May 1982, when the Port of San Francisco lost out to the Port of Oakland as the dominant bay port and the need for the bridge diminished. The swing span was welded open to allow boat passage. In 1993, the San Mateo County Transit District bought the bridge. The train line may be revived in the future as part of the Dumbarton Rail Corridor Project, which proposes a 21-mile commuter rail connection between Redwood City and Union City.

Dumbarton Bridge pathway

HETCH HETCHY WATER PIPES

Also visible south of the Dumbarton Bridge is the Hetch Hetchy aqueduct. Managed by the San Francisco Public Utilities Commission, these pipelines carry water from the Hetch Hetchy Reservoir in Yosemite to San Francisco and the peninsula, a distance of 167 miles. The system, completed in 1934, is a gravity-driven network of dams, reservoirs, tunnels, aqueducts, and pipelines that serves over 2.4 million residential, commercial, and industrial customers in the Bay Area. In 2010, construction began on a new tunnel under the bay to carry the aqueduct flow.

RAVENSWOOD OPEN SPACE PRESERVE

The Ravenswood Open Space Preserve consists of 370 acres of leveed marsh, on both sides of the Dumbarton Cutoff, managed by the U.S. Fish & Wildlife Service and the Midpeninsula Regional Open Space District. In the preserve's northern portion, accessible from the parking area at the western end of the Dumbarton Bridge, a 0.7-mile gravel levee trail runs between

Sharing the Bay: Can Birds and Trail Users Coexist?

Studies conducted by Dr. Lynne Trulio of San Jose State University and Jana Sokale, environmental consultant, investigate whether people using trails at the edge of the San Francisco Bay are disturbing birds that depend on the bay for survival. Birds face

Scientists studying shorebirds

many challenges, from bay pollution to climate change; trail use could be another stressor in birds' lives. Of concern are migratory shorebirds and waterfowl that spend the winter foraging in ponds and tidal wetlands located adjacent to trails. Also under study is the snowy plover, a threatened shorebird that nests in dry ponds and needs protection during the sensitive breeding season. Do trail users scare birds away from their foraging or nesting site—or are birds tolerant of trail use? The answers to such questions are likely to vary by species and situation. In addition to studies of birds, the researchers and their field team also collect data on what people think about their bayside trail experiences. Information gathered about the birds and about the perspective of trail users gives managers tools to design bayside trails that can protect birds from trail use disturbances while allowing people the opportunity to enjoy the beauty of the San Francisco Bay.

the bay and a restored pond with shorebird nesting islands and a dry nesting habitat for threatened snowy plovers. This restored pond is part of the South Bay Salt Pond Restoration Project (see p. 170). Two viewing platforms provide elevated vantage points for birdwatching. The preserve's southern portion is a former salt pond that's been restored to a salt marsh. It has a parking area, 1.5-mile trail, and two observation platforms with views of Palo Alto Baylands Nature Preserve's vast marshland to the south, Cooley Landing, the East Palo Alto Baylands, the Dumbarton Cutoff, and the southeast bay. Small planes drone overhead as they lift off from the Palo Alto airport to the immediate south. Enormous transmission towers high-step across the preserve north and south after detouring to a substation on Bay Road. Although the preserve's southern part is hemmed in by railroad tracks, housing, and a confusion of industrial uses, its vibrant, bird-filled marsh is a joy to behold. Park at the end of Bay Road.

Ravenswood Open Space Preserve

COOLEY LANDING

Cooley Landing, a 9-acre former landfill on the shoreline's edge, is a waterfront nature park, complete with trails, open space, and picnic areas. Surrounded on three sides by water, Cooley Landing is East Palo Alto's first access to the open waters of San Francisco Bay. For many years, this was the place where trash and debris were dumped, and in some cases burned. A former boat repair shop and remnants of a historic dredge vessel will become part of the hands-on educational programming at Cooley Landing. Future plans include a community and education center, viewing platforms, and interpretive displays.

PALO ALTO BAYLANDS NATURE PRESERVE

In the 1960s, local activists and the city of Palo Alto preserved 1,400 acres of neglected and abused salt marsh. In subsequent years, more wetlands were revitalized and restored. Today, the Baylands encompasses some 1,940 acres, including a duck pond, 15 miles of scenic trails, and a seasonal freshwater marsh fed by treated wastewater. Many consider this area to be one of the best bird-watching destinations on the West Coast. The marshlands are host to a sizable local population of shorebirds and serve as an important migratory stopover on the Pacific Flyway.

Collecting Brine Shrimp

The bay's tiny brine shrimp, known to many children as the "sea monkeys" in mail order kits, occur naturally from Saskatchewan, Canada, southward throughout western North America. The minute eggs of the half-inch shrimp are transported by winds and birds and can lie dormant for years until covered with saltwater. They hatch within 18 hours to two days, depending on water temperature. About three weeks after hatching, brine larvae quickly grow into adult shrimp, a favorite food of migrating and resident shorebirds and ducks. About 1 million pounds of brine shrimp are collected commercially in active and former salt ponds around San Francisco Bay, where shallow, warm waters and high salt concentrations create optimal conditions for shrimp production. Two South Bay companies with specially equipped boats skim the shrimp from the upper layers of salt ponds. Frozen shrimp are sold internationally as aquarium fish food; live shrimp are sold for science research projects and fish food.

Brine shrimp

Faubermeister Marsh in Palo Alto

Ravenswood, a Short-Lived Town

State House, San Jose, 1849

During the Gold Rush years of 1849–50, San Francisco was California's unchallenged civic and commercial center, but San Jose was the state's capital. Stagecoach service started between the two cities in 1849, and steam boats maintained regular service. At Ravenswood Point, travelers could switch from coach to steamer, or the other way around, depending upon weather and road conditions. This was one of the few sites along the peninsula where dry land was accessible from deep water. A long wharf was built, and the town of Ravenswood began to grow. In the 1850s, however, after a prominent citizen absconded with the municipal funds, Ravenswood went into sharp decline. Its demise was expedited by the rise of Redwood City and its port to the immediate north. Today, not one building, nor even a wharf piling, remains. The old town site is now within the city of East Palo Alto.

Lucy Evans Baylands Nature Interpretive Center

Boardwalk toward open water in the baylands

Dogs are permitted on leash, unless posted in special nesting areas. The preserve extends inland past Byxbee Landfill Park to East Bayshore and a 15-acre seasonal freshwater marsh dedicated to Emily Renzel, an activist who fought for its revival as a member of the city council and of the San Francisco Bay Conservation and Development Commission. The marsh was created with the aid of the State Coastal Conservancy and is one of several on the bay to use treated wastewater to enhance wildlife habitat. The runoff from the marsh flows into Matadero Creek, which empties into the bay. In summer, this wetland is allowed to dry out to minimize mosquito problems, bird diseases such as avian botulism, and excessive vegetative growth.

Lucy Evans Baylands Nature Interpretive Center

♿ 🚶

Opened in 1969, this unique, many-sided building was the first interpretive center on the bay. It stands on pillars above pickleweed at the end of Embarcadero Road and is a good place to begin a visit to the Baylands. The Lucy Evans Baylands Interpretive Center has a host of interesting interactive educational displays that inspire people of all ages to learn more about wetland ecology. The dis-

Ring-Necked Pheasant

This native of Georgia, near the River Colchis in Asia, was introduced throughout the United States in the 19th century as a game bird. It is now common around farmlands and in the upper zones of bay marshes. The male has brilliant colors and a boisterous "kork-kok" call. The Palo Alto Baylands are home to a healthy population of this exotic species: the flood control ponds north of the interpretive center were part of a pheasant farm until the 1960s.

Ring-necked pheasant

Western Sandpipers

The salt ponds, wildlife ponds, tidal flats, marshes, and seasonal wetlands of San Francisco Bay provide important habitat for over a million resident and migrant shorebirds each year. The most abundant species in the bay is the western sandpiper, which arrives here each autumn from breeding grounds in the Russian and Alaskan tundra. Many sandpipers winter in Panama, and some 100,000 winter on the bay. Western sandpipers are precision flyers. Flocks lift off together from the mud flats to perform flawless patterns, and then settle again to search for food. Biologists are only beginning to learn about these "peeps." In one study, 110 were captured in mist nets in the South Bay, tagged with tiny radio receivers, and tracked for five weeks as far as the Copper River Delta in Alaska. While in the South Bay, these small birds were found to stay within an area as small as 1.4 square miles. In migrating north along the coast, some have been known to fly 1,200 miles in 24 hours.

Western sandpiper

plays offer information about bat rays and tide cycles and allow visitors to listen to recordings of bird calls from several shorebirds that call the baylands their home. A self-service Open Ecology laboratory provides microscopes, mounted bird specimens, educational leaflets, guide booklets, and other tools to visitors who wish to explore what's around. A .2-mile boardwalk extends from the center over the salt marsh to the edge of the bay. Nature walks and programs on ecology and natural history are presented for all age groups and are offered on weekends throughout the year. Lucy Evans, for whom the center is named, was a historian, conservationist, and teacher who worked hard to save Palo Alto's baylands, first as a private citizen and then as a member of the Palo Alto City Council. South of the center, the former marina (now silted-in) and an area of diked-off baylands have been restored to marshland.

Byxbee Park sculptures

Palo Alto Baylands EcoCenter

In partnership with the city of Palo Alto, Environmental Volunteers, Inc. has transformed the boat-shaped former Sea Scouts building into an environmental education center. Rehabilitated in 2012, the EcoCenter incorporates "green building" elements within the context of historic preservation and provides hands-on learning about environmental stewardship for visitors of all ages.

Byxbee Park

This park has taken shape atop the eastern portion of Palo Alto's landfill, next to a recycling center and the regional water quality control plant. A 34-acre portion of the

park opened in 1991, with some interesting site sculptures. The landfill's western section is still active, though it will soon be capped and Byxbee Park will be expanded to 146 acres. The park section completed thus far—a cooperative effort by the city, landscape architects George Hargreaves Associates, and artists Peter Richard and

Red-Winged Blackbird

The boisterous spring display of male red-winged blackbirds, with their shining red epaulets and throaty "kong-ka-ree" and "o-ka-lee-onk," signals that freshwater is near. On the south side of Byxbee Park, freshwater creeks join in Mayfield Slough. The tule reed and cattail here provide excellent blackbird nesting habitat.

Red-winged blackbird

Michael Oppenheimer—features artwork designed to emphasize the transition from artificial and controlled environments to natural and self-regulating ones. *Chevrons*, a sculpture made from concrete highway barriers, is visible to pilots landing at the Palo Alto airport. *Pole Field*, a collection of poles of varying heights, symbolizes the transition from park to marshland. Those nearest the park are in rows, while those closer to the marsh appear to be more random. *Hillocks* are grassy mounds atop the park's higher points. They are meant to suggest Ohlone Indian shell mounds while adding topography and creating micro-habitats for wildlife. *Keyhole* provides a clue to what lies below: methane from the buried garbage burns off through a vertical pipe set in white gravel.

Bay Access Ramp

A pier and ramp allow windsurfers and hand-carried boats to launch in the channel to the former yacht harbor. This launch site will become part of the Bay Area Water

Palo Alto Baylands boat ramp

Trail system. For more information, see p. 7.

Palo Alto Regional Water Quality Control Plant

The Regional Water Quality Control Plant is owned and operated by the city of Palo Alto and serves the communities of Los Altos, Los Altos Hills, Mountain View, Palo Alto, Stanford University, and the East Palo Alto Sanitary District. The plant is an advanced treatment facility that uses gravity settling, biological treatment with microorganisms, and dual media filtration to remove unwanted organic materials and toxins from the approximately 22 million gallons a day of wastewater generated by the service area's 220,000 residents. The plant's treated effluent meets all of the stringent requirements for discharge to the sensitive South San Francisco Bay. Reducing the amount of treated wastewater discharged into the South Bay decreases the impacts on saltwater marshes and helps preserve saltwater and tidal marshland habitats. When treated wastewater is discharged

into South Bay marshes, it can decrease the salinity and alter the plant communities that grow there. Using treated water for irrigation helps preserve Palo Alto's saltwater marshlands, the sensitive habitat of two endangered species, the California clapper rail and the salt marsh harvest mouse.

Duck Pond

The Baylands' duck pond was originally a saltwater swimming pool constructed in the 1930s. Due to issues with bird guano, the area was turned into a refuge for waterfowl. Several species of gulls, ducks, and geese can be seen at the duck pond. Feeding wildlife is strongly discouraged as it disrupts

Palo Alto Baylands Duck Pond

migration, spreads disease, and causes overcrowding and competition.

SHORELINE AT MOUNTAIN VIEW

"Shoreline," as it is commonly called, is a well-groomed 750-acre waterfront park that provides over 10 miles of paved and unpaved trails, a sailing lake, a lakeside café, an 18-hole golf course, and Michaels at Shoreline restaurant, all beside sloughs and marshes alive with shorebirds and waterfowl. Lawns and open hillsides around the lake are perfect for picnicking, and a small playground is a great location for kids to explore. While enjoying the trails alongside marshes, you will pass locations with interpretive signs, including

Shoreline at Mountain View

Mountain View tidal marsh

Charleston Slough and the historic Rengstorff House. Kite-flying is also a popular activity in the designated area near the entrance to Shoreline.

Mountain View and Stevens Creek Tidal Marshes

Two creeks enter the bay at Shoreline at Mountain View—Permanente and Stevens creeks. The tide brings saltwater into these creeks, and salt marshes line their banks. Since tidal action was restored in 1983 to Mountain View Marsh, the marsh has reshaped itself, and pickleweed has grown in its mud flats. Cordgrass, which grows more slowly than pickleweed, has taken hold with the help of planting programs. At Stevens Creek Marsh, a culvert system was installed to help increase tidal flow, and more cordgrass was planted. Hundreds of birds now feed on the mud flats here. You can watch from numerous benches. To the southeast are the Stevens Creek Shoreline Nature Study Area, owned by the Midpeninsula Regional Open Space District, and Moffett Field. The Stevens Creek Trail, which links downtown Mountain View to the bay, extends south from the Bay Trail, crossing

beneath Highway 101. The trail continues over Central Expressway, under El Camino Real, and extends to Sleeper Avenue. Since the winter of 2012, the Stevens Creek Trail has extended over Highway 85 to Dale/Heatherstone Avenue.

Charleston Slough

Popular with bird watchers, Charleston Slough is a habitat dotted with tiny islands and edged with pickleweed. Over 130 different bird species have been seen in the course of a year along the slough, which snakes north from the foot of San Antonio Road and ends at a levee that cuts it off from the bay. Water from the bay flows in through a tidal gate, is pumped into the lake, and then flows out into Permanente Creek and back to the bay. Ducks, terns, and hundreds of white pelicans frequent these shallow waters, as well as Palo Alto's marshy flood control basin to the north. Look for the northern shoveler, a duck with a spoonlike bill, dark head, white belly, and rust-striped wings. When feeding, these ducks often form a tight clump, paddling round and round in a circle, heads underwater. Great flocks of migrating ducks arrive in the fall

en route to wintering grounds to the south. In summer, white pelicans and terns feed in open water, while hundreds of avocets breed and raise young along the banks of the slough.

Charleston Slough

Northern shoveler

Rengstorff House

Permanente Creek

Common Pickleweed

Pickleweed, also known as glasswort, is abundant along the edges of salt marshes and grows throughout coastal California. Unlike cordgrass and salt grass, pickleweed does not have special salt-excreting glands. It concentrates salt in its end segments (two modified leaves, fused together around a stem) until they turn red, dry up, and fall off. Its genus name, *Salicornia*, is derived from Greek and means "salt-horn," referring to the plant's salt-concentrating abilities. Break a green stem open, and you'll find salty juices. Flower-bearing scales are visible from April through September. In late summer and fall, dodder, a spidery, bright orange parasitic plant, grows atop pickleweed, highlighting sections of the shoreline.

Common pickleweed

Rengstorff House

The restored Rengstorff House is one of the finest examples of Victorian Italianate architecture remaining on the West Coast. Built by Henry Rengstorff in 1876, the house stood along Stierlin Road (now Shoreline Boulevard) until it was moved to Shoreline Park in 1980. Rengstorff was a poor German immigrant who started out as a farm laborer and eventually acquired six farms. He built this fine home for his wife and seven children. Made of Douglas fir and shingled with redwood, the home has 15 rooms, four marble fireplaces, and a staircase railed with hand-turned spindles. The hip roof, widow's walk, and front portico were popular features in

the 1800s. Several docent-guided tours are offered weekly; call for the tour schedule. The house is also a great location for private events, including weddings, business meetings, and other special events.

Meadowlands

Believe it or not, the softly undulating hills of this upland area are made of household refuse. In 1968, the city of Mountain View bought a 500-acre shoreline site and prepared a series of landfill cells lined with clay to prevent the leaching of pollutants. San Francisco then paid for the privilege of disposing its refuse into these cells for the next 13 years. Mountain View also installed a gas

Cordgrass

One of the tallest salt marsh plants, with long, durable leaves, cordgrass can stand 4 feet in low zones of coastal California marshes. Between July and November, it produces a 6-inch spike with dense seed heads. Cordgrass needs to be inundated by saltwater daily. It has adapted to the harsh salt marsh habitat: specialized glands eject excess salt from its system, and specialized leaves help transport oxygen to its waterlogged roots. Both cordgrass and pickleweed are visible from the trails within Shoreline.

Cordgrass

recovery system to extract landfill gas, which includes methane, produced from the decay of organic wastes in refuse. The city sells the gas to Google, which generates electricity to power up to three of their buildings. By 1983, Mountain View closed the Meadowlands section of the landfill, capped the cells, began landscaping, and started restoring nearby wetlands. Today, the only hint of landfill in Shoreline's protective green veneer is a small hidden flare station, which burns off excess gas not utilized by Google.

"Some of our landfills are now richer in resources than some of our mines."

DENIS HAYES, 1989

Landfills

Ever since towns began springing up around the bay in the 1850s, the seemingly useless muddy zone between them and the water has been visited by an endless stream of vehicles hauling refuse, debris, and soil to be dumped near the bay. Today, countless landfills have been capped with clay and vegetative soil along the entire bayshore per regulatory requirements. Some are still active landfills, while others sit idle, but some have been capped and converted into parks such as Shoreline. Other local landfills include Candlestick Point State Recreation Area in San Francisco, Sunnyvale Landfill, Oyster Bay Regional Shoreline in San Leandro, San Mateo's Shoreline Park, Bayfront Park in Menlo Park, Byxbee Park in Palo Alto, Berkeley's North Waterfront Park, and the West County Landfill in Richmond.

Shoreline Golf Links

Shoreline Golf Links is an 18-hole, championship-level golf course. Designed by Robert Trent Jones II and Associates and constructed in 1982–83, the course is nestled within Shoreline at Mountain View. The links offer some excellent vistas of coastal mountains and San Francisco Bay, particularly on holes 7 through 12.

Michaels at Shoreline

Adjacent to the golf course pro shop, Michaels at Shoreline serves as the clubhouse for the golf links and offers patio dining and refreshments daily. Outdoor seating overlooks the golf course and ponds. Michaels is also a full service banquet facility for special occasions and events.

Shoreline Lake Aquatic Center and Café

Shoreline's 50-acre man-made salt lake attracts small-craft sailors, paddle boat enthusiasts, and windsurfers. Whether you're looking for a day on the lake paddling and sailing or you just want to enjoy a view with your meal, head to the Shoreline Lake Aquatic Center and Café.

Kite-Flying

Shoreline, with its large expanse of open space and favorable

Shoreline's sailing lake

California Ground Squirrels

These native squirrels are inordinately common in developed parks around the bayshore. Why? They are masters of disturbed short-grass habitats. No matter how beautiful a park is, in the world of bayshore ecology, it is a disturbed habitat. Most important to the squirrels, grasses are kept low in many parks, allowing them a clear view of approaching trouble. They are colonial nesters (i.e., they live in colonies) and chirp in loud alarm to warn others around active nests. Squirrels play an important role at Shoreline because they create burrows that the burrowing owls utilize as habitat. These two species do not compete for burrows; rather, the owls use vacant burrows left behind by squirrels.

wind conditions, is an ideal location for flying all kinds of kites, from basic models to the more advanced stunt kites. The designated kite-flying area is located near the main entrance. Due to the nearby Palo Alto and Moffett Field airports, the air space above Shoreline is regulated by various governmental agencies. Flying kites unsafely or too high is prohibited under state and federal regulations.

Dog Park

Although dogs are not permitted within Shoreline at Mountain View, there is a dog park located just outside the entrance gates. The dog park, approximately two-thirds of an acre, is open every day from 6 a.m. until half an hour past sunset. The park is designed to provide separate fenced open areas for both small and large dogs, along with a shade structure. Animals may run off-leash while inside the park; however, they are required to be leashed while going to and from the parking area. Park amenities include

Stevens Creek Trail over Caltrain tracks

drinking fountains, animal waste bags, trash receptacles, a disabled-accessible restroom, and seating benches. See the "References/Resources" section for a list of dog parks along other sections of the Bay Trail.

MOUNTAIN VIEW TRAILS

Shoreline at Mountain View trails extend a total of approximately 10 miles from the Palo Alto border

and continue to the south, where the trail system connects to the Stevens Creek Trail. The Stevens Creek Trail extends south from Shoreline for approximately 5 miles to the Dale/Heatherstone access point. Stevens Creek Trail is a paved all-weather pathway and contains six undercrossings; five pedestrian bridges; a major quarter-mile overcrossing structure that spans Central Expressway, Evelyn Avenue, light rail, and the Caltrain tracks; and a 350-foot pedestrian/bicycle overpass spanning Highway 237. A new overcrossing takes the trail from Sleeper Avenue over Highway 85 to the Dale/Heatherstone access point.

The trail passes through woodlands, tidal marshes, and city neighborhood parks. In addition to offering a unique creekside experience to urban residents and workers, Stevens Creek Trail provides easy connections to major bus routes, Caltrain, and light rail, which makes it ideal for bicycle commuting and connecting to the city's North Bayshore businesses. Dogs are allowed on leash on the Stevens Creek Trail, but they're

Burrowing Owls

The burrowing owl is the only owl species that lives underground and is active during the day. About 9 inches tall, brown, and long-legged, it makes its home in the burrows of ground squirrels. Look for owls standing at their front doors or atop fence posts along the shoreline trail to Stevens Creek. Burrowing owls have been monitored for years within Shoreline at Mountain View. In 1998, the city formally implemented the first of two burrowing owl management plans to ensure the safety and success of this "species of special concern." The city also plans to implement a new burrowing owl preservation plan in order to increase the population. Currently, a part-time burrowing owl specialist monitors the birds, improves their habitat, and evaluates maintenance projects to make sure these projects limit human impacts on the owls according to state and federal regulations.

Burrowing owl

"When we try to pick out anything by itself we find it hitched to everything in the Universe."

JOHN MUIR, 1911

Stevens Creek Shoreline Nature Study Area

not allowed in Shoreline at Mountain View. Parking is available at the Crittenden Lane, La Avenida, Whisman, Landels, and Yuba Drive trailheads. The trail is open from 6 a.m. to half an hour after sunset.

The Permanente Creek Trail access point can also be accessed next to Vista Slope within Shoreline at Mountain View. This trail now reaches from Shoreline to the south side of Old Middlefield Way, following construction of a pedestrian/bicycle bridge over Highway 101 and a tunnel under Old Middlefield Way, which was completed in the spring of 2012.

STEVENS CREEK SHORELINE NATURE STUDY AREA

Cross Stevens Creek on one of two bridges, and you'll be in the Stevens Creek Shoreline Nature Study Area, managed by the Midpeninsula Regional Open Space District and set against the backdrop of Moffett Field. As you move bayward on the levee trail through this 55-acre property, you'll see a wide variety of shorebirds and waterfowl, such as black-necked stilts, mallards, snowy and great egrets, great blue herons, cormorants, and pintails.

MOFFETT FIELD

This shoreline airfield located between Mountain View and Sunnyvale, known as Moffett Field,

has been here since 1933. Most nearby residents and visitors recognize the three gigantic hangars on the site. Hangar One, one of the world's largest freestanding structures, covers over 8 acres and was built for the construction of the airship USS *Macon* in 1933 (now resting on the ocean floor off Monterey Bay); the other two hangars were constructed for blimps in the early 1940s. Functioning as a joint civil-military airfield for many years, Moffett Field was formerly a U.S. Navy facility that's now owned and operated by the National Aeronautics and Space Administration (NASA) Ames Research Center. The property also includes expansive marshes and habitat for shorebirds and waterfowl.

The sale and conversion of Cargill's salt ponds and levees, part of the South Bay Salt Pond Restoration Project (see p. 170), initiated the completion of a 2.4-mile gap in the Bay Trail. In September 2010, after many years of work, bicyclists and pedestrians were allowed access along the levee behind Moffett Field, which links Sunnyvale Baylands and Shoreline at Moun-

tain View. Completion of this gap opened a 26-mile continuous stretch of Bay Trail between East Palo Alto and San Jose. The section of the trail behind Moffett Field is managed by the U.S. Fish & Wildlife Service as part of the Don Edwards San Francisco Bay National Wildlife Refuge, and no dogs are allowed on the refuge. Seasonal waterfowl hunting is permitted. See pp. 50–51 for more information about hunting along the shoreline.

GETTING AROUND

From the Ravenswood Pier parking lot, a gravel levee trail moves south into the Ravenswood Open Space Preserve for 0.7 miles along restored wetlands; it terminates at an observation platform. The Bay Trail route goes west on Bayfront Expressway. To reach the southern portion of Ravenswood Open Space Preserve, continue on streets until the end of Bay Street. From here, the Bay Trail runs through the southern portion of the preserve for 1.5 miles on dirt levee trails and extends out to the bay at Cooley Landing. The Bay Trail continues south along levees to the Palo Alto Baylands,

Bay Trail behind Moffett Field

the Lucy Evans Baylands Nature Interpretive Center, Byxbee Park, and miles of dirt trails. One Bay Trail route runs along the bay to Charleston Slough and Shoreline at Mountain View. The other route runs along the shoulder of East Bayshore Road for about 1.5 miles, then turns bayward on a paved bike path at Charleston Slough and continues through Shoreline at Mountain View. At the junction of the Stevens Creek Trail, the Bay Trail continues south along the gravel levee adjacent to Moffett Field to Sunnyvale Baylands Park. No dogs are allowed in Shoreline at Mountain View, on the trail behind Moffett Field, or in Sunnyvale Baylands Park. The Stevens Creek Trail extends over 5 miles to downtown Mountain View and beyond.

Moffett Field hangars

SUNNYVALE BAYLANDS PARK TO NEWARK SLOUGH

This portion of the shoreline is the true southern arm of the bay and constitutes the heart of the 30,000-acre Don Edwards San Francisco Bay National Wildlife Refuge. Its freshwater creeks and marshes, salt marshes, mud flats, sloughs, and shallow bay water (from the Dumbarton Bridge south, bay waters average 6 feet) support an estimated 250 resident and migratory bird species. Other native wildlife, including the reclusive harbor seal, also flourishes here. Nestled among the region's expansive marshes, the historic sites of Alviso and Drawbridge are visible reminders of the human imprint on the land.

Marshes near Alviso

SUNNYVALE BAYLANDS PARK

Sunnyvale Baylands includes 105 acres of seasonal wetland and 72 acres of grassy uplands that feature grounds for picnicking and hiking, a children's play area, wildlife habitat, and several miles of Bay Trail. To the north on Caribbean Drive are the Sunnyvale refuse transfer station and recycling center, the Sunnyvale Water Pollution Control Plant, trails on the former landfill, and the trail exten-

Sunnyvale Baylands Park

sion behind Moffett Field. No dogs are allowed in the park.

SUNNYVALE WATER POLLUTION CONTROL PLANT

In 1959, when fruit canneries flourished in the area, this plant was opened to provide primary treatment for 7.5 million gallons of wastewater daily. Ever since the valley that had been known for its orchards became Silicon Valley, heartland of the electronics industry, sewage treatment has become more difficult as well as more important. About 16–21 million gallons a day now undergo a three-step process here. From the north side of the plant, a dirt levee trail ventures along the wastewater ponds toward the bay.

Subsidence

Some Santa Clara County Water District engineers believe that many wells were dug near the southwestern edge of the bay just before 1900 to accommodate a growing population. By 1915, the first serious drop in the water table was noticed, and well water pressure decreased. The land above the aquifer slowly began to subside across a wide area as increasing amounts of groundwater were extracted for the irrigation of countless fruit trees and for use in canneries. By the time the district began importing water in 1969, halving its groundwater extraction, the land had sunk an average of 11 feet, a particularly messy problem for flood-plagued towns such as Alviso that were built at or near the level of the bay. The "epicenter" of subsidence is just southeast of downtown San Jose, where the land surface has fallen 13 feet. Since 1969, the land appears to have stabilized. The district maintains an active groundwater recharge program.

Canning local fruit in the 1950s

Alviso boat landing, 1895

Alviso Marina County Park boardwalk

Laine General Store in Alviso

ALVISO

A historic waterfront town at the bay's southernmost extremity, Alviso is part of the city of San Jose. Offshore are the wetlands of the Don Edwards San Francisco Bay National Wildlife Refuge and former salt ponds undergoing restoration as part of the South Bay Salt Pond Restoration Project (see p. 170). Onshore, in the 160-year-old town, you can view relics of what was once the busiest port on the bay, enjoy a waterfront stroll, and study today's environmental challenges. Listed in the National Register of Historic Places, Alviso presents an intriguing mixture of past and present issues.

Town and Marina County Park

Alviso's marina silted up years ago, leaving derelict boats stuck in the mud. The Santa Clara County Parks and Recreation Department has restored the former marina to

wetlands, in addition to improving trails and constructing a boat launch at Alviso Slough. A 9-mile dry season loop trail extends around the former marina.

Downtown Alviso is not much more than a post office, a library, and a handful of restaurants. Weather-beaten shacks roofed with corrugated iron, patched with odd bits of wood, and sunken in by a 1983 flood, stand amid renovated Victorians, modern split-level homes, and historic landmarks. The Tilden-Laine Residence on Elizabeth Street is the finest remnant of Alviso's heyday. Built in 1887 by Susan Tilden, a pioneer who rounded Cape Horn and managed her own general store (located next door), it was still home to her descendants in the 1990s. Wade Warehouse, the handsome brick building

on El Dorado, has been owned by a succession of Wades, beginning with Henry Wade in the mid-19th century, the first person to bring wagons safely through Death Valley in 1849. Unpaved streets run through neighborhoods that have subsided as much as 4 feet since their founding. Amtrak runs right through town along El Dorado Street. Former salt ponds and wetland wildlife habitats border nearby landfills.

Alviso Marina County Park

Wetlands

The wetlands around Alviso include some of the southernmost reaches of the wildlife refuge. Some are seasonal wetlands, flooded by winter rains; others are brackish and freshwater marshes, flushed by both tides and wastewater from the San Jose/Santa Clara Water

Bird-watching at Mallard Slough in Alviso

Pollution Control Plant to the east. Salt ponds, formerly managed by Cargill Salt, are being transformed into tidal wetlands and other habitats. See p. 170 for more information about wetland restoration throughout the bay.

San Jose/Santa Clara Water Pollution Control Plant

The sustainability of the South Bay relies heavily on the San Jose/Santa Clara Water Pollution Control Plant—since 1956, the facility has worked to protect the region's health by removing pathogens and pollutants before discharging wastewater into the bay. One of the largest advanced wastewater treatment facilities in California, the plant cleans an average of 110 million gallons of wastewater per day from eight cities with 1.4 million residents and a business sector of more than 17,000 main sewer connections. The facility seeks to achieve resource efficiency: it's on track to meet 100 percent of its 11-megawatt energy needs, primarily using the methane generated in on-site digester tanks and at the adjacent landfill. It also recycles 10 percent of its wastewater for use in irrigation, cooling towers, and toilet systems, and plans are in place to double this by 2020. In addition, the biosolids (solid material extracted from wastewater) are treated for reuse as a soil amendment or for daily cover in landfill operations.

Located on 2,600 acres at the South Bay shoreline and in the Pacific Flyway, the plant site is home to bay wildlife and migratory birds each year. A master plan addresses how to best rebuild the aging plant and how to use its large site to benefit the South Bay region, including expanded Bay Trail access. Tours of the plant are available with advance reservations.

HERON ROOKERY

Great egrets, great blue herons, and black-crowned night herons nest in alkali marshlands around Alviso. Each pair lays two to five eggs a year. The trail to the heron rookery is open mid-August through March. Though very shy, herons can also be seen from other refuge trails, particularly in the early morning. Flocks of egrets appear at the end of June.

Great blue heron

DON EDWARDS SAN FRANCISCO BAY NATIONAL WILDLIFE REFUGE

The refuge encompasses some 30,000 acres of bay sloughs, salt ponds, marshes, mud flats, vernal pools, open water, and uplands. It circles the South Bay from Redwood City's Bair Island to Coyote Hills in Fremont. Though the refuge is specifically preserved as wildlife habitat, visitors are welcome to explore its 37-mile network of trails, and waterfowl hunting is allowed seasonally. In

Alviso Yacht Club, 1914

Black-necked stilt

Coyote Creek Trail

Alviso Environmental Education Center

addition to offering access, the extensive network of refuge trails invites reflection on the South Bay environment. Here, it's the natural landscape, rather than the human landmarks, that prevails: still waters, rich mud flats, tide-stirred marshes, distant foothills—a golden blur of water, land, and sky.

COYOTE CREEK

In 1986, tidal action was restored to 260 acres of former marshland along this section of the Bay Trail. A 2.75-mile paved section of the Bay Trail extends along the eastern side of the creek through Milpitas between Highway 237 and Dixon Landing Road. There are several access points from North McCarthy Road and a rest area midway along the route.

ALVISO ENVIRONMENTAL EDUCATION CENTER

The refuge's Environmental Education Center in Alviso is open to the public Saturday and Sunday, 10 a.m. to 5 p.m., and irregularly on weekdays. Call first. The gate is closed when the center is closed. Trails are open sunrise to sunset.

MOWRY SLOUGH

Up to 168 harbor seals haul out on the remote shores of Mowry Slough during the pupping season from March through June, making this location the bay's largest harbor seal haul-out. Harbor seals need dry ground to rest, warm up, give birth, and nurse. Mothers sometimes stay out of the water 23 hours a day so their pups can suckle at will. To protect these highly sensitive pinnipeds, Mowry Slough is strictly off-limits to visitors during this time. For the public, a more accessible place to get a distant view of these spotted marine mammals is in Marin County, at the Corte Madera State Ecological Reserve (see p. 193–94). Other bay haul-out spots include Coyote Creek, Greco Island, Bair Island, Yerba Buena Island, and Castro Rocks, and under the Richmond Bridge.

Drawbridge, a Ghost Town

Out in the mists and bogs of the refuge stands the ghost of a town where "you wouldn't go if you weren't a different breed of cat," as one old resident put it. Drawbridge got its start on Station Island when the South Pacific Coast Railway built two hand-operated drawbridges and a cabin there in 1876.

Historic Drawbridge

Abundant waterfowl attracted trainloads of hunters, some of whom put up cabins on stilts along the railroad tracks. By 1906, Drawbridge had 79 buildings, two hotels, and a house made of a 50-passenger Matson Line lifeboat. Besides stalking mallard and pintail in the marsh, residents and visitors enjoyed swimming, fishing, boating, and "high-tide parties," when the water level allowed revelers to dock at one another's back porch. Drawbridge began to decline in 1936 because of overhunting, freshwater depletion, and sewage contamination from nearby cities. It wasn't until 1979, however, that the last "different breed of cat" left Drawbridge. Today, it's off-limits to visitors.

Sportsfield Park

Newark Slough

GEORGE M. SILLIMAN RECREATION COMPLEX AND SPORTSFIELD PARK

Near the Newark shoreline, adjacent to salt ponds, the 21-acre George M. Silliman Recreation Complex includes a fenced softball field and soccer fields. In 2004, the city of Newark completed the Family Aquatic Center adjacent to the park, which features a pool, water slides, spas, a gymnasium, and a fitness center.

NEWARK SLOUGH

Newark Slough curves around hills and meanders through the refuge's reclaimed salt ponds until it reaches the bay. The head of the slough has been an important local access point to the bay since the early 1800s, first as the main embarcadero for Mission San Jose and later as a landing for the growing port community of Newark. Today, it serves as a launch ramp for canoes and kayaks near the junction of Marshlands and Thornton roads.

GETTING AROUND

At the Sunnyvale Water Pollution Control Plant, a dirt levee trail of about 4 miles runs between the wastewater treatment ponds and wide marshes. The levee trail continues through Sunnyvale Baylands Park and along Highway 237 to Gold Street. From Alviso, a seasonally accessible dirt levee trail loop, approximately 9 miles long, leads into the Don Edwards San Francisco Bay National Wildlife Refuge. A 1.5-mile loop trail leaves the refuge's Environmental Education Center off Grand Boulevard. To reach the Bay Trail in Milpitas along Coyote Creek (2 miles of paved trail), use streets or the parking areas just off N. McCarthy Boulevard. Use streets to reach Cherry Street to the northwest; the Bay Trail route, paved, continues on Cherry, past Sportsfield Park, to Thornton Avenue. Go left on Thornton toward the Don Edwards San Francisco Bay National Wildlife Refuge Headquarters and Visitor Center.

INFORMATION

Public Transit
Call 511 or visit 511.org.

Transit & Trails
www.transitandtrails.org

Alviso Environmental Education Center
www.fws.gov/desfbay
408-262-5513

Don Edwards San Francisco Bay National Wildlife Refuge
www.fws.gov/desfbay
510-792-0222

Lucy Evans Baylands Nature Interpretive Center
www.cityofpaloalto.org/recreation/enjoy
650-329-2506

Newark Recreation Department
www.newark.org
510-578-4620

Ravenswood Open Space Preserve and Midpeninsula Regional Open Space District
www.openspace.org
650-691-1200

San Francisco Bay Bird Observatory
www.sfbbo.org
408-946-6548

San Jose/Santa Clara Water Pollution Control Plant
www.rebuildtheplant.org
408-535-8550

Shoreline at Mountain View
www.mountainview.gov
650-903-6392

Sunnyvale Baylands Park
sunnyvale.ca.gov
408-730-7751

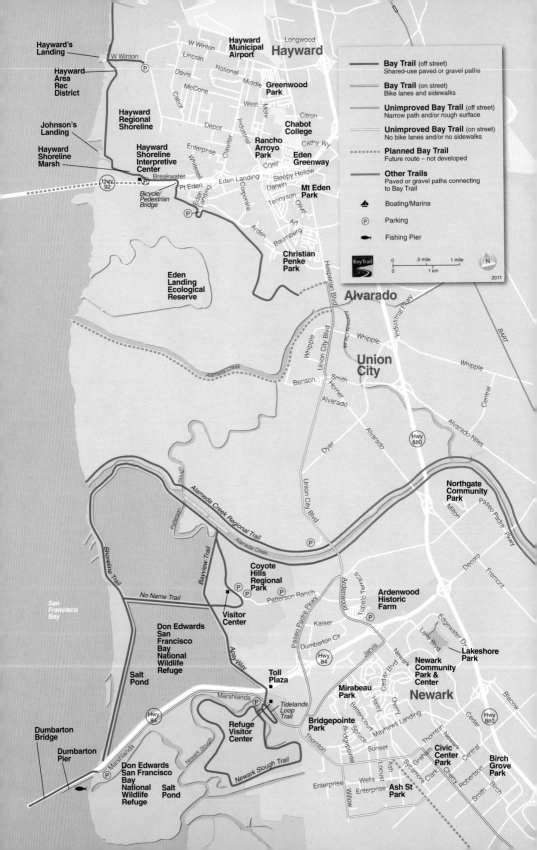

DON EDWARDS SAN FRANCISCO BAY NATIONAL WILDLIFE REFUGE TO COYOTE HILLS REGIONAL PARK

This stretch of bayshore offers lessons in human history, natural history, and history in the making. Two centuries ago, the Ohlone people maintained large encampments here. You can learn about them, and about the region's plants and wildlife, at the visitor centers for the Don Edwards San Francisco Bay National Wildlife Refuge and Coyote Hills Regional Park.

Don Edwards San Francisco Bay National Wildlife Refuge Headquarters

Overlook at the Refuge Visitor Center

DON EDWARDS SAN FRANCISCO BAY NATIONAL WILDLIFE REFUGE VISITOR CENTER

The visitor center overlooks LaRiviere Marsh, named after environmentalist Florence LaRiviere, who played a pivotal role in establishing the refuge. The 1.3-mile Tidelands Loop Trail leads to Newark Slough, winding through uplands covered with sweet-smelling sagebrush, which offers habitat for sparrows, ground squirrels, cottontail rabbits, and gray foxes. The Newark Slough Trail branches off the Tidelands Loop Trail and reaches closer to the bay, circling around salt ponds for some 5 miles. Visitor center exhibits describe endangered species and

Tidelands Loop Trail near Refuge Headquarters

migratory birds, and there is a media room with videos on the Don Edwards Refuge, the San Francisco Bay National Wildlife Refuge Complex, and the South Bay Salt Pond Restoration Project. A touch-screen computer features flora and fauna that can be found in the refuge, and natural history items are for sale. You can reach the slough by boat from a small ramp nearby, at the intersection of Marshlands Road and Thornton Avenue.

Bird-Watching

Take any trail from the visitor center and headquarters area into the refuge, and you'll see many different birds. Don't just watch, however; listen. By tuning in to their peeps, cracks, chirps, and warbles, you can tune out the roar of traffic from nearby Dumbarton Bridge. The center publishes a checklist of birds found on the refuge. Bring binoculars or check out a pair for free when the visitor center is open.

California Clapper Rail and Red Fox

In the early morning or evening, you might hear the endangered California clapper rail. Its sound resembles that of hands clapping. Although these rails are very secretive, you can sometimes glimpse one at high tide, when they retreat to

California clapper rail

higher, more exposed, habitat. Your chances are best during a daytime high tide between November and January. The California clapper rail walks like a chicken (and kind of looks like one), prefers to swim rather than fly across water, and builds its nest in cordgrass. The nest rises and falls with the tide, but the grass keeps it from floating away. This brown bird is one of two federally endangered bird species living along the bayshore. The other is the California least tern. Tens of thousands of clapper rails populated the bay's shore in the 19th century. During the Gold Rush era, they were a popular menu item in San Francisco restaurants. By 1975, however, after decades of hunting, loss of habitat, and bay contamination by mercury and selenium, only an estimated 4,000 were counted; in 2009, approximately 1,400 clapper rails were counted throughout the estuary.

Aside from habitat destruction, one of the greatest threats to the rail's survival is the red fox, native of the East Coast, which was introduced to the West to be hunted and raised in captivity for its fur. Some foxes escaped or were released from fox farms in the Sacramento Valley and became established along the coast and San Francisco Bay. Unlike the native gray fox, which prefers uplands and dry regions, the introduced red fox prospers in marshland and can swim. It kills clapper rails, California least terns, and other birds, and eats their eggs. In 1986, the red fox population exploded throughout the marshes of the South Bay. The U.S. Fish & Wildlife Service began to trap foxes in the wildlife refuge and other trouble spots in the 1990s. Where this predator was removed, clapper rail populations rebounded.

Common Tule

Common tule is an abundant plant in brackish and freshwater marshes. There are nine species of tule in coastal California, 17 in the state. The round stems of common tule can shoot up 15 feet, and produce pale-brown to reddish flower clusters. For the Ohlone, tule had many uses. Now scientists have found yet another: tule removes metals (copper, zinc, lead) from marsh waters and retains them in its root systems, making marsh habitats safer for both wildlife and humans.

Salt Marsh Harvest Mouse

The salt marsh harvest mouse, a federally listed endangered species, lives in dense pickleweed on San Francisco Bay. It does not burrow like other mice, but builds nests of dry grasses and sedge on the marsh surface and sometimes in abandoned swallows' nests. If you part the pickleweed, you may see a network of passages, but you are highly unlikely to see the mice that made them. Only during the highest tides do they emerge from cover, to swim to higher ground and find shelter among gumplant, Australian salt bushes, fat hens, and other unsubmerged salt-tolerant plants. Its unique physiology allows this little mouse (about 3 inches long) to survive on plants with a very high salt content. Biologist Howard S. Shellhammer, who spent more than 30 years studying the salt marsh harvest mouse, says it appears to eat pickleweed. But because it is endangered, it may not be captured for studies that could show what else it eats. It has big brown eyes and fur that ranges from blackish brown to cinnamon on the back, with a tawny stripe, and a cinnamon to white belly. Its scientific name is *Reithrodontomys raviventris.*

Salt marsh harvest mouse

Wagon ride at Ardenwood Farm

Patterson House

ARDENWOOD HISTORIC FARM

More than a hundred years ago, George Patterson turned 3,000 acres of shoreline grasslands and marshes into one of Alameda County's most prosperous farms: Ardenwood. The heart of Patterson's farm remains in operation today as part of a 205-acre historic regional park west of Fremont. Visitors can participate in turn-of-the-century farming activities, take a wagon ride, wander around orchards and wooden barns, and meet chickens, goats, sheep, Belgian draft horses, and other farm animals (for a fee). Dogs are not allowed in the park.

Ardenwood uses the farming and food processing methods characteristic of an East Bay farm between 1890 and 1920. Horses draw plows over fields; a blacksmith mends tools in a forge; and a cook churns butter, cans fruit, and flips corncakes over a wood-burning stove. Park staff—and visitors who sign up—farm 30 acres; other lands are leased to a local organic farmer.

House & Grounds

The city of Fremont operates the Patterson House Museum, a classic example of Queen Anne architecture with steep roofs, a corner turret, and 15 rooms. Outside, every window, wall, and corner is adorned with carved wood, stained glass, or scalloped shingles. Inside, every piece of furniture, scrap of rug, and strip of wallpaper harks back to the Victorian era. Formal grounds surround the house with lawns, flowers, a gazebo, and a fountain. Tours are available April through mid-November.

Eucalyptus Forest

Patterson started to plant eucalyptus in the 1880s, when many California farmers were experimenting with growing these Australian natives for lumber, ship masts, and railroad ties. Unfortunately, the wood proved impossible to cut, plane, or work. Patterson's 35-acre grove now provides an excellent

Monarch butterfly

windbreak, an overwintering site for Monarch butterflies (November through February), and a forest of fragrant silver-green alleys.

"Time was when education moved toward soil, not away from it."

ALDO LEOPOLD, 1949

The Pattersons, A Farming Family

George Patterson went into farming in 1851, after prospecting for gold along the American River. He worked his way up from field hand at Mission San Jose to owner of 6,000 acres in scattered locations around the bay. After his death in 1895, Patterson's wife, Clara, took over. She not only kept the lands productive, but she also championed women's rights. Her sons and grandchildren continued farming the land until 1970.

George Patterson   Clara Patterson

The Bay's Breadbasket

California agribusiness got its start a century ago with East Bay farms like George Patterson's. His was one of several large and lucrative agricultural enterprises in southern Alameda County to profit from the rich alluvial soils, cheap land and labor, and direct access to urban markets via the bay. These farms quickly became the breadbasket of the entire state and developed an international reputation for outstanding grains, wines, hops, and other products.

Coyote Hills Regional Park

COYOTE HILLS REGIONAL PARK

Ohlone legends describe the bay as a giant coyote paw print. The Ohlone lived along the East Bay shore for at least 4,000 years and considered themselves neighbors to coyotes and all other creatures. In the area of today's 1,064-acre Coyote Hills Regional Park—with saltwater on the bay side and tule marshes, creeks, and grasslands on the inland side—lay the bounty that sustained humans and others for some 22 centuries. The reconstructed Ohlone village here provides a tangible link to the bay's past. Trails invite exploration of the park's varied landscape.

Ohlone Village

Built on the shell mound is an outdoor architectural museum of traditional village structures. The Ohlone cut willows along creeks, bent them into frames, and then wove long spongy strands of tule or cattail through the willow branches to build domed dwellings. These kept out wind and rain, and lasted for several years. Reconstructed here are a tule hut, a sweat house, a shaded arbor for cooking and chores, a dance circle, and a pit house.

DUST Marsh

In a 55-acre artificial freshwater marsh in the northeast corner of the park, the natural ability of wetlands to remove waterborne pollutants is being put to the test. Since 1983, this DUST (Demonstration Urban Stormwater Treatment) Marsh, a joint effort of the Association of Bay Area Governments and the East Bay Regional Park District, has been receiving the urban runoff (residential and commercial) from a 4.6-square-mile area of Fremont. Most urban runoff enters the bay without any processing. Such runoff and illegal industrial dumping are the biggest pollution sources on the bay, sending heavy metals, hydrocarbons, PCBs, and other contaminants

Ohlone Life

Over 2,000 years ago, there were four villages at the foot of today's Coyote Hills. The Tuibun, a community of the Ohlone people, collected mussels and oysters along the shore and fished for salmon in Alameda Creek. They wove dwellings, blankets, and baskets (some, made of sedge, held water and were used for cooking). The men hunted while women collected firewood, seeds, and berries in the fields and hills, and mashed acorns into the mush that was the staple of every meal. Great storytellers and singers, the Ohlone embraced their interdependence with all other creatures and the land. In the late 1700s, they welcomed Europeans as guests in their land. The Europeans, however, did not see themselves as guests and forcibly relocated many of the Ohlone to Mission San Jose.

Shell Mounds

A 1910 survey found more than 400 mounds of debris from indigenous settlements around the bay. Today, very few remain. Shell mounds contained bones, beads, shells, broken tools, and blackened rock from fire pits. One of the few shell mounds the public can visit in the Bay Area is at Coyote Hills. To do so, you must join a naturalist-led tour. (Call ahead for reservations.)

DUST Marsh in background with North Marsh in foreground

> "Civilization began around wetlands; today's civilization has every reason to leave them wet and wild."
>
> EDWARD MALTBY, 1986

into the aquatic environment each year. Many marsh plants and organisms are highly efficient at removing organic waste and toxins from water, by either storing these substances in their root systems (thereby keeping them out of the food cycle) or transforming them into less toxic components. Heavy metals bond with clay in a marsh and fall to the bottom. Hydrocarbons tend to float to the water's surface, where they are stirred up by winds and can more readily be broken down by bacteria and absorbed by plants. Therefore, marshes have been used in sewage treatment for some time, in some cases to the benefit of wildlife. The DUST Marsh, however, is California's first experiment with urban stormwater runoff. Studies that have tracked toxins through this marsh indicate that the quality of urban runoff can be vastly improved before it is released into the bay.

Coyote Hills

The Coyote Hills are stragglers of a well-worn north-south mountain range older than the East Bay hills. Other stragglers appear farther north, at Albany Point and Point Richmond. After making the steep climb to the summit of Coyote's Red Hill, you will come upon outcrops of chert pushed up from the ocean floor. From these rocky stacks, rusty-red with iron and silver-green with lichen, you can view the shallows of the bay, a tapestry of inland marshes, and the cities of Newark and Fremont to the east. When California was part of Mexico, this entire area was a large land grant called Potrero de los Cerritos (Pasture of the Little

Marshes

West of Coyote Hills lie salt marshes and diked salt ponds swept by bay breezes. Most of this wetland is part of the Don Edwards San Francisco Bay National Wildlife Refuge. To the east, freshwater marshes and seasonal wetlands are sheltered from the wind and from the

Freshwater marsh at Coyote Hills

rumblings of the Dumbarton Bridge. At the turn of the century, high tide reached far inland, turning the hills into islands and flushing marshes with saltwater. The wetland mixture seen today is a result of dike building, duck pond construction, farming, flood control projects, and park development.

In the freshwater marshes, the tules and cattails grow tall and thick, turning from green to gold with the seasons. A summer stroll along the boardwalk is like a walk through a sweet-smelling, rustling, fertile wheat field. The boardwalk also traverses quiet ponds where waterfowl and other birds abound, especially during fall and spring migrations. Other wildlife includes muskrats that eat plants and underwater roots, helping keep the marsh clear of debris.

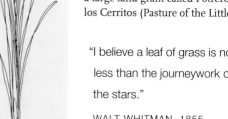

Cattails

> "I believe a leaf of grass is no less than the journeywork of the stars."
>
> WALT WHITMAN, 1855

Hills). On the slopes below, fragrant sage and fennel grow among the grasses. Halfway down, in the forested cleft known as Hoot Hollow, great horned owls have been known to nest. Glider Hill is a favorite with local remote-control glider enthusiasts.

Grasslands

Along the park's eastern perimeter, grasslands provide habitat for mule deer, black-tail jackrabbits, snakes, meadowlarks, and other wildlife. These are some of the fallow fields of a former 3,000-acre shoreline ranch owned by the Patterson family, whose home further inland is now a historic park. Willow trees meander across the grassland, marking the paths of streams and underground water.

Coyote Hills Visitor Center

The center features an information desk and gift shop, as well as exhibits on the birds, wildlife, and wetlands of the park. A separate room dedicated to the Ohlone Indians serves as the media center, where slides, films, and videotapes are shown.

Coyote Hills

GETTING AROUND

The Bay Trail route splits as it leaves the Don Edwards San Francisco Bay National Wildlife Refuge Visitor Center: one branch goes to Coyote Hills Regional Park; the other, on bike lanes along Paseo Padre Parkway, leads to Ardenwood Historic Farm. Before leaving the visitor center, explore the 1.3-mile Tidelands Loop Trail. There are benches and trailside exhibits along the way as the loop moves through upland areas, salt marshes, and salt ponds. The Tidelands Loop Trail connects to the Newark Slough Trail, a 5-mile trail that loops around the salt ponds. You will be surrounded by American avocets, black-necked stilts, and Forster's terns. Allow several hours for this walk. If time is a factor, you can visit some restored salt ponds and see an abundance of bird life by taking the 1-mile Avocet Marsh Trail. Pick up this trail about a quarter mile beyond the entrance of the refuge on Marshlands Road. It starts at the head of the bridge and goes about a mile before returning to Marshlands Road.

To reach Ardenwood, use streets. For Coyote Hills, the Bay Trail leaves the refuge visitor center on Quarry Trail (paved and dirt), goes over Highway 84 on a bridge, and then continues into the park for approximately 3 miles along the edge of Coyote Hills' southwest slope, reaching the Alameda Creek Trail (Quarry Trail quickly becomes Apay Way Trail on the north side of Highway 84, then Bayview Trail after about 1 mile). Several miles later, it continues east on the Alameda Creek Trail for 1.5 miles until Union City Boulevard.

Trail along marshlands at Coyote Hills

ALAMEDA CREEK TO HAYWARD REGIONAL SHORELINE

This 8-mile stretch of shore begins and ends at parks managed
by the East Bay Regional Park
District. In between, the California Department of Fish and
Game manages acres of former
salt ponds and wetlands. If you
want to see broad mud flats, this
is the place. From the Hayward
Regional Shoreline Interpretive
Center, about 7.5 miles of well-

Hayward shoreline with the Interpretive Center and Highway 92 to the left

maintained unpaved trail provide for fine continuous hiking and biking. As you follow the levee trail and view the skylines of San Francisco and Oakland framed by the Hayward Hills to the east and the San Mateo Bridge to the southwest, you can envision what this landscape once looked like and see what it is becoming.

ALAMEDA CREEK REGIONAL TRAIL

The 12-mile, multi-use Alameda Creek Trail runs from the foothills to the bayshore along Alameda Creek, connecting Vallejo Mill Historic Park with Coyote Hills Regional Park. Along the way, you'll find picnic sites and fishing ponds at Niles Community Park and Alameda Creek Quarries Regional Recreation Area. Alameda Creek once meandered between lush greenery that shaded salmon spawning grounds. In the 1840s, Kit Carson trapped beaver along its banks. A branch of the creek still enters the bay along its historic course, but most of its flow has been diverted to a concrete flood control channel banked by high levees 2 miles to

Alameda Creek Regional Trail

the south. You can hike on either side of the channelized creek. The north levee also accommodates horseback riders, while the south levee is paved for cyclists. There are numerous access points to this trail. Between 1910 and 1915, the area around Niles Boulevard and the old train station (at the end of I Street) was a pre-Hollywood movie production site. It was here that Bronco Billy (Gilbert) Anderson became the first cowboy star of the silver screen. He starred in some 150 pictures shot in this area, and his movie studio

produced a total of 450 pictures in or near Niles. Some Charlie Chaplin films, including *The Tramp*, were also filmed here. On the first Saturday in June, Niles celebrates Charlie Chaplin Day with nonstop Chaplin films (and a few of Bronco Billy) and displays of memorabilia.

EDEN LANDING ECOLOGICAL RESERVE

More than 600 acres of former salt ponds are being transformed into managed ponds and tidal wetlands in this area south of Highway 92. Part of the 15,100-acre South Bay Salt Pond Restoration Project (p. 170), Eden Landing provides new habitat and public access. The area is open to waterfowl hunters between November and January. In the future, a trail to the bay, interpretive displays, and a kayak launch will be constructed. Volunteers with Save the Bay have been working with the California Department of Fish

Eden Landing Ecological Reserve

Marshlands at Hayward Shoreline

and Game to restore habitat by establishing native vegetation and controlling non-natives along the perimeter levees. Once restored, Eden Landing will provide habitat for many different species, including California clapper rail and the salt marsh harvest mouse (both endangered species), black rail (a state-listed threatened species), steelhead trout, starry flounder, Pacific herring, western snowy plover, and thousands of shorebirds and migrating waterfowl. The gravel trails planned for this area will stretch from the Hayward Shoreline north of Highway 92 to the Alameda Creek Regional Trail and allow bicyclists and hikers to experience the restored salt ponds and view the variety of shorebirds and other wildlife that are already congregating in the new habitat. The East Bay Regional Park District has already opened almost 3 miles of trail that you can access from either the bicycle/pedestrian

Making Salt on the Bay

Bright pink, chartreuse, and yellow may seem strange colors for ponds that line the South Bay shoreline, but the striking hues of the salt ponds, caused by naturally-occurring algae are a familiar sight to airline passengers flying into the San Francisco Bay Area. Making salt via solar evaporation requires shallow salty water, lots of sun and wind, little rain, and flat impermeable soil. Since the bay's shore has all of these, plus a major market, local entrepreneurs have been harvesting salt near the bay-shore since the 1850s. By 1880, dozens of family-owned salt companies were working the shoreline from San Leandro to Newark. Earlier, Native Americans, Spaniards, and Mexicans collected naturally occurring salt deposits along the bay's edge.

Today, Cargill is the sole remaining salt maker, operating on 9,000 acres of salt ponds owned by the Don Edwards San Francisco Bay National Wildlife Refuge and harvesting salt on another 4,500 acres in Newark and Redwood City. Solar saltmaking today begins when Cargill pumps baywater into intake ponds. Over five years, the sun and wind evaporate

Cargill Salt plant, salt mountains, and salt ponds

Three-dimensional shapes of salt crystals

the water, concentrating the brines, which Cargill slowly moves through its series of concentrator ponds (200 to 800 acres each) until the brines reach saturation, now called "pickle." Each spring, the pickle is pumped into clean, graded, and planed crystallizer beds, where crystals of pure salt begin to grow. By fall, the salt is ready for harvest. Each year, Cargill's San Francisco Bay Area operation produces about 500,000 tons of pure solar sea salt for industry, agriculture, water conditioning, food, and medicine, serving customers throughout the West Coast.

Hayward Shoreline Interpretive Center

American avocets

bridge over Highway 92, the staging area at the end of Eden Landing Road which has dedicated parking for trail users, or the gated trailhead near Eden Shores Park in Hayward.

SOUTHERN HAYWARD SHORELINE

The 1,713-acre Hayward Regional Shoreline provides habitat for hundreds of species of birds and other wildlife, including the endangered salt marsh harvest mouse. At first glance, this shoreline looks like many other stretches of marshy waterfront. Wet fields of nubby pickleweed and lush cordgrass extend out to the bay, divided by straight levees and snaky sloughs. Egrets fish the shallow waters, sandpipers forage across mud flats, waves crash on the breakwater, and northwesterly breezes build into gales across miles of open water and marsh. Upon closer inspection of one sector of

the freshwater marsh north of the Hayward Regional Shoreline Interpretive Center, however, you'll find that water flows in not from a creek, but from a municipal pipe. The sweeping tides enter the marsh through tiny gates, and the channels look a little too straight to be natural. This wetland has been engineered by humans, first by creators of the early salt ponds and more recently by marsh restoration experts. Between 1980 and 1991, 600 acres were transformed from fallow salt ponds into freshwater, brackish, and saltwater marshes.

Hayward Regional Shoreline Interpretive Center

Perched on stilts above a salt marsh, the Hayward Shoreline Interpretive Center is your introduction to the ecology of the San Francisco Bay Estuary. Operated by the Hayward Area Recreation and Park District, the Interpretive Center features an art gallery,

animal exhibits, and programs and activities designed to inspire a sense of appreciation, respect, and stewardship for the Bay. After getting an overview of the park and its features, join a naturalist on one of the many weekend programs offered. The Interpretive Center is a great starting off point to explore over 8 miles of trail along the Hayward shoreline.

NORTHERN HAYWARD SHORELINE

The northern reaches of the park, between Sulphur and San Lorenzo creeks, include extensive pickleweed marshes, seasonal wetlands, and acres of mud flats teeming with wading birds. Old pilings stand out against the water. Access is easiest from West Winton and Grant avenues. The West Winton trail passes a retired landfill. The Grant Avenue route skirts the Oro Loma Wastewater Treatment Plant.

Johnson's Landing

Poking out of the water northeast of the interpretive center are the remains of a landing built in the 1850s by John Johnson and once used to ferry passengers, fruit, vegetables, and grain to San Francisco. Johnson was the first commercial salt farmer on the bay. He built levees around 14 acres of salt marsh. The landing was the linchpin of his property, which also included a hotel popular with sportsmen. Many a guest enjoyed a hunt on the marsh, followed by an evening next to the hotel fire listening to Johnson's tales of whale hunting, pirates, and his near-fatal tangle with a local grizzly bear.

GETTING AROUND

From the Alameda Creek Trail, use Union City and Hesperian Boulevards to reach the Eden Landing Ecological Reserve. Take Eden Shores Boulevard through the Eden Shores housing development to the Gordon E. Oliver Eden Shores Park. To the north of the park, turn left on Dune Circle to access the trail. Cross a bridge over the channel to reach the re- serve. A gravel levee trail follows the edge of the marsh. Continue north to the bicycle/pedestrian bridge over Highway 92 to access the Hayward Shoreline Interpre- tive Center. From the Interpretive Center, the Bay Trail follows a gravel levee for approximately 5 miles to the regional shoreline's northern limit at San Lorenzo Creek. The trail continues from this point to a paved trail at the San Leandro Marina and golf course. The entire stretch from the Eden Landing Trail to the marina is about 13 miles. In order to protect wildlife, dogs are not allowed at Eden Landing or south of the West Winton Avenue flood control channel.

Oro Loma Wastewater Treatment Plant

The Oro Loma plant, on the bayshore alongside Bockman Channel, provides secondary treatment for 11 million gallons of sewage daily, on average, but has the capacity to treat up to 20 million gallons of sewage daily. A small per- centage of the treated water irrigates nearby Skywest Golf Course; the rest is transported into the bay. To the south and inland about a mile is the Hayward Sewage Disposal Plant, providing secondary treatment for some 13 million gallons a day, with a maximum capacity of 18.5 million gallons a day.

California Horn Snail

This snail, one of the few native species of invertebrates left in the South Bay, lives in salt pans that only fill with water at high tide. It is adapted to withstand high temperatures and strong salinity. When waters retreat, the horn snail draws its foot into its convoluted shell, pulls up its operculum (a kind of shell door), and waits for the next high tide.

INFORMATION

Public Transit
Call 511 or visit 511.org.

Transit & Trails
www.transitandtrails.org

**Alameda Creek
Regional Trail**
www.ebparks.org
888-327-2757, option 3,
ext. 4501

**Ardenwood
Historic Farm**
www.ebparks.org/parks
/ardenwood
888-327-2757, option 3,
ext. 4504

**Coyote Hills
Regional Park**
www.ebparks.org
888-327-2757, option 3,
ext. 4519

**Don Edwards San
Francisco Bay National
Wildlife Refuge**
www.fws.gov/desfbay
510-792-0222

**Eden Landing
Ecological Reserve**
www.dfg.ca.gov/lands/er
/region3/eden.html

**Hayward Regional
Shoreline**
www.ebparks.org
888-327-2757, option 3,
ext. 4531

**Hayward Shoreline
Interpretive Center**
www.haywardrec.org
/hayshore.html
510-670-7270

**Patterson House
Museum tours**
www.fremont.gov
510-791-4196

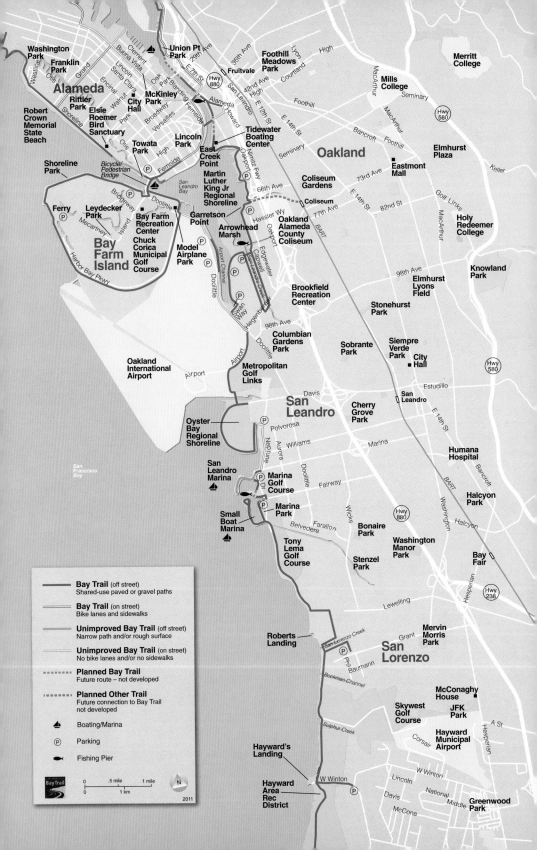

MARINA PARK TO BAY FARM ISLAND

Moving north from the wildlife refuge and extended parklands of the South Bay, the shoreline becomes increasingly sinuous, urbanized, and wonderfully complex. Here, between distinct neighborhoods, restaurants, corner stores, and the Oakland Airport, the bayshore is shaped by parks, piers, and sheltered embayments.

Marina Park

Shoreline Trail at Marina Park

MARINA PARK

San Leandro's Marina Park is one of the busiest shoreline parks in the East Bay. Here you will find marinas, waterfront restaurants, picnic tables, and a landscaped lawn area. Two playgrounds offer children a chance to swing, whirl, tumble, balance, and climb. Adults can exercise by taking a turn on the grassy point jutting out from the shore. The point (a breakwater, really) features a 1-mile paved loop, a dirt horse trail, and 18 fitness stations coached by gulls and plump ground squirrels. Dogs must be leashed.

Those interested in a more challenging hike or bicycle ride will find few stretches of the Bay Trail more scenic and extensive than the one between Marina Park and the Hayward Shoreline Interpretive Center to the south. A 7-mile levee-top trail runs briefly alongside a golf course and past a small building in which wastewater is dechlorinated before discharge into the bay. The trail continues past pickleweed marshes and bird-filled mud flats the rest of the way down the Hayward Shoreline.

Roberts Landing

In the late 19th century, the slough at Roberts Landing was important to agricultural shipping. Hay, vegetables, fruit, and other products from local farms were loaded aboard scow schooners that sailed into the slough on high tides. On a subsequent high tide, the schooners returned to San Francisco. Unlike Johnson's or Hayward landings to the south, which were constructed on fill, Roberts Landing, owned by Captain William Roberts, was a natural inlet. What remains of the slough today receives tidal action only during exceptionally high tides. A sandy beach fronts the area, and pickleweed gives way to annual grasses as the land rises

Roberts Landing

slightly away from the shore. From 1900 to 1965, the Trojan Powder Works manufactured explosives on this slough. After extensive clean-up of contaminated soil, this former manufacturing site now boasts a residential development, restored historic marshlands, and a part of the Bay Trail.

Oyster Bay Regional Shoreline

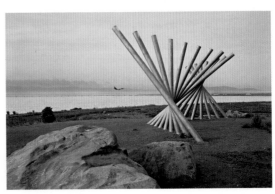

Rising Wave sculpture

To the north of Marina Park, two more miles of trails wind along two breakwaters past the San Leandro Marina and pier (a favorite of windsurfers) and the Spinnaker Yacht Club. At the tip of the northern breakwater, look for *Still On Patrol*—a memorial for the 3,515 men who died on the 52 U.S. submarines lost during World War II.

OYSTER BAY REGIONAL SHORELINE

Less than a mile north of popular Marina Park is the 157-acre Oyster Bay Regional Shoreline, dedicated in 1980. At the Shoreline's southern entrance, at the end of Neptune Drive, a trail moves south, then slowly climbs the hill-

West Coast painted lady

side through fields of fennel and mustard. In late spring, so many swallowtails, painted ladies, and California sisters frequent these host plants that you might feel as though you're walking through a butterfly tunnel. The trail continues (for about 1.5 miles) over the hill and then continues along the shoreline, turning north until it reaches the Bill Lockyer Bridge,

which crosses the San Leandro Slough toward Oakland. Northern harriers, white-tailed kites, and red-tailed hawks patrol the slopes for mice; snowy egrets and ducks fish in the shallows below. You'll also see and hear much bigger birds—jets. There's no better spot than atop this park's summit to watch planes approaching Oakland Airport from the south. Beyond the airport, across the water, San Bruno Mountain rises from the bay's western shore. Also at the top of the park is *Rising Wave*, a sculpture by Roger Berry consisting of seventeen 10-foot poles set on end. This entire park is built on top of a former landfill.

SAN LEANDRO WATER POLLUTION CONTROL PLANT

This secondary treatment plant, directly behind Oyster Bay Regional Shoreline, processes some 5 million gallons of sewage daily, using 1,000 pounds of chlorine daily for disinfection. Before the effluent is discharged into the bay, chlorine is removed by adding sulfur dioxide. Across Davis Street from the plant are the San Leandro Public Rifle and Pistol Range and the Davis Street Recycling and Transfer Station.

Bay Scow Schooner

During the 19th century, hundreds of two-masted scow schooners plied the bay and delta, hauling food and supplies. These solid working boats, built with heavy timbers, were flat-bottomed, wide, and capable of sailing with 80 tons of cordwood or 1,000 bales of hay onboard, passing through tule grass and marshes. They were called "scows" after similarly shaped *schouw* boats of the Netherlands, and "schooners" because of the type of rigging they used. The crew sometimes consisted of families who both owned and operated the vessel.

Bay scow schooner

Shoreline Park

BAY FARM ISLAND'S
SHORELINE PARK

Bay Farm Island (formerly known as Asparagus Island) is actually the northern half of the peninsula shared with the Oakland Airport. The island, on which farmers once grew vegetables and fruit, has been expanded considerably by fill and linked to the mainland. The Harbor Bay Island development, which includes luxury homes and a business park, occupies most of the peninsula's northern tip. The northern waterfront is bordered by the nicely landscaped Shoreline Park. From the Bay Farm Island Bridge, the well-groomed trail (both paved and dirt) on Bay Farm Island encircles it

and creates an almost 6-mile-long loop trail. The shoreline portions of the trail offer a clear view (except for occasional fog) to the northwest, beyond gigantic cargo ships anchored mid-bay, to San Francisco and Mt. Tamalpais. During your bike ride on the shoreline, you'll also pass the Happy Isle Ferry Terminal for the Alameda Harbor Bay Ferry. The East Bay Regional Park District has future plans to create a new park entrance and parking lot at the end of Davis Street in the northeastern part of the park.

GETTING AROUND

From Marina Park, the Bay Trail route follows streets to Oyster Bay Regional Shoreline. At Oyster

Bay, the Bay Trail is paved for the 1.5-miles from the Neptune entrance to the Bill Lockyer Bridge at San Leandro Slough. From the Bill Lockyer Bridge, the Bay Trail heads north and then east on paved trails until the corner of Airport Boulevard and Doolittle Drive. The Bay Trail then continues on Doolittle until it reaches Martin Luther King Jr. Regional Shoreline at Swan Way, where it continues on paved trails through the park. Farther north, at the corner of Doolittle and Harbor Bay Parkway, the Bay Trail route circumnavigates Bay Farm Island for almost 6 miles on paved trails and travels through Shoreline Park. At Bay Farm Island's Happy Isle Ferry Terminal, you can catch an Alameda Harbor Bay Ferry to San Francisco, or step aboard an AC Transit bus with limited service to the Oakland Airport and Fruitvale BART station.

INFORMATION

Public Transit
Call 511 or visit 511.org.

Transit & Trails
www.transitandtrails.org

AC Transit
www.actransit.org
510-891-4700

Alameda Harbor Bay Ferry
www.eastbayferry.com
510-769-5500

Bay Area Rapid Transit (BART)
www.bart.gov
510-465-2278

**Alameda Recreation
& Park Department**
www.cityofalamedaca.gov
/Recreation/
510-747-7529

Oyster Bay Regional Shoreline
www.ebparks.org
888-327-2757

**San Leandro Recreation &
Human Services Department**
www.sanleandro.org
510-577-3462

Oakland International Airport

This 3,000-acre airfield, built mostly on tidelands and marshes, is tacked onto the southern end of Bay Farm Island. When it opened in 1927 as the Oakland Municipal Airport, Colonel Charles Lindbergh was present for the ceremonies, flying the *Spirit of St. Louis*.

Amelia Earhart

On May 20, 1937, Amelia Earhart and navigator Fred Noonan lifted off from here on their final voyage. Their plane vanished in the South Pacific one month later. Today, the site of the original airport, known as North Field, services general aviation and cargo planes, while the modern passenger terminal serves some 9.5 million travelers yearly. More than 900 flights depart weekly for domestic and international destinations. The entire airport complex is operated by the Port of Oakland.

MARTIN LUTHER KING JR. REGIONAL SHORELINE TO ROBERT CROWN MEMORIAL STATE BEACH

Along some 10 miles of bayfront straddling the border between Oakland and Alameda, the shoreline has so many faces it could take days to explore. But even an hour or two is sufficient to bait a hook and drop a fishing line, run along winding shoreline paths, go birding in a sanctuary, or wriggle your toes into the sands of Alameda.

Arrowhead Marsh looking north

MARTIN LUTHER KING JR. REGIONAL SHORELINE
(Includes Doolittle Area, Arrowhead Marsh, Creek Junction, Garretson Point, Damon Marsh, and East Creek Point)

San Leandro Bay bears little resemblance to its historic form. Massive filling and development projects have reduced its 2,000 acres of tidal marsh to 70 since 1900, shifted its southward draining mouth northwest, and surrounded it with an airport, a freeway, cities, and industry. And yet the bayshore here remains green and open while offering fishing piers, paved trails, picnic areas, and wildlife habitat. Visitors can relax, stretch out on grass, and survey the skylines of Alameda, Oakland, and San Francisco. Egrets hunt in the shallow bay waters, and cinnamon teals find shelter along the edges of inflowing creeks. The endangered California clapper rail nests in the cordgrass. A two-lane launch for non-motorized boats is at the south parking lot along Doolittle Drive.

Doolittle Area
San Leandro Bay's grassy western shore has three picnic areas (phone to reserve for large groups), a boat launch, and the Shoreline Center, which can be reserved for large events for a fee. The Shoreline Center features floor-to-ceiling windows and a large deck that overlooks Airport Channel and Arrowhead Marsh. A pier at the channel's edge incorporates part of an old wharf where schooners, clipper ships, and speedboats tied up during the bay's century of waterborne commerce.

Arrowhead Marsh
From above, this 50-acre marsh resembles an arrowhead aimed at the heart of San Leandro Bay. Pickleweed and salt grass grow thick here. A short boardwalk extends over the marsh, and a fishing pier is nearby. If you're very lucky, you might see a California clapper rail flushed by high tide onto the joists of the boardwalk. Upslope are a large lawn, picnic sites, a Whale Garden for children (two fiberglass gray whales swimming in sand), and a wooden structure of wheelchair-accessible ramps and decks featuring informational

Wooden observation platform at Arrowhead Marsh with views of the bay

panels and good bay views. On the lawn below this structure, you can't miss Roger Berry's *Duplex Cone*, a sculpture indicating the sun's path at summer and winter solstices.

Creek Junction

Bridges at the confluence of the Elmhurst and San Leandro creek culverts inspire musings on the sinuous meanders that must have passed below before people manipulated the course of these waters. Striped bass can be caught here. A well-equipped exercise station invites you to stretch, and waterfowl rest along the shore.

Garretson Point

A good place to start a bayshore walk is the point dedicated to Skip Garretson, a reporter whose articles in the *Oakland Tribune* played a major part in the struggle to win protection for San Francisco Bay. From the point, you can take the 1-mile Elmhurst Creek Trail down a strip of shore planted with trees and poppies, and scattered with picnic tables and exercise stations, past Creek Junction to Arrowhead Marsh.

Damon Marsh

North of Garretson Point, the shoreline is fringed with salt grass, pickleweed, and the flotsam and jetsam deposited by currents and tides. When the tide is out, shorebirds frequent the mud flats on this 20-acre marsh. When it's in, you may see brown pelicans, cormorants, and other birds drying their wings on a derelict boat marooned in the mud nearby. Just north of Damon Slough at the end of Zhone Way, there's a sculpture park where you can sit and enjoy the nature-inspired artwork and Damon Marsh.

East Creek Point and Tidewater Boating Center

This former 48-acre business lot became part of the Martin Luther King Jr. Regional Shoreline in 1992. A 1.5-mile trail from here connects Damon Marsh with East Creek Point and the Tidewater Boating Center. This trail will eventually continue north to the High Street Bridge. Opened in 2011, the Tidewater Boating Center is a 12,300-square-foot boathouse complex where local youth and the public can go kayaking

and canoeing. Fishing and picnic areas are also available near the boathouse.

FRUITVALE BRIDGE PIERS

Piers stick out into the dredged shipping channel here at both ends of the Fruitvale Bridge. Fishermen regularly catch perch and striped bass (some close to 50 pounds) here and also land starry flounder, white croaker, various sharks, skates, bat rays, and other fish.

Leopard shark

TOWATA PARK

Although this park consists mostly of parking spaces and a few tables, it is strategically placed (off Otis Drive) as a jumping-off point to explore both Bay Farm Island and the island of Alameda.

ROBERT CROWN MEMORIAL STATE BEACH

Speeding through Oakland on Highway 880, few think to take the Alameda exit. On the west side of this 12-square-mile island, however, is the bay's largest and warmest beach. Along the 2.5-mile-long Robert Crown Memorial State Beach, you'll find sand, shallow warm water, picnic tables, a paved trail, and a visitor center. You can take to the water or head to Crab Cove, where mud flats and rocky shores invite exploration. At the southeastern end of the beach is the Elsie Roemer Bird Sanctuary and several observation platforms.

Crab Cove Visitor Center

At the Crab Cove Visitor Center, you can see bay creatures in an 800-gallon aquarium, use interac-

Gulls

Every bit of bayshore has its gulls—the bullies of the bayshore bird world. You can't miss them soaring overhead, resting on old pier pilings, scavenging around garbage cans, or harassing other birds until they drop their food. Unlike other aquatic birds, gulls can eat in any position—whether flying, swimming, swooping, or walking. At San Leandro Bay, they've developed a taste for mollusks, as evidenced by the purplish shells littering trails. The gulls take mollusks high up into the air, then drop them on the hard pavement to crack their shells. To identify gulls, it's best to concentrate on adult birds because young gulls take two to four years to mature while changing plumage, bill, and leg color almost constantly.

ROGUE'S GALLERY OF BAY GULLS

Western gull
This year-round resident is one of the largest gulls on the bay, measuring some 27 inches from bill to tail. You'll see it walking up and down beaches, and in great flocks near garbage dumps. The adult has a white head, yellow eyes, a yellow bill with a red dot on the lower mandible, dark wings with white spots at the tips, and pink legs and feet. Some 16,000 western gulls nest on the Farallon Islands, and an unknown number on bay islands and bridges. During the winter season (between October and April), more arrive on the bay from outlying nesting sites.

California gull
Another permanent resident, the California gull looks like a slightly smaller version of the western gull, except that it has dark eyes, the wings are lighter gray, and the legs and feet are yellow-greenish. This bird has mastered diverse habitats, including schoolyards. It ranges throughout the interior of the western United States and Canada, nesting on islands in saltwater, alkaline, and freshwater lakes, such as the salty Mono Lake—180 miles (as the gull flies) due east of this bay, where some 65,000 breeding birds have been recorded. In 1981, this gull began to nest in the South Bay as Mono Lake's water was diverted by Los Angeles, causing the lake levels to drop and allowing coyotes to reach nesting grounds on Negit Island. The population of California gulls in the South Bay has since exploded to some 46,000 breeding birds, and this is now the most common gull on our bay.

Herring gull
To distinguish the herring gull from the California gull, look at the eyes, legs, and feet. The herring gull's eyes are white, and its legs and feet are pink. This winter visitor is a scavenger, but it also has a taste for mollusks. It's another landfill patron and frequent boat follower. You may see it soaring in circles high above the water or shore, calling loudly. It nests in northern Canada and Alaska.

Glaucous-winged gull
This gull is abundant around harbors and occasionally visits landfills. It is one of the lighter-colored gull species, with light gray wings and gray spots on the wing tips. It has dark eyes, and its legs and feet are pink. It nests along the shoreline of the Pacific Northwest and visits the bay in winter.

Ring-billed gull
The most common small gull on the bay (about 18 inches), this winter visitor has a yellow bill with a complete black ring toward its tip, and yellow legs and feet. It nests in the interior of the western United States.

Mew gull
This gull's name comes from its call, a low mewing. The mew gull is small (16 inches), and a winter visitor from nesting grounds in Alaska and northern Canada. The adult has a white head, a short and plain yellow bill, white spots on black wing tips, and yellow legs and feet.

Heermann's gull
Of all the bay gulls, this one is easiest to identify. The adult has a white head, dark gray body, black tail, red bill, black legs and feet, and a white triangle on its wings. It is common here in winter, but unlike all other visiting gulls, the Heermann's gull nests as far south as Baja California and the Sea of Cortez (April to June).

Bonaparte's gull
A very small (about 14 inches), almost tern-like bird, the Bonaparte's gull has a black bill and orange legs and feet. Its head is black in summer, but in winter it is white with conspicuous black dots behind each eye. This gull is rare here in summer, but common near salt and managed ponds in winter. It nests in the Alaskan and Canadian interior.

water. Between 1982 and 1986, some 200,000 cubic yards of sand were dredged from the bay bottom between Alcatraz and Angel islands—enough sand to fill the Oakland Coliseum—then brought by barge to Alameda and hosed onto the beach. This beach replenishment project, called Operation Sandpour, was a joint effort by the California State Department of Boating and Waterways, the city of Alameda, and the East Bay Regional Park District. Though sand had been imported to Crown Beach for a century, this was the first time large-grained sand was used. The result has been reduced erosion. Do go for a swim. Summer water temperatures tend to hover around the mid-60s here. Showers and changing rooms are available at the beach house.

Robert Crown Memorial State Beach

tive stations to view microscopic animals, build a crab from the inside out, or get a lug worm's view of the mud flats. There's a waterless plunge which is a display case showing a cross-section of the bay, with lifelike models of shoreline and underwater animals. The visitor center's classroom is designed to resemble an old wharf, and naturalist-guided programs teach kids about bay ecology in the classroom and outdoors.

Beach

The beach extends south from Crab Cove, beyond banks of man-

made dunes. Take your shoes off and stroll around barefoot. You'll find the sand coarse, since this is an artificial beach with sand that was carefully chosen for its heavy, large-grained particles in order to minimize erosion by wind and

Sand castle competition

Crab Cove

Forming a small arc between the beach and a rocky promontory to the northwest, Crab Cove shelters grassy fields and a marine reserve with mud flats and shallow waters. Low tides pull the cove's water back like a bed sheet, exposing a wavy bay bottom. Here on the mud flat, you can peek at golden, single-celled diatoms migrating to the surface to catch the light, ghost shrimp sifting nutrients out of the mud, and pea crabs scurrying from one borrowed burrow to another—places where bat rays and flounder will feed with the rising tide. No collecting or digging is allowed in the reserve. (Note: Most crabs are found on rocky shores, not in mud flats.)

Borrow an Adventure Pack from the visitor center for a close look at the mud flat. The pack includes a magnifying glass, bug boxes, and laminated cards that describe mud flat organisms and suggest learning games and activities.

Crab Cove

Wheelchair ramp into tidepool at McKay Avenue

Please examine organisms carefully (pick crabs up by the back, not the legs) and return them unharmed to the exact place where you found them. Be sure to return rocks to their original position, as overturned rocks strand many animals, leaving them exposed to drying sun and predatory birds. Naturalist-led tours of the shoreline and mud flats are also available.

The promontory, edged with riprap, marks the northwest side of the cove. This artificial rocky shore provides habitat for crabs, mussels, barnacles, and other intertidal organisms equipped with the shells and suckers necessary to survive the daily deluge of sun and saltwater. Inland lies a large lawn area. There was a saltwater swimming pool here at the turn of the 20th century, but it's been filled. Scattered over the grass and under trees are seven major picnic areas. A paved trail meanders between beach and lawn, connecting restrooms, parking, showers, changing rooms, and a small, inaccessible brackish-water lagoon.

The city of Alameda has been holding its annual Sand Castle

and Sculpture Contest at Crown Beach every June since 1967. Hundreds of people participate, sculpting sand into shapes ranging from elaborate cathedrals to fanciful mermaids.

Wheelchair Ramp

At the end of McKay Avenue, a ramp offers wheelchair access to the water. With the help of a guard rail, wheelchair users can move down to the water's edge, or into the water, for a close view of tide pool creatures. During high summer tides, the central 100-foot section of the ramp is sometimes under 2 or 3 feet of water.

Elsie Roemer Bird Sanctuary

At the southeastern end of Crown Beach, sand yields to cordgrass, and beachcombing gives way to bird-watching. This small sanctuary, named for dedicated Alameda birder Elsie Roemer, shelters ducks, egrets, gulls, and wading birds, including the American avocet. In spring during breeding season, you may see the gorgeous peachy hues of the avocet's head from one of the sanctuary's three observation decks. Even more distinctive is the side-to-side sweeping motion the avocet makes through the water with its bill as it feeds.

Elsie Roemer Bird Sanctuary

World War II Memorial

A modest granite memorial stands on the Crab Cove lawn "in memory of graduates of this station who gave their lives in service of country 1941–1945." The "station" refers to the U.S. Maritime Service Officers School, where thousands of officers learned how to run the Liberty Ships built by nearby Kaiser Shipyards during World War II. The school served the entire western United States. Its eastern counterpart was in New London, Connecticut. Today's visitor center was the school's infirmary.

WASHINGTON PARK

⛺ ♿

Just inland from Crab Cove, Washington Park offers more lawn and picnic facilities, plus two well-groomed baseball fields; outdoor fitness equipment; courts for basketball, volleyball, and tennis; and a playground with swings, jungle gyms, and sand pits.

GETTING AROUND 🚶‍♀️🚶

From Bay Farm Island, the Bay Trail route splits. One fork returns south to the Doolittle Area of Martin Luther King Jr. Regional Shoreline, traveling partly on streets and partly on paved trails. From the intersection of Doolittle and Swan Way, the route continues on paved trails through the park, where it terminates at East Creek Point and the Tidewater Boating Center. To reach the Bay Trail route at the High Street Bridge and Fruitvale Bridge, use streets. The other fork crosses Bay Farm Island Bridge to Towata Park and from there heads to the paved trail at Crown Memorial Beach. A section of the Bay Trail goes south from Towata Park, under the bridge, past the Aeolian Yacht Club, and along the shore for 1 mile. It then continues along Fernside Boulevard to the High Street Bridge.

Coney Island of the West

Between 1879 and 1939, the Alameda shoreline was known as one of the finest beach resort areas in the West. Millions visited its beaches, spas, pools, gardens, and amusement park. California's first professional baseball game was held here, and famous local prizefighters gathered to

Neptune Beach, ca. 1920

spar on the sand. For 10 cents, you could enter Neptune Beach Amusement Park (opened in 1917) and take a dip in a saltwater pool; sample the world's first "Sno cones" for 5 cents; dare a roller coaster ride on the *Whoopee;* or attend gypsy balls, seances, swimming marathons, and beauty contests. The amusement park went bankrupt in 1939 and was closed. During World War II, the site was used by the U.S. Maritime Service Officers School. Eventually, it was reshaped into today's park.

Neptune Beach, ca. 1920

INFORMATION

Public Transit
Call 511 or visit 511.org.

Transit & Trails
www.transitandtrails.org

AC Transit
www.actransit.org
510-891-4700

Alameda Recreation & Park Department
www.cityofalamedaca.gov
/Recreation/
510-747-7529

Crab Cove Visitor Center
www.ebparks.org
510-544-3187

Martin Luther King Jr. Regional Shoreline & Robert Crown State Beach:

East Bay Regional Park District
www.ebparks.org
888-327-2757

Sand Castle and Sand Sculpture Contest
www.cityofalamedaca.gov
/Recreation/
510-747-7529

COMMON PLANTS AND PLANT COMMUNITIES

The San Francisco Bay Area has many distinctive native plants that grow nowhere else. You will see many of these, as well as plants that have arrived from elsewhere, as you take trails around the bay. Twelve of the most common plants are pictured here; ten of them are natives. Plants grow in groups called communities. All the members of a given community can tolerate a particular set of physical conditions. Some thrive in the salt and moisture of a salt marsh, others in the salt, wind, and sand of a coastal beach strand or the hot, dry, windy areas where chaparral occurs. It is easy to learn the most common plants and their communities as you travel around the bay.

Coastal salt marshes occur where tidal waters meet the land. Plants growing here, called *halophytes*, have adapted to wet and salty soils.

Pickleweed
Salicornia virginica, the most common salt marsh plant, stores salt in its joints and has vestigial leaves.

Gumplant
Grindelia humilis, grows on the upper edge of a marsh and has longlasting bright yellow flowers.

Seasonal wetlands, although not tidal, usually have ponded rainwater in winter and spring. The varying degree of saltiness in these ponds limits the plant species that can grow in this habitat.

Saltbush
Atriplex spp., with several representatives growing in wetlands, is in the goosefoot family. This family is also well represented in the desert.

Coastal strand is the first terrestrial plant community above the high tide line. Plants here respond to loose shifting sand, sometimes piled into dunes, by developing deep roots and a sprawling growth form.

Bush lupine
Lupinus arboreus, a shrubby lupine, blooms profusely in spring with yellow or purple flowers.

Coastal scrub, dominated by a maritime climate, is characterized by low shrubs intermixed with grassy meadows. Coyote brush is the most common plant.

Coyote brush
Baccharis pilularis var. consanguinea, blooms in winter on separate male and female plants.

French broom
Cytisus monspessulanus, though pretty in spring with its bright yellow flowers, is a **nonnative weedy species** that eliminates native plants by its aggressive growth.

Oak woodlands are often considered the most typical Bay Area landscape. Three species of oak are most common here: coast live, interior, and canyon live oaks. Grassland grows between trees in oak woodlands.

Coast live oak
Quercus agrifolia, is a handsome feature on the San Francisco Bay Area landscape and supports a great deal of wildlife: insects, birds, squirrels, and deer.

Chaparral, one of the most characteristic of California plant communities, occurs mostly on south-facing slopes that are dry in summer. It is made up of hard, thick- and small-leafed evergreen shrubs that are dense and often impenetrable.

Manzanita
Arctostaphylos spp., one of the most beautiful of our shrubs, blooms in winter months with pretty white or pink bell-shaped flowers.

Toyon
Heteromeles arbutifolia, is called Christmas berry because its bright red berries ripen in December.

Mixed evergreen forests grow only where coastal fog occurs in summer months. Here, hardwood trees such as tanoak, California bay, and bigleaf maple grow together with redwood, Douglas fir, and other conifers.

California bay
Umbellularia californica, is a common tree in Bay Area forests. Its fragrant leaves are used in cooking.

Madrone
Arbutus menziesii, is a medium sized tree with smooth, reddish bark, evergreen leaves, and clusters of urn-shaped flowers that mature into orange-red fruit.

Grasslands often occur where the ground has been disturbed or overgrazed, or near outcrops of toxic soil derived from rocks such as the greenish serpentine. Most of the grasses are nonnative annuals that came from Europe with cattle in California's early years.

Rattlesnake grass
Briza minor, is a **nonnative weedy** species of grass that has spread rapidly during the past 20 years. Its flower looks like the tail of a rattlesnake. It also rustles when dry.

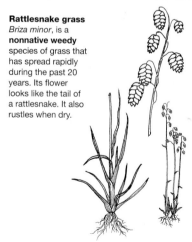

HIGH SPOT GEOLOGY

You can enjoy sweeping views of the bay and surrounding landscape from the peaks and elevated sites listed below. At the same time, you can also get a sense of local geology. Before visiting any of these "High Spots" you might want to read "How Rivers, Mountains, and the Ocean Made the Bay" (see p. 3), which will help you read land contours and rocks. Look for the most common rocks of the Franciscan Complex, the mixed bedrock that underlies the sediments of the bay and surrounding hills. The bedrock consists mostly of graywacke (sandstone), serpentine, chert, pillow basalt, and metamorphic rocks.

From Edgewood County Park, in south San Mateo County, you can look out over Redwood City and beyond, to the San Mateo Bridge and the middle of the bay. Look also at

the greenish-gray, soapy-textured rock abundant in this park. It is serpentine, an altered rock from the Earth's mantle and also California's official state rock. Serpentine is low in nutrients and high in metals toxic to most vegetation, yet it supports a large variety of native plants, many of which have evolved at individual sites of serpentine. You will see serpentine in many places, including Mt. Diablo, Mt. Tamalpais, and Ring Mountain. (Ring Mountain and Angel Island are also known for unique metamorphic rocks.)

Ancient volcanic pillow basalts (formed on the ocean floor) can be found in the Marin Headlands, while relatively young (non-Franciscan) volcanic rocks are dramatically displayed here.

Mt. Tamalpais in Marin County

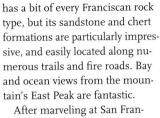

has a bit of every Franciscan rock type, but its sandstone and chert formations are particularly impressive, and easily located along numerous trails and fire roads. Bay and ocean views from the mountain's East Peak are fantastic.

After marveling at San Francisco's skyline from H. Dana Bowers Memorial Vista Point, follow the stairs under the Golden Gate Bridge's northern anchor and move downhill. Watch for the contorted layers of chert exposed by road cuts and erosion. Red-brown Franciscan chert can be found throughout Marin County, on San Francisco's Twin Peaks, and down the peninsula east of the San Andreas Fault.

Sandstone

Serpentine

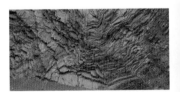

Chert

High Spots

SAN FRANCISCO
- Telegraph Hill/Coit Tower
- Twin Peaks (910 feet)

NORTH SAN MATEO COUNTY
- San Bruno Mountain (1,314 feet)
- Sweeney Ridge Trail* (1,200 feet at highest point)

SOUTH SAN MATEO COUNTY
- Hill One (800 feet), Edgewood County Park
- Windy Hill Open Space Preserve* (1,900 feet)

FREMONT/HAYWARD
- Mission Peak (2,517 feet), Mission Peak Regional Preserve*
- Red Hill Top (300 feet), Coyote Hills Regional Park

- Vista (934 feet), Garin (948 feet), and Tolman (900 feet) peaks, Garin/Dry Creek Pioneer regional parks
- Dinosaur Ridge (1,000 feet), East Bay Municipal Utility District*

OAKLAND/BERKELEY
- Volmer Peak (1,913 feet), Tilden Regional Park*
- Nimitz Way Trail (approx. 1,200 feet), Tilden Regional Park*
- Mt. Diablo (3,849 feet), Mt. Diablo State Park

RICHMOND
- Nicholl Knob (368 feet), Miller/Knox Regional Shoreline

NORTHEAST BAY
- Franklin Ridge Loop Trail (750 feet), Carquinez Strait Regional Shoreline

NAPA/SONOMA
- Sugarloaf Peak (1,686 feet), Skyline Wilderness Park

NORTH MARIN COUNTY
- Mt. Burdell (1,558 feet), Olompali State Historic Park*
- Nike Site (1,000 feet), China Camp State Park

SOUTH MARIN COUNTY
- East Peak (2,571 feet), Mt. Tamalpais State Park
- Ring Mountain (602 feet), Tiburon
- Mt. Caroline S. Livermore (781 feet), Angel Island State Park
- H. Dana Bowers Vista Point, Marin Headlands, Golden Gate National Recreation Area*

*On the Bay Area Ridge Trail

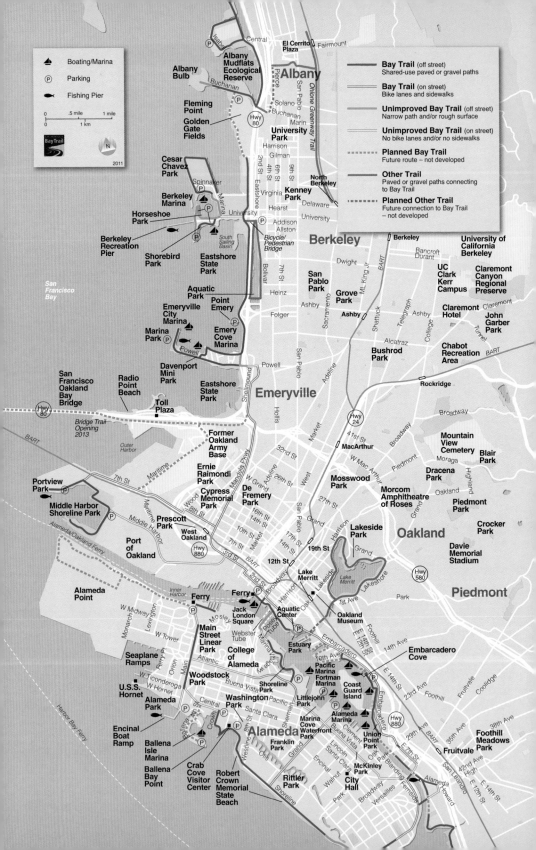

NORTH ALAMEDA AND OAKLAND

Many longtime Bay Area residents know very little of the Alameda and Oakland shorelines, and few visitors explore them. Yet there is much to discover here, including the bay's largest active port, historical sites better known across the world than they are at home, stretches of trail with delightful views, and some of the oldest city homes in the region.

Oakland Estuary with Fruitvale Bridge in the foreground and High Street Bridge in the background

NORTH ALAMEDA

Alameda Island, known primarily in the past for the now-closed Alameda Naval Air Station, is also the site of one of the Bay Area's oldest cities. Alameda was incorporated in 1854, following San Francisco by four years and Oakland by two. The 2-by-6-mile island was a peninsula before the Oakland Estuary was connected to San Leandro Bay in 1901. Ohlone people lived here for at least 4,000 years before Europeans arrived. In the late 19th century, settlers passing through San Francisco built boats on the estuary's shores, and sea captains and sailors retired here in Victorian houses.

PARKS

Aside from Robert Crown Memorial State Beach (see p. 91) and adjacent Washington Park, several neighborhood parks grace the Bay Trail route as it moves north across Alameda. McKinley Park, at Walnut Street and Buena Vista Avenue, has a playground, recreation center, picnic area and basketball court shaded by old trees. At Littlejohn Park, between Benton and Sherman streets on Buena Vista Avenue, a large lawn surrounds a baseball diamond. Pine trees shade the children's playground and picnic areas. There are also basketball courts and a recreation center. The park is named after Elector Littlejohn, an activist for social justice, whose children played on the park site when it was only a vacant lot.

GRAND STREET BOAT RAMP, FORTMAN MARINA, MARINA COVE WATERFRONT PARK, AND SHORELINE PARK

Where Alameda's Grand Street ends at the Oakland Estuary, directly across from Coast Guard Island, you'll find a public boat ramp and a small fishing pier with cleaning sinks. You don't need a boat or a pole, however, to enjoy the view: the East Bay hills, downtown

Alameda, ca. 1910

Grand Street boat ramp

Shoreline Park

Oakland, and the 9th Avenue Marine Terminal are all clearly visible. Fortman Marina, off Entrance Road, is tucked between the large brick Encinal terminals and an industrial storage tank facility. The Marina Cove Waterfront Park overlooks Fortman and Grand marinas. As you walk along the shoreline trail, you'll see a children's playground, several picnic tables, and a large lawn area where you can watch the marina activities. To the immediate north is Alaska Basin. Mostly empty and run-down today, it was the overwintering site for Alaska Packers Association sailing vessels from the late 1800s until the late 1920s. Dozens of square-rigged fishing boats waited here for the ice to break in the northern Pacific.

Shoreline Park arcs around Marina Village Yacht Harbor and is bordered by restaurants, condominiums, and office buildings. To the immediate south is Pacific Marina, home to the Encinal and Oakland yacht clubs. There are public exercise stations just off the Bay Trail that invite you to work out while gazing beyond anchored pleasure craft to downtown Oakland.

ENCINAL BOAT RAMP AND BALLENA BAY POINT

The concrete-covered breakwater at the Encinal Boat Ramp, at the south end of Main Street, offers a view across the bay to South San Francisco and Hunters Point. In summer and spring, you can watch endangered California least terns diving into the bay for small fish just offshore (see sidebar on p. 103). You can also put in boats here, fish off the breakwater, or have a picnic. To the north is Pier 3, which was built by the Navy to accommodate huge aircraft carriers. The USS *Hornet* is docked here as a floating museum, and you can board the aircraft carrier that both participated in the battle for the Pacific during World War II and recovered the Apollo 11 command module and crew after the first manned landing on the moon.

Just south of the boat launch is Ballena Bay Point, offering a unique perspective on Crown Memorial State Beach and Bay Farm Island. You'll pass a few restaurants, small

stores, condominiums, and the Ballena Isle Marina to get to the dirt parking lot at the end of the point.

ALAMEDA FERRY GATEWAY TERMINAL

In addition to being a good place to hop a ferry to San Francisco, this terminal, at the northern end of Main Street, is popular with local anglers and is perhaps the best site for watching the towering gantry cranes load and unload enormous container ships just across the channel at the Oakland Inner Harbor. To the northwest, out beyond the channel's opening where small yachts dash between container ships, you can see the Golden Gate Bridge under the deck and between two spans of the San Francisco–Oakland Bay Bridge.

Gantry cranes at the Port of Oakland

Bay Terns

Caspian tern

The stocky Caspian tern is the largest North American tern and an uncommon spring nester and summer visitor on the bay. It's about the size of a California gull, measuring some 21 inches from head to tail. The adult has a brilliant orange bill, a black cap (which fades in winter), and black legs and feet. The body is light gray on top and white below; the tail is moderately forked. This tern nests in small colonies along coasts and inland lakes, rivers, and marshes. It dives for fish in bay waters. Its distinctive and raucous calls—*kowk* and *ca-arr*—are not easily forgotten once heard.

Elegant tern

Small numbers of this tern visit the central and southern portions of the bay between July and October. Slightly smaller than the Caspian tern, it has a long, thin orange bill. Its cap, legs, and feet are black, and its tail is much more deeply forked than the Caspian's. When the elegant tern is at rest, a small tuft of feathers can sometimes be seen on the back of its head. This tern nests in the Gulf of California and, to a lesser extent, southern California. Its call is a sharp *kee-rick*.

Forster's tern

The Forster's tern looks like a 14-inch version of the Caspian, except that its bill is thinner and orange-red, its legs and feet are orange-red, and its tail is deeply forked. This is the most common tern on the bay during the spring nesting season and summer. It dives for fish, and also eats insects. In the bay, the Forster's tern nests in colonies in salt and managed ponds and in saltwater marshes. Its most common call is a coarse-sounding *kyarr*.

California least tern

The endangered California least tern is the smallest North American tern, measuring only 9 inches from head to tail. It resembles the Forster's tern except that its bill, legs, and feet are orange-yellow instead of orange-red, and its wing beat is quicker. Also, the least tern has black wing tips during breeding season. It once nested farther south on California's coast, but ventured north and began nesting in the Bay Area in the late 1960s as rapid coastal development destroyed traditional southern nesting sites. The California least tern population dropped precipitously during this period. The species was listed as endangered in 1970. Today, it is making a slow comeback. Approximately 300 pairs nested in 2010 at the former Alameda Naval Air Station, where they are now protected. Smaller colonies have occasionally appeared at several other Bay Area sites. The least tern's calls are a high-pitched *kip* note and a harsh *zree-eek*.

OAKLAND WATERFRONT

Oakland is the East Bay's largest and most diverse city, yet it is also one of the least discovered. Its 19-mile waterfront is a dynamic mix of world trade and local industry, old warehouses and modern condominiums, yachts and container ships. The nation's fourth-busiest container port and the transcontinental railroad's western terminus are here.

The working waterfront runs from the San Francisco–Oakland Bay Bridge to Oakland International Airport but is only sporadically accessible to the public between the bridge's toll plaza and Jack London Square, where ship berths and rail yards give way to pedestrian plazas, restaurants, and shopping complexes. Farther south, parks, condominiums with yacht marinas, and occasional restaurants alternate with warehouses and rusty boat-repair yards. The estuary narrows before joining San Leandro Bay, where parks and marshlands make up some of the southernmost reaches of the Oakland waterfront.

Bay Trail along the Oakland Estuary

Sunday farmers' market at Jack London Square

In 2002, Oakland developed a plan to reclaim its southern waterfront for the public, and its citizens passed a bond measure with the vision that the funding would be used to complete the Bay Trail and people would eventually be able to walk or ride their bicycles along the Oakland Estuary from Jack London Square to Martin Luther King Jr. Regional Shoreline. Work to realize this vision is expected to continue for several years to come.

JACK LONDON SQUARE

Jack London Square is the public hub of the Oakland waterfront. Plazas and white-railed boardwalks lead to shops, restaurants,

The *Potomac*

and the ferry that links Oakland with San Francisco. Benches invite you to linger by the water and reflect on views of Oakland, Alameda, and San Francisco. Beneath the square's concrete cobbles lie the pilings of Oakland's first wharf, built in 1852. At the northwest edge of the main plaza are the Oakland Ferry Terminal, the city's fireboats, as well as President Franklin D. Roosevelt's official yacht, the *Potomac*.

If you follow Water Street into

the square, you will pass a full-figure statue of Jack London at the end of Broadway en route to his favorite waterfront haunt—Heinhold's First and Last Chance Saloon—and the tiny sod-roofed cabin in which he lived in Alaska during the Klondike Gold Rush. (The cabin was brought here in 1969.) In the saloon, look on the back wall—you'll see many old, yellowed cards left by visitors from Eastern Europe who came here because they love London's books.

The Alameda-Oakland ferry runs several times a day between Jack London Square, Alameda, and San Francisco's Ferry Building and Pier 39. It offers a dramatic and exhilarating approach to San Francisco's downtown waterfront

An Altered Shore

Looking out over Oakland's waterfront region 150 years ago, you would have seen the landscape of low hills and oak trees that inspired this city's name. At that time, Alameda was a peninsula, not an island; Lake Merritt a salt marsh, not a lake. Today's tidal channel between the lake and the Oakland Estuary was a meandering tidal slough, and the estuary was a shallow creek. Water covered the 120 acres where the 7th Street marine terminals stand today. What is now Broadway—Oakland's major street—was a dirt path to the only spot on this marshy shore dry enough for boarding a boat.

Painting of Oakland waterfront in the 1870s

Jack London's cabin

Heinhold's First and Last Chance Saloon

and Financial District. For some cross-bay commuters, the ride is a mini-vacation, a chance to watch the sunset reflected on the water and listen to gulls instead of automobile traffic. For visitors, the ferry is an inexpensive alternative to tourist cruise boats, offering a good offshore view of the Port of Oakland, the Alameda shoreline, Yerba Buena Island, and the underside of the Bay Bridge. The Oakland ferry terminal is at Clay Street and the Embarcadero.

ESTUARY PARK

Five blocks southeast of Jack London Square is the Oakland waterfront's only park with a sizable lawn. To get there from the square, use the shoreline path or the Embarcadero. From the park's parking lot (off Embarcadero), a path bordered by sycamores leads to the shores of the estuary. The path parallels the Oakland Estuary, which is also known as San Antonio Creek. Giant concrete steps provide places to fish and sit. Next to the lawn, checkered daylight filters through a large arbor onto picnic tables. Palm trees reach skyward along the shoreline path. The city operates sailing, kayaking, and rowing programs for adults, youth, and people with special needs at the Jack London Aquatic Center in Estuary Park, as well as at its Lake Merritt Boating Center.

Estuary Park

Jack London

Writer Jack London was born in 1876 in San Francisco, but he grew up in Oakland and Alameda. He began poking around the bay in a small rowboat as a boy and, a few years later, bought a sloop and named it *Razzle Dazzle*. It is said that he used this sloop for midnight raids on private oyster beds in the South Bay, sometimes making more money in one night than he could from a week's work in a cannery.

As a young man, London moved with a rough waterfront crowd, drank heavily, and spent hours listening to tales of the sea at Heinhold's First and Last Chance saloon. Here he met the infamous seal poacher Alexander McLean, captain of a vessel sailors knew as the "Hell Ship" and the inspiration for Wolf Larsen in *The Sea Wolf* (1904). In 1884, London put his first-hand experience as an oyster pirate to work for the other side by joining the bay's Fish Patrol. He later wrote of his experiences in *Tales of the Fish Patrol*, and of the Oakland waterfront in *John Barleycorn* and *The Cruise of the Dazzler*.

Jack London

Embarcadero Cove

Union Point Park

There is also a small public boat ramp and fish cleaning station near where the Bay Trail meets Embarcadero. See p. 7 for information about the Bay Area Water Trail.

EMBARCADERO COVE

Beyond Estuary Park, the Oakland Estuary widens around Coast Guard Island, headquarters for the captain of the port and the 11th U.S. Coast Guard District. Across the eastern channel from Coast Guard Island is Embarcadero Cove. Starting just south of the 9th Avenue Terminal, there's a short section of shoreline trail that passes in front of a hotel and a small commercial building with a café. Portions of the trail run along boardwalks that take you over the Estuary waters, and there are benches along the trail where you can linger to watch the activity at Embarcadero Cove Marina. Farther south, you'll find the San Antonio Fishing Pier and picnic tables where you can enjoy a snack. Barbecue stands lie at the end of the path near the entrance to the Embarcadero Cove Marina. Most of the cove's shore is lined

with marinas, and the air is full of their sounds—the whip and snap of windblown flags, the clang of bells, and the creak of wooden masts. Throughout this area, you'll find intermittent access to the shoreline via paved walkways, roads, and marina parking lots.

A large wooden sign, "Embarcadero Cove," announces an odd collection of displaced buildings. Crammed on this patch of waterfront are Victorian gardening sheds and a little red schoolhouse, old train cars converted for use by a yacht club, historic mansions joined to water towers, and Quinn's Lighthouse, built in 1903 at the mouth of the estuary to guide ships into Oakland's harbor. After a new Coast Guard lighthouse replaced it, Quinn's Lighthouse was moved here in 1965 and converted into a restaurant. The cove's gardens are delightful,

Quinn's Lighthouse

with climbing roses, weeping willows, and miniature white picket fences.

UNION POINT PARK

As you pass the southern tip of Coast Guard Island, you'll see one of Oakland's newest shoreline parks. Union Point Park is a shining example of the transformation of the Oakland waterfront from its industrial legacy to a shoreline that includes trails and parks which provide access to the bay's water. Opened in 2005, Union Point Park is the result of collaboration among many public, private, and community groups. With nine acres, the park has many amenities, including expansive lawn areas, a large playground, picnic areas with barbecue stands, restrooms, and a trail that spirals up a 21-foot-high hill, providing breathtaking views of the Bay Bridge and the San Francisco

San Antonio Fishing Pier

Port of Oakland, California's third-busiest container port

Middle Harbor Shoreline Park, Port of Oakland

skyline. You'll also find the *Oculus Wave* art piece by Ned Kahn which takes you over the waters of the Oakland Estuary.

SOUTHEAST SHORELINE

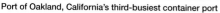

At Alameda's Park Street, the Oakland Estuary narrows, and the first of three drawbridges crosses the waterway. Along the Oakland shore are industrial areas and modest neighborhoods. As Oakland pieces together its vision of a waterfront trail that connects Jack London Square to Martin Luther King Jr. Regional Shoreline, the trail between the drawbridges has mostly been completed, and the city continues to work on making the trail connections underneath

the bridges. On the Alameda side are picturesque houses and cottages, many with boats docked alongside. Take the steps down to the Fruitvale Pier from the Bay Trail, and Oakland recedes behind the trees on the bank, leaving you in a green-brown world of leaves and slow-moving water. Farther south, the estuary opens into San Leandro Bay.

PORT OF OAKLAND

The Port of Oakland manages and operates maritime ports along Oakland's northern shoreline. West of Clay Street, you'll find a trade and transportation zone of daunting proportions. Steel-limbed gantry cranes loom along the shore like Trojan horses, stretching their

necks to hoist containers on and off ships, three football fields long, docked at sprawling truck, rail, and storage yards. Thousands of detached cabs, trailers, and containers clutter the concrete landscape.

In 1962, Oakland berthed one of the world's first container ships—a tanker converted to carry 474 truck trailers. The use of intermodal containers soon reduced loading time from a week to a day, and handling costs from

Port Vocabulary

BREAK BULK: Cargoes such as coffee, grains, sugar, lumber, and steel that are transported in the ship's hold, rather than in containers.

RO-RO: Roll-on, roll-off cargoes, such as large vehicles, are loaded on and off via large ramps.

GANTRY CRANES: Rail-mounted cranes on wharves.

POST PANAMAX: Ships too big to pass through the locks of the Panama Canal.

INTERMODAL CONTAINERS: Boxes 20 to 40 feet long, in which cargo is moved mechanically between ship and rail or truck.

STACK TRAINS: Trains equipped to carry two stacked containers per car.

Dredging

Most San Francisco Bay harbors must be dredged regularly to stay navigable. The U.S. Army Corps of Engineers scoops up millions of cubic yards of sediment from bay channels each year and dumps most of that off Alcatraz. With careful management and limits on the amount of sediment dumped at Alcatraz, it continues to be a sustainable dumping site for dredged material.

In the mid-1990s, the Port of Oakland, seeking to deepen its main channels to 50 feet in order to accommodate the newer generation of cargo ships, had an additional problem. The amount of sediment that needed to be removed could not all be accommodated at Alcatraz. Before proceeding, the Port of Oakland needed to find alternative sites for the disposal of sediments. A partial solution was devised: some of the material may be used to restore tidal marsh habitat in the North Bay (see p. 174).

Middle Harbor Shoreline Park with views of the Bay Bridge and San Francisco skyline

Main picnic area at Middle Harbor Shoreline Park

$24 to $4 per ton. Oakland went on to become the nation's fifth-busiest container port, after Long Beach, Los Angeles, Newark, and Savannah. Today, the port has ten terminals equipped with a total of 20 deepwater berths, 36 gantry cranes, and 759 acres of terminal space, all of which serve 27 shipping lines and about 2,000 vessels a year.

MIDDLE HARBOR SHORELINE PARK AND PORTVIEW PARK

Two waterfront parks offer close-up views of port activities, as well as fishing opportunities, places to rest, and picnic areas with barbecue stands. They are connected to each other by over 2 miles of Bay Trail, which loops around the shoreline of Middle Harbor Basin.

Both parks can be reached via 7th Street. Middle Harbor Shoreline Park is located where 7th Street intersects with Middle Harbor Road and sits on a 38-acre site that was formerly the Oakland Naval Supply Depot. The park has an abundance of amenities including several picnic areas equipped with barbecue stands, an open-air natural amphitheater, a small beach,

A New Bridge on the Bay

A major transformation is in the works high above San Francisco Bay with the construction of the new East Span of the San Francisco–Oakland Bay Bridge. Rising over the bay between Oakland and Yerba Buena Island, a self-anchored suspension span with a single signature tower will extend for 2.2 miles. After the bridge's eastern span was damaged by the Loma Prieta earthquake in 1989, state authorities determined that the existing span would have to be completely replaced. Under construction since 2002, the new bridge is scheduled to open in 2013.

An almost 16-foot-wide bicycle and pedestrian path is being built on the south side of the new bridge next to the eastbound traffic lanes. The path, which will be slightly higher than the roadway, is the result of a cooperative effort among bicycle and pedestrian groups and participating agencies and will be wheelchair-accessible. Completing a section of the Bay Trail between Oakland and San Francisco, the path will link the existing trails in Emeryville and Oakland to Yerba Buena and Treasure islands. The trip along the path will offer new views and sweeping vistas of the bay and surrounding hills.

Where the bridge lands in Oakland, a new Gateway

Artist's rendering of the pathway on the new eastern span of the Bay Bridge: opens 2013

Park is being planned to welcome travelers to the East Bay and to serve as an entry point for the bridge pathway. Public ideas for park design and activities include a transportation museum, bridge artifacts, art installations, bicycle and pedestrian trails, a great lawn, a festival venue, restaurants, shops, a shoreline train, bicycle rentals, kayaking, and an interpretive center. The park will be constructed in phases over several years after the bridge has been completed.

Walking paths along Lake Merritt's shore

Children's Fairyland

restrooms, and several large lawn areas. Breathtaking views of the Bay Bridge and the San Francisco and Oakland skylines can be seen from almost everywhere in the park, with the observation tower offering the most spectacular birds-eye views. Free viewing scopes to help you enjoy the scenery are available at the observation tower and Point Arnold. At the south-western part of the park near the observation tower at the Western Pacific Mole (a large breakwater/pier originally created to transfer passengers and goods between ships and rail cars), you'll have a close-up view of the largest cranes at the Port of Oakland moving cargo containers on and off ships at the Hanjin Terminal. These cargo cranes were built in Shanghai and cleared the underside of the Golden Gate Bridge by only a few feet when they were brought into the bay by ship.

Portview Park lies at the tip of an artificial peninsula extending far out into the bay at the foot of 7th Street. It can be reached from Middle Harbor Shoreline Park by following the Bay Trail north and then west along the Middle Harbor Basin. The park was extensively renovated after the 1989 Loma Prieta earthquake. From Portvew Park, you can survey the

Port's Outer Harbor terminals to the north, or scan Bay Area sky-lines. Beyond the small lawn, anglers use the park's octagonal pier (which most call the 7th Street Pier) and riprap shore to haul in striped bass, sharks, and other species. There's also a children's playground, picnic tables with barbecue stands, and restrooms.

LAKE MERRITT

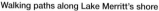

Lake Merritt, with its surrounding 30-acre Lakeside Park, is to Oak-land what Central Park is to New York, and the Seine with its banks is to Paris—a beautiful, free, and open space in the heart of the city, with attractions for everyone. People of all ages stroll along the lake's shores, while children enjoy feeding ducks in the duck pond, romping in the playgrounds, or taking rides at Children's Fairyland. Plants from around the world grow in the park, and birds that abound on the lake can be identified at the city-run Rotary Nature Center, which also provides nature walks and other programs. Offerings at the Lake Merritt Boating Center include boat rentals, lessons, wheelchair-accessible boat tours, and an adapted boating program designed for people with disabilities. An amazing array of boating programs

is available from the Boating Center, such as sailing, dragon boating, and whale boat rowing. The Lake Merritt Boathouse has been transformed into a restaurant where you can enjoy the lake perched at key seats in the restaurant or enjoy open-air dining at the tables on the restored boat docks, where you can also hire a gondola to take you on a romantic ride around the lake. At night, Lake Merritt glitters with a necklace of lights.

Lake Merritt was an estuary, marshy at low tide and a saltwater lake at high tide, until 1869, when Oakland Mayor Samuel Merritt personally funded the building of a dam at 12th Street that turned the estuary into a permanent 150-acre lake. (The mayor owned considerable land on the lake.) A year later, he persuaded the state legislature to declare the lake a game refuge, the first state wildlife refuge in the nation.

The avian life on Lake Merritt is extraordinary. Some 50 waterbird species rest or nest on five "duck islands," built of dredge materials. Many diving ducks stop by during annual migrations, while other waterbirds—including a large number of Canada geese that no longer migrate long distances—can be seen year-round.

Lakeside Park is at the northern

109

end of the lake, as are Fairyland, the Lake Merritt Boating Center, the Rotary Nature Center, and the Junior Center of Arts and Science, which are open to the public. Along the southwestern reach of the heart-shaped lake, on Lakeside Drive, the Camron-Stanford home stands alone, one of the last of the elegant Victorian mansions built around the lake in Mayor Merritt's days. Peralta Park and Channel Park follow the lake's outlet to the bay. The city of Oakland is working toward connecting these parks with Estuary Park in the future and is already making changes along Lake Merritt Channel that will improve access for bicyclists, walkers, and kayakers, as well as improve water quality to Lake Merritt.

GETTING AROUND 🚶🚶

On Alameda, the Bay Trail route follows streets along the bay side of the island, from Towata Park to the Encinal Boat Ramp. Another portion of the route shadows the Oakland Estuary by following Buena Vista and Atlantic avenues, although the city of Alameda has long-range plans for a shoreline trail along the Estuary. The Bay Trail route leads to Oakland by turning off Atlantic onto Triumph Drive; then it follows a paved shoreline path for a half mile toward the northwest. To continue to the Webster Street Tube and Oakland, take streets. For the Alameda Gateway Ferry Terminal, continue along Atlantic Avenue until it turns into Ralph Appezzato Memorial Parkway; then

turn north on Main Street until it bends toward the west. The ferry terminal is just to the north near the bend.

In Oakland, the Bay Trail route gets complicated. It joins a branch of the trail moving up from the south along Embarcadero, with paved trail portions running through the Embarcadero Cove Marina and along the waterfront to Estuary Park and Jack London Square. From Jack London Square, use city streets to reach Middle Harbor Shoreline Park and Portview Park. You can also continue to Emeryville along city streets via Mandela Parkway. Bikers, be alert throughout the port area: drivers of large trucks may not see you. Railroad tracks can catch a bike tire.

INFORMATION

Public Transit
Call 511 or visit 511.org.

Transit & Trails
www.transitandtrails.org

AC Transit
www.actransit.org
510-891-4700

Alameda-Oakland Ferry
www.eastbayferry.com
510-522-3300

Alameda Recreation and Park Department
www.cityofalamedaca.gov
/Recreation/
510-747-7529

East Bay Regional Park District
www.ebparks.org
888-327-2757

Junior Center of Arts and Science
www.juniorcenter.org
510-839-5777

Lake Merritt Boating Center and Jack London Aquatic Center
www.oaklandnet.com
/parks
510-238-2196

Oakland Parks and Recreation Department
www.oaklandnet.com/
parks
510-238-7275

Port of Oakland
www.portofoakland.com
510-627-1100

The *Potomac* Association
www.usspotomac.org
510-627-1215

Rotary Nature Center
www.oaklandnet.com
/parks
510-238-3739

EMERYVILLE AND BERKELEY TO POINT ISABEL

In 1913, the U.S. Army Corps of Engineers proposed to build parallel seawalls from the Emeryville Crescent area to just north of Point Isabel, creating a 5-mile-long shipping channel to accommodate a shipping boom projected for the entire East Bay. Obviously, the plans came to naught. Today, pockets of beautiful marshes and important wildlife habitat survive along this stretch of shore—little jewels of open space that also provide recreation sites for thousands of East Bay residents and visitors.

Emeryville Marina

Emeryville Fishing Pier

EMERYVILLE MARINA

The artificial 1-mile-long peninsula was one of the last major fill projects permitted on the bay. It shelters marinas and parks at its tip and provides a foundation for high-rise apartment and office buildings, condominiums, and restaurants near Interstate 80. The peninsula is ringed by some 3 miles of paved trails, which can be rough in places.

MARINA PARK

At the tip of the peninsula, small public lawns face the bay, screened on their landward sides by rows of cypress and pines. The sweeping view is superb: Angel Island, the remnants of the Berkeley Ferry Pier, and most of the central bay are before you. On the park's leeward side, the Emeryville Fishing Pier is calmer (and less frequented) on windy afternoons than the Berkeley Pier. Cleaning sinks and benches make it that much easier to haul in the flounder, kingfish, and rubberlip perch this pier is known for.

DAVENPORT MINI PARK AND BEYOND

Don't blink as you stroll on Powell Street toward Interstate 80, or you'll miss Davenport Mini Park—a tiny lawn, with benches, that looks out over the boats in the Emery Cove Marina. The Bay Trail route splits by the mini park. One arm swings north past a restaurant and follows the edge of the peninsula on a wide boardwalk for a half mile. Look for the windproof boardwalk turnout with benches. No biking or fishing is allowed along the length of this boardwalk, which ends at a grassy strip near another restaurant and two public piers. Where the route moves to West Frontage Road, miniature sculptures adorn abandoned pilings in the water. The other arm of the route from the mini park continues down Powell Street.

Davenport Mini Park

Radio Point Beach

Point Emery

RADIO POINT BEACH, EMERYVILLE CRESCENT, AND EASTSHORE STATE PARK

As you hustle east off the San Francisco–Oakland Bay Bridge by car and turn north on Interstate 80, look for Oakland's Radio Point Beach hidden at the end of a single-lane road near the bridge's toll plaza. This strip of shore is highlighted by three radio transmission towers and graced by a fringe of beautiful marsh. Public access is at the end of the road, but the road can only be accessed by taking the last Oakland exit on your return trip toward the San Francisco–Oakland Bay Bridge on westbound Interstate 80.

East of Radio Point Beach is the Emeryville Crescent, a sliver of marsh that has survived decades of sculpture-making, political protests, illegal garbage dumping, and development proposals. Despite the constant roar of cars, thousands of birds stop here in fall and early winter. In spring, nesting avocets prance about and join the killdeers in their plaintive calls.

The stretch of shore that begins at Radio Point Beach and swings around into the Emeryville Crescent has been included in Eastshore State Park. This park extends along more than 8 miles of East Bay shoreline from the Bay Bridge in Oakland through Emeryville and Berkeley to the Marina Bay development in Richmond. The park was created to preserve and protect this area of the East Bay shoreline for open spaces, recreation, and habitat. The East Bay Regional Park District manages and operates Eastshore State Park and is continuing the planning, acquisition, and restoration work needed to realize this park vision. The park already includes 1,854 acres of uplands and tidelands.

EMERYVILLE TO TREASURE ISLAND

In 2013, the newest stretch of Bay Trail, which connects Emeryville and the rest of the East Bay to Treasure Island, will be opened when the new eastern span of the Bay Bridge is completed. Over 4 miles long, this part of the trail will provide a unique experience for the adventurous bicyclist or walker, taking them from Shellmound Street in Emeryville, underneath the freeway overpasses at the MacArthur Maze, past the East Bay Municipal Utility District's main treatment plant and the Caltrans maintenance yard, to the new eastern span of the Bay Bridge. Those who continue onto the new bridge trail will be treated to a bicycling and walking experience that rivals that of the Golden Gate Bridge. Once on Yerba Buena Island, a path will guide you to Treasure Island. The realization of this trail is a result of the collaboration between countless agencies and stakeholders. A new regional park is also being planned for the area where the Bay Bridge lands in the East Bay (see p. 108).

POINT EMERY AND WEST FRONTAGE ROAD

Point Emery is one of those unexpected pleasures you can discover by patiently poking around the bayshore. In the 1960s, the city of Emeryville planned a huge fill project from here to the Emeryville Peninsula, but the Bay Conservation and Development Commission refused to permit the filling. Instead, the city was required to provide public access, including a parking lot, benches, and landscaping. On the north shore, a small beach is used by windsurfers and kite surfers to assemble gear. From its tip, Alcatraz seems to float mid-span against the Golden Gate Bridge.

West Frontage Road, between Point Emery and University Avenue, is well used by locals for fishing, birding, windsurfing, bay

Bay Trail near the Berkeley bike-ped bridge

Berkeley Marina Berthing Basin

watching, lunching, and naps. Along its western edge is perhaps one of the most popular 3-mile stretches of the Bay Trail. From Emeryville to the Berkeley Marina, the lucky bicyclist or walker is treated to iconic views of the San Francisco skyline, Golden Gate Bridge, and Bay Bridge. Many people stop at the deli market at the corner of University Avenue before continuing north to Gilman Street, where the trail currently ends, but there are plans to connect to the trail at Buchanan Street in the future. At Gilman Street, the Tom Bates Regional Sports Complex features fields for team sports such as soccer, lacrosse, rugby, and more. Just south of University Avenue is the architecturally stunning Berkeley bicycle and pedestrian bridge, which crosses Interstate 80 to Aquatic Park and the rest of Berkeley.

BERKELEY MARINA

This 52-acre peninsula at the end of University Avenue is highly popular. Created partly on a land-fill, it has some 5 miles of trails, a pier, parks, restaurants, playgrounds, a berthing basin, small boat launch, and good windsurf-ing and kite-flying conditions. You might begin your exploration at tiny Horseshoe Park, just south of the marina entrance.

SOUTH SAILING BASIN AND SHOREBIRD PARK

If you follow the shoreline trail at the South Sailing Basin, it will lead you to a small craft launch-ing dock (with a nice view of the East Bay hills), Cal Adventures and the Cal Sailing Club (both of which offer sailing and windsurf-ing classes), and eventually to Shorebird Park, where you'll find picnic areas, barbecue stands, and a playground.

The Shorebird Park Nature Center is full of educational displays and packed with the bones, shells, skins, and feathers of bay animals. A large saltwater tank contains bay

Small watercraft launching dock at South Sailing Basin

Shorebird Park playground

Adventure Playground

fish, anemones, crabs, and other bay creatures. Classes for children are offered. The straw-bale building at the Center incorporates green building design concepts and acts as an educational tool on sustainable design, which utilizes recycled and energy-efficient materials. Behind the center is the Adventure Playground, designed to allow children to experiment with building materials.

BERKELEY RECREATION PIER

Despite the brisk afternoon breezes that blow across the Berkeley Recreation Pier, this is probably the most visited pier in the Bay Area. Crowds of anglers hook striped bass, bullhead, and shiner perch here; others enjoy the fresh air while walking out the 3,000-foot length of the pier to take in the view. When you hike to the end of the pier, you'll see the remnants of an older pier stretching out across the water. In 1927, the Berkeley Ferry Pier was extended 3.5 miles out into the bay, to water deeper than 10 feet, so large ferry boats could dock. When the San Francisco–Oakland Bay Bridge was completed in 1936, ferry service stopped, and the pier fell into disrepair. The city of Berkeley acquired it in 1938 and rebuilt the first 3,000 feet in 1958, and again in 1961. Although some complain that the old pilings interfere with small craft navigation, local activists have shown that they serve an important role as micro-habitats for bay life and as perches for birds.

BERTHING BASIN

The Berkeley Marina's 52 acres of water can accommodate 1,100 watercraft. Some of the vessels nestled in its Berthing Basin may be houseboats that stay put much of the time. The legality of their presence here is a matter of chronic contention. You'll find good lookout points at both sides of the basin entrance, but the northern side seems to be the favorite with shoreline visitors. The Berkeley Yacht Club is at the southern side of the entrance.

CESAR E. CHAVEZ PARK

Believe it or not, this popular, attractive park was a landfill until 1983. Now, just about the only visible evidence of its past is a small metal shed and chimney located mid-park, which vents methane gas. The western shore of the park rivals San Francisco's Wave Organ jetty for the best view of the Golden Gate Bridge. A paved perimeter trail is punctuated by small turnouts with benches. Several dirt trails crisscross the hilly top of the park, leading to picnic areas, lawns

You can walk 3,000 feet out over the bay on the Berkeley Recreation Pier.

for kite-flying, and great views. You can usually rent a kite at this park, and on breezy weekends you'll almost always see people performing dazzling aerial acrobatics. The entire park has been seeded with native grasses. On the hilltop closest to the point, planted with native shrubs and grasses, you can see how attractive a water-saving native garden can be. The northeast corner of the park has been redesigned to protect the habitat for migratory burrowing owls when they visit between October and April every year. Urban dwellers can view and learn about one of our native species that is being impacted by loss of habitat.

Kite-flying at Cesar E. Chavez Park

Aquatic Park

BERKELEY'S AQUATIC PARK

🪑 🐦 ♿ ⛵ 🚶 🚴

This unique park centers on a body of water that is located between Ashby and University avenues on the east side of Interstate 80. Construction of Aquatic Park began in the early 1930s, when the original shoreline here was filled to create the highway. It was completed in 1935 by the Works Progress Administration. The city of Berkeley acquired the park the following year. The southern basin has been designed for model yacht racing, the middle basin for water skiing, and the north basin for sailing, rowing, and canoeing. The basins are still connected to the bay via tidal gates operated by the city. On the 33 acres of land surrounding the basins, people can jog (numerous exercise stations line the shore), watch birds, or try some disc golfing.

FLEMING POINT AND ALBANY BULB

🐦 🚶 🚴

This stretch of shore directly behind Golden Gate Fields was home to J. J. Fleming in the late 19th century, but not much is known about him. Remnants of old piers can still be seen in the waters by the rocky point—the only reminders of the original shoreline along this stretch of the bay's edge. Small beaches are tucked up against the base of the

The East Bay Regional Park District

In 1934, the East Bay Municipal Utilities District (EBMUD) announced the sale of some 10,000 acres. Citizens in Alameda and Contra Costa counties saw the sale as an opportunity to preserve lands and natural communities and joined in an effort that led to the creation of the East Bay Regional Park District (EBRPD). The park district acquired watershed lands that are now Tilden, Temescal, and Sibley parks and then went on to secure an extensive park system for the East Bay. Today, 65 parks (totaling over 100,000 acres) and 29 regional trails are scattered across the district's two-county jurisdiction.

In 1992, the state legislature gave EBRPD the responsibility for acquiring the land, including tidelands, for Eastshore State Park, which runs along more than 8 miles of shoreline from Oakland to Richmond. The district is also responsible for cleaning up toxic or hazardous materials and planning for the park. As this new park is developed, the Bay Trail and shoreline facilities will expand and improve.

Beach at Albany Bulb

bluff, and from on top, the views of the central bay and southern Marin County are spectacular. In 2002, the Albany Bulb (located at the end of Buchanan Street) became part of Eastshore State Park. Its informal trails lead to the point, which offers amazing views of San Francisco and the Golden Gate Bridge. One of the longest continuous stretches of the Bay Trail begins at Buchanan Street and continues north to Point Isabel, the Richmond Marina, and finally the historic Ford Building, site of the future Rosie the Riveter World War II Home Front National Historical Park Visitor Center. As you travel north from the Albany Bulb, look for an interpretive sign erected by Caltrans. It describes the 270 acres of tidal mud flats and 10 acres of

Well-behaved dogs are welcome at Point Isabel Regional Shoreline.

salt marsh between Golden Gate Fields and Central Avenue, an area commonly referred to as the Albany Shoreline. More than 90 species of resident and migratory birds have been seen here.

POINT ISABEL REGIONAL SHORELINE

If you are a dog person, you'll love this park, and so will your dog: it's an off-leash area for canines. While dogs are chasing balls, wrestling, and cavorting about, their owners huddle in informal groups telling doggy stories. They keep a sharp eye out for anyone who doesn't pick up a pet's poop and are likely to reprimand offenders. But even if you're a cat person, Point Isabel is a great place for a walk (sans cat), with marvelous bay vistas. At the Isabel Street parking lot near the picnic area, there's a building that houses a dog washing service for your pooch and a café next door for your dog's best friend to get a well-deserved snack.

GETTING AROUND 🚶🚶

To reach Radio Point Beach by car, travel west on Interstate 80 toward the Bay Bridge and take the last Oakland exit. (Watch out: If you miss it, you will have to take the bridge to San Francisco!) After you exit, take the first right turn onto a small, unmarked, one-lane frontage road. (Don't go toward the former Oakland Army Base.) This small frontage road dead-ends near Radio Point Beach. Radio Point Beach isn't accessible when traveling east from San Francisco on Interstate 80. When you leave Radio Point Beach, follow the turnoff onto the ramp toward the former Oakland Army Base. When you reach Maritime Street, turn right and take Maritime south to 7th Street. Follow the signs to Middle Harbor Shoreline Park along 7th Street. The Emeryville Marina can be accessed from the Powell Street exit off Interstate 80. Between the Emeryville Marina and Fleming Point, the Bay Trail route follows West Frontage Road, with a branch leading down University Avenue to the Berkeley Marina. From the Albany Bulb, the Bay Trail moves north to Central Avenue and Point Isabel Regional Shoreline.

INFORMATION

Public Transit
Call 511 or visit 511.org.

Transit & Trails
www.transitandtrails.org

AC Transit
www.actransit.org
510-891-4700

Aquatic Park, Berkeley
www.ci.berkeley.ca.us
510-981-5150

Berkeley Marina
www.ci.berkeley.ca.us
510-981-6740

California Adventures
www.recsports.berkeley
.edu
510-642-6400

Cal Sailing Club
www.cal-sailing.org

East Bay Regional Park District
www.ebparks.org
888-327-2757

Emeryville Marina
www.emeryvillemarina
.com
510-654-3716

Emeryville Marina Park
www.ci.emeryville.ca.us
510-596-4353

Shorebird Park Nature Center and Adventure Playground
www.ci.berkeley.ca.us
510-981-6720

INDIGENOUS PEOPLE

THE BAY'S ENDURING NATIVE PEOPLE

On November 2, 1769, a group of soldiers from the Portolá expedition climbed a ridge and, to their utter amazement, looked down upon *"un inmenso brazo de mar"*—an immense arm of the sea. Beyond it, they reported, lay beautiful plains studded with trees, and from the columns of smoke everywhere they concluded that this land was *"bien poblada de ranchería de gentiles"*—well populated by the villages of native people.

Indeed, at the time of this first contact, scores of villages rimmed the bay, inhabited by an astounding diversity of people. Those who lived on what would be called the San Francisco Peninsula spoke a language called Ramaytush; those in the South Bay, Tamyen; those in the East Bay, Chochenyo; those along the southern shores of the Carquinez Strait, Karkin. These four languages, perhaps as different from each other as French is from Italian, were part of the Ohlone group of languages. In what is now Marin County, the native people spoke a dialect of the Coast Miwok language. At the mouth of the Napa River and along the north shores of the Carquinez Strait lived Patwin speakers, while east of the Strait were the villages of the Bay Miwok speakers.

The richness of languages only hints at the diversity and cultural complexity of the people who had lived along the shores of the bay for over 10,000 years before the arrival of Europeans.

At the time of European contact, the native populations lived in dozens of interrelated but politically independent communities. Each community centered on

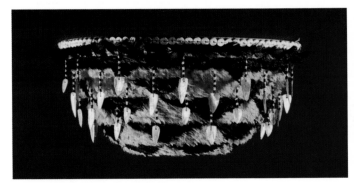
Feathered basket with abalone pendants, Pomo

Wife of Chief Huyumhayum and unknown man, Coast Miwok, 1905

118

a main village, led (rather than ruled) by a member of a prominent family who would likely be linked to other prominent families in the area by ties of marriage and trade.

While trading was an important part of life—clam-shell "money" beads, abalone shells from the ocean, and cinnabar ore (used for paint) from the San Jose area were traded out, while obsidian and pine nuts flowed in—the peoples of the Bay Area were by and large self-sufficient. Their dwellings were generally constructed of willow frames thatched with tule—readily available, easily gathered materials. Food was likewise plentiful for a people who had the skills and sense of timing needed to take advantage of the great flocks of geese and ducks that darkened the sky each fall, the salmon and steelhead that crowded the creeks at spawning season, and the inexhaustible beds of clams and oysters that extended into the clean waters of the bay.

At various times of year, people left the shores of the bay to harvest acorns, nuts, berries, roots, seeds, or other goods in the foothills, returning to permanent villages to winter—to tell wondrous stories of how the world was created and how Coyote conducted himself with such divine foolishness and to celebrate with games, dances, and songs of the joy of being human in a land of ample beauty and great plenty.

It is easy enough to cast a nostalgic look back upon this "lost" world. But it isn't gone altogether: in fact, many of the languages and stories and much of the knowledge of the people who lived here before us have been recorded. Also, the descendants of the bay's original inhabitants live among us today. Many of them still hold onto parts of their heritage, while some are even relearning languages that have not been spoken for generations, reacquiring and practicing skills that have been long neglected. The world of the Bay Area's native people is not entirely "lost"; more to the point, it is generally ignored by a different culture that seems to be going too fast to notice it.

Pomo man

"The Ohlones can provide us with a vision of how a Stone-Age people, a people whom we have so long belittled, had in fact sustained a life of great beauty and wisdom."

MALCOLM MARGOLIN
THE OHLONE WAY, 1978

Richmond/San Pablo

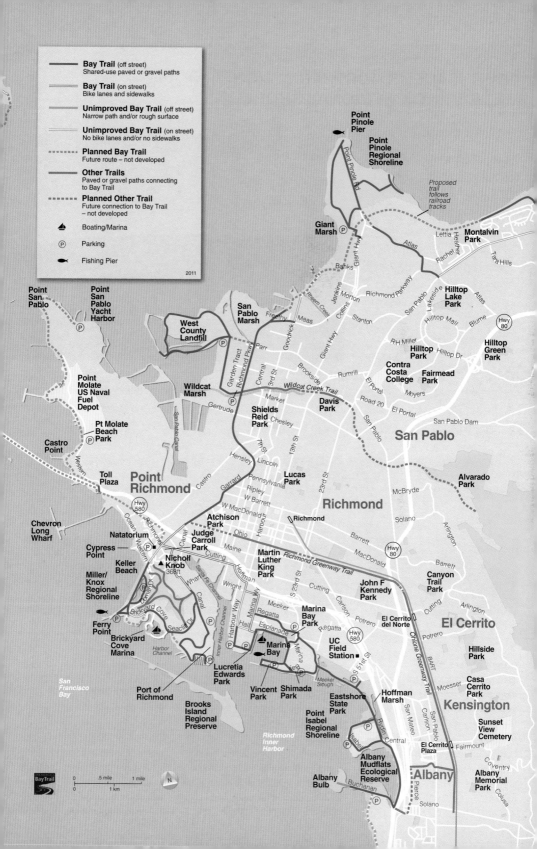

POINT ISABEL'S NORTHERN SHORELINE TO MILLER/KNOX REGIONAL SHORELINE

Interstate 580 channels motorists through Richmond's industrial heart while obscuring a segment of bay shoreline rich with history, expansive views, and parklands. Pull off, and slow down. Railroads, the oil industry, the Port of Richmond, and World War II shipbuilding left their legacies on the shore here. Oil, shipping, and some manufacturing remain, but where acrid smoke once drenched the air, condominiums are now spreading, pleasure

Meeker Slough wetlands

boats sail among tankers and cargo ships, and former ferry slips and corporation yards are now public parklands. The departure of heavy industry has, however, left many Richmond residents jobless and has dealt a devastating economic blow to the city.

Trail between Marina Bay and Meeker Slough

View of Potrero Point with the Red Oak Victory and the Whirley Crane in the background

POINT ISABEL TO SHIMADA FRIENDSHIP PARK AND BARBARA AND JAY VINCENT PARK

With the exception of the Cypress Point bluffs to the north, this entire shoreline has been molded and shaped during a century of industrial use. From Point Isabel Regional Shoreline, the Bay Trail route moves north 1 mile on an old railroad levee—now owned by the East Bay Regional Park District—to an intersection by Meeker Slough. A varied pattern of marshes and mud flats extends on both sides of the levee. Inland, the densely vegetated marshes are seasonal—they fill with water after winter storms and exceptionally high tides. Hoffman Marsh, a tidal marsh between the levee and the highway north of Point Isabel, is strictly off-limits to protect wildlife. Bayward, strips of marsh grasses and mud flats extend from the levee's base. Both areas are important wildlife habitat, particularly for resident and migrating birds.

At the Meeker Slough trail intersection, one arm of the Bay Trail moves to the northwest and Marina

Barbara and Jay Vincent Park with Angel Island in the background

Bay Park. The westward arm hugs the riprap shore for a half mile and leads to Shimada Friendship Park and Marina Bay. This park is named for Shimada, Japan, Richmond's sister city, and, together with the nearby housing development, exemplifies the shift toward a different use of this waterfront. From Shimada's manicured lawn and large picnic tables, you can see Brooks Island stretching across the near horizon only a half mile away. The view to the west is of tankers docked along Potrero Point on Harbor Channel, and the Tiburon Peninsula across the bay. To the south, in the distance, is Berkeley's North Waterfront Park.

Beach at Barbara and Jay Vincent Park with the Ford Building in the background

Continuing westward from Shimada Friendship Park, you'll arrive at Barbara and Jay Vincent Park which is named after two local activists who worked to create a number of parks and trails along the East Bay shoreline. This six-acre park features many amenities including an observation platform over the bay, two small beaches, a large picnic area with tables and barbecue stands, an expansive lawn area, restrooms, and an ADA-accessible playground.

BROOKS ISLAND

When San Francisco Bay was first mapped in 1775 by José de Cañizares, this sliver of an island was labeled Isla de Carmen. Later it was variously known as Rocky, Bird, and Sheep Island before being named Brooks Island. Ohlone people lived here for perhaps 4,000 years, and two Ohlone shell mounds and burial sites have been preserved here. By the 1860s, and into the 20th century, the island was used for fruit growing, oyster cultivation, rock quarrying, yachting, and hunting.

Brooks Island viewed from Shimada Friendship Park

Richmond Marina

Today, as a 375-acre preserve of the East Bay Regional Park District (75 acres of land and 300 acres of water), Brooks Island retains much of its native vegetation and wildlife. Although exotic guinea fowl and pheasants once existed here when crooner Bing Crosby and friends used the island as a private hunting reserve, some 100 native species of birds have been recorded here, and over 18 species of birds nest here, including Caspian terns and Canada geese. Portions of the island are closed year-round for the Caspian terns, and another section is closed from March to August for the returning heron and egret colonies. Access to this island preserve is by reservation only.

RICHMOND MARINA TO SHERIDAN OBSERVATION POINT

This marina, located on the former site of Kaiser Shipyard No. 2, seems remote from the economic struggle that faces much of Richmond as a result of the departure of industry, which took many blue-collar jobs with it. Here, rows of glistening white sailboats rock gently at berth, orderly clusters of homes flourish adjacent to the shoreline trail that leads from Vincent Park to the marina's northern shore, and large parks offer a place to run or rest.

The trail around the marina, constructed of patterned concrete and sections of boardwalk, connects with the Marina Bay Park, Marina Green, Lucretia Edwards Park, and the wharf around the Ford Building. Marina Bay Park starts at the marina with a small sandy beach, then moves inland toward a playground and picnic area. Fishing, with a state permit, is allowed off the marina's riprap shore. Access and conditions are good for intermediate and advanced windsurfing. The Marina Green is a large lawn with benches near the water.

Lucretia Edwards Park was named after a local community activist who worked to create a variety of shoreline parks. The park was created to honor the shipbuilding efforts of the Bay Area during World War II. It has a low wall seating area, restrooms, and two stairways that lead to the water, allowing you to sit close to the bay. Traveling west from Lucretia Edwards Park, the trail continues along the wharf that skirts the historic Ford Building. Just west of the Ford Building is the Sheridan Observation Point, where you'll often find locals fishing in the bay.

It's hard to believe that most of the shoreline between the marina and Potrero Point was occupied by Kaiser Shipyards and heavy industry during World War II, but it was. A few blocks inland from the tidy marina are remnants of the old waterfront: enormous warehouses, industrial facilities, scrap yards, and marine businesses.

ROSIE THE RIVETER WORLD WAR II HOME FRONT NATIONAL HISTORICAL PARK

Established in 2000, this National Park was created to tell the story of the home-front efforts during World War II by highlighting Richmond, which played a critical part in building ships, jeeps, and tanks during the war. Today, it is hard to imagine the magnitude of the war industry here during the 1940s, but remnants of that era are strewn all around the city. Today's Richmond Marina, the Port of Richmond at Potrero Point, Inner Harbor Channel, and Santa Fe Channel were the sites of four massive Kaiser Shipyards, where Victory and Liberty ships were built around the clock in order to transport supplies, equipment, and troops to the war. All told, these yards constructed 747 ships, with an average construction time of less than a month. One ship,

Watching a kayaker from the steps at Lucretia Edwards Park

Ford Building

the SS *Robert E. Peary Liberty*, was built in less than five days.

If you ride down Canal Boulevard to the Kaiser Shipyard III at the Port of Richmond, you'll be treated to a spectacular view of San Francisco across the bay and find the last remaining Victory ship that was made in the Kaiser shipyards, the SS *Red Oak Victory*. A dedicated group of volunteers is constantly refurbishing the ship, which is open to the public. From the deck, you can view the Whirley Crane on the adjacent dock. Although this crane was moved here from a different shipyard, the same type of crane was used here to move large ship sections during construction.

Walk or ride the Bay Trail from Barbara and Jay Vincent Park through the Richmond Marina to Sheridan Observation Point, and you'll find eight interpretive exhibits along the way that discuss different aspects of how the war effort transformed Richmond and our society. Along the way, make sure to stop at the Rosie the Riveter Memorial, Lucretia Edwards Park, and the Ford Building.

At Marina Bay Park, the *Rosie the Riveter Memorial* is an art sculpture designed to represent a Liberty ship and dedicated to the men and women who worked in

the Kaiser shipyards. Part of the sculpture allows you to experience the small spaces ship welders had to crawl through to do their work. When you arrive at Lucretia Edwards Park, look for the boot prints embedded in the trail and the low seating walls that orient you toward important wartime shipyards in San Francisco Bay. Afterward, head a short distance to the newly renovated Ford Assembly Building, featuring a restaurant where you can grab a snack and reenergize. Before World War II, cars were manufactured here, but when the war broke out, the plant was converted to manufacture jeeps and put finishing touches on tanks and other armored vehicles. During this period, the plant turned out 49,000 jeeps and 91,000 tanks and armored vehicles. The Ford Building is also the planned site

African Americans

During World War II, Richmond became a major shipbuilding center (as did Sausalito in Marin County and Hunters Point in San Francisco). Workers were recruited throughout the country, especially in the South and the Midwest, for jobs building Liberty Ships. (You can visit the last unaltered Liberty Ship, the SS *Jeremiah O'Brien*, at Pier 45 in San Francisco's Fisherman's Wharf.) Richmond's population quadrupled, from 25,000 before the influx began to 100,000 at the end of the war. The number of African American residents jumped from 270 in 1940 to 5,673 in 1943 and to 13,780 by 1947.

Suburban-style homes were built with federal funds for whites only. African American families were either quartered in temporary housing or squeezed into already crowded non-white neighborhoods.

When the war ended and the shipyards closed, African Americans, the last to be hired during the Great Depression, were again among the last to be reemployed in peacetime jobs. Poverty and despair took root in Richmond's African American community, as it did in Hunters Point and Marin City.

Richmond shipyard workers, 1942–43

The Natatorium

Downtown Point Richmond today

of the future Rosie the Riveter National Historical Park Visitor Center.

POINT RICHMOND

The community of Point Richmond began as a railroad town in 1897. Santa Fe Railroad purchased the area just north of the small peninsula called Ferry Point, and the town of Santa Fe soon flourished. The town eventually changed its name to Point Richmond, and today it is a distinct neighborhood in the city of Richmond. Point Richmond's famous indoor swimming pool, the Natatorium (more popularly known as the Richmond Plunge) began in 1911 as an exploratory oil well one block off Richmond Avenue. Instead of an oil geyser, water was discovered. A pool was built, and the community gained a swimming facility that has entertained generations since 1924. After many renovations, the Natatorium is still in operation and is a guaranteed lively spot throughout the year. Call ahead for hours and fees. Across Richmond Avenue from the Natatorium is Washington Park, which features a baseball diamond edged by picnic tables and large trees. Several blocks northwest on Richmond Avenue, you'll locate downtown

Downtown Point Richmond, 1897

Point Richmond with its small shops and specialty stores.

Today, Point Richmond's hilly enclave of beautiful old homes, renovated downtown, and small neighborhood park is a welcome break from the surrounding industrial landscape. The Garrard Boulevard tunnel leads to Miller/ Knox Regional Shoreline and bay vistas. Richmond is working to develop a trail that will connect Point Richmond to Point Molate.

MILLER/KNOX REGIONAL SHORELINE AND KELLER BEACH

This open, often windy park is perfect for kite-flying, Frisbee-tossing, or picnics. There are three parking lots here. The north parking lot is a good takeoff point to start the steep hike to the top of Nicholl Knob (370 feet) and its 360-degree vista. From the picnic grounds

(at water level), you can glance beyond the lagoon and old railroad tracks westward to the Chevron Long Wharf, the Richmond–San Rafael Bridge, Red Rock, Angel Island, and Mt. Tamalpais. The park's lagoon attracts egrets, herons, and resident Canada geese. The 318-acre park is named after Congressman George Miller and former Assemblyman John Knox, longtime supporters of the East Bay Regional Park District.

A fence along the railroad tracks currently blocks shoreline access except at Keller Beach, at the northern end of the park, where a sandy beach and ample picnic grounds are popular with swimmers on warm summer weekends (no lifeguard). The Park District plans to remove the railroad tracks and

Golden Gate Model Railroad Museum

This unique museum of working miniature trains (open only on Sundays, April through December, 12 p.m.–5 p.m.; also open Saturdays, 12 p.m.–5 p.m., in December only) is located in the Miller/ Knox Regional Shoreline. To make sure it's open before you visit (it's staffed by volunteers), call on Friday or Saturday.

Miller/Knox Regional Shoreline

Brickyard Cove

fence in the future to open up the shoreline. No bikes are allowed into the Keller Beach area. Atop the riprap seawall extending from the beach, anglers catch fish from the bay as railroad cars rumble by only a few yards beyond a security fence.

FERRY POINT FERRIES

The old pump house building and the pier of the Santa Fe Ferry Terminal can still be seen at Ferry Point. This was the western terminus of the Atchison, Topeka, and Santa Fe Railroad. Starting in 1900, ferries, tugs, and barges transported railcars, merchandise, and people from this spit of land to San Francisco's Ferry Building and China Basin terminals. Santa Fe continued barging freight cars from Ferry Point to San Francisco's China Basin until the early 1980s.

The Southern Pacific Golden Gate Ferry Terminal was at the foot of Dornan Drive, just west of Richmond Terminal No. 1. These ferries operated in the late 1920s and early 1930s. The East Bay Regional Park District now owns the ferry terminal and adjacent land, and the entire 5 acres at Ferry Point have become part of the Miller/Knox Regional Shoreline. The Park District has rebuilt a portion of the old Santa

Fe Pier, and much of the old pier can still be seen while anglers haul in starry flounder, cabezon, leopard shark, and other fish from the new pier.

BRICKYARD COVE

This development of condominiums, shoreline homes, the Brickyard Cove Marina, and the Richmond Yacht Club is clustered around the former site of the Richmond Pressed Brick Company, which made many of the bricks used in rebuilding San Francisco after the 1906 earthquake and fire. The brick kilns were preserved by the developers of the condominium complex nestled in the hills behind them.

GETTING AROUND

From Point Isabel Regional Shoreline, the Bay Trail route moves north for 1 mile along a former railroad levee, then divides at an intersection: to the left, the Bay Trail goes half a mile to Shimada Friendship Park, then continues to the Richmond Marina and Ford Assembly Building at Harbour Way; to the right, the Bay Trail route moves half a mile along Meeker Slough to Marina Bay Park. About halfway between Point Isabel and this intersection, a side trail con-

Santa Fe Ferry Terminal, 1900s

nects with the Bay Trail from a parking area on South 51st Street.

At Marina Park, you can either go directly to the Richmond Marina through the park, or continue on Regatta Boulevard and Marina Way to the west end of the marina. A 0.6-mile section of the Bay Trail follows the shore of the marina.

The Bay Trail route then follows streets to Kaiser Shipyard III and the community of Point Richmond. From Cutting Boulevard, one arm of the Bay Trail travels south on Canal Boulevard, which takes you to Kaiser Shipyard III. You can also turn onto a paved trail at Seacliff Drive, which takes you through Brickyard Cove to the Miller/Knox Regional Shoreline. From Cutting Boulevard, the other arm continues on city streets to Garrard, where you turn south to Point Richmond and then continue through Ferry Point Tunnel to the Miller/Knox Regional Shoreline.

Tides In The Sky

"There is nothing on earth exactly like the fog of San Francisco Bay. None of the thousand evanescent forms of air and water that move across the globe between the equator and the poles is as fantastic in shape and motion yet as tangible and intimate as the thick white vapor that rolls through the Golden Gate in summertime like an airborne flood and spreads to the farthest reaches of the bay and its shores.

In most parts of the earth, fog traditionally is a dark, disagreeable smudge that comes from nowhere, hides the sun, obscures the vision, afflicts the lungs, and casts a damp pall over the land. In San Francisco the fog is a thing of beauty and wonder, a daily drama of the elements with the wide bay itself as the central stage."

HAROLD GILLIAM,
SAN FRANCISCO BAY, 1957

Fog

Summer fog (typically present between May and August) occurs only in the few regions of the world that enjoy a Mediterranean climate, with long dry summers; cold upwelling coastal waters; and steady onshore winds. The beautiful white coolant that pours through the Golden Gate on hot summer days is experienced most directly by those who walk across the Golden Gate Bridge as it comes in. But to gain a macroperspective, and to understand the geography and mechanics of fog, go to the East Bay shoreline.

Fog at the Golden Gate

Here you can observe the various moods of fog as it slips through the Golden Gate, eases over bay waters, and gathers against the East Bay hills.

San Francisco Bay's fog forms when summer temperatures soar in the Central Valley. The hot air rises, creating a "vacuum" below. Marine air moves toward the coast to fill that vacuum with the help of northwesterly winds. As this moist marine air passes over the cold (average 55°F), upwelling waters offshore by the continental shelf, it condenses into fog and is then both pulled and pushed inland. Marine air is dense, and often capped by a warm summer inversion, so it usually stays low, probing coastal valleys for inland routes. The Golden Gate—which acts as a type of "fog funnel"—is the only large breach of the coastal mountains for hundreds of miles in central California, so the fog typically enters the bay and moves toward the East Bay en route to the hot valley. When the ranges of moisture-loving coastal redwoods and fog are mapped and compared, their similarity is striking: fog not only cools, but it can also produce measurable quantities of precipitation below trees and shrubs in the form of "fog drip."

Fog has many shapes, depending on climatic conditions. It can blast into the bay as a wall hundreds of feet tall, creating a regional whiteout in a few hours. It can slither in underneath the Golden Gate Bridge just 30 feet off the water's surface, flick the ramparts of Alcatraz Island, retreat, and then inch its way to Berkeley or San Pablo Bay. Or it can cap the coastal mountains for days, unwilling either to advance or to retreat.

INFORMATION

Public Transit
Call 511 or visit 511.org.

Transit & Trails
www.transitandtrails.org

AC Transit
www.actransit.org
510-891-4700

Brooks Island Reservations
www.ebparks.org
888-327-2757

East Bay Regional Park District
www.ebparks.org
888-327-2757

Golden State Model Railroad Museum
www.gsmrm.org
510-234-4884

Natatorium
www.richmondplunge.org
510-620-6820

Richmond Marina Bay
www.marinabayyacht
harbor.com
510-236-1013

Richmond Museum of History
www.richmondmuseum
ofhistory.org
510-235-7387

RICHMOND–SAN RAFAEL BRIDGE TO POINT PINOLE

Most Bay Area residents view the meandering shore from the Richmond–San Rafael Bridge northward to Point Pinole Regional Shoreline as an industrial area with unsightly oil refineries and chemical plants. But this shoreline also has a patchwork of colorful flower nurseries, stables, marshland, preservation areas, historical sites, trails, and open space. This region is accessible, culturally and ecologically diverse, and full of surprises. Take a while to explore the unknown shore of Contra Costa County.

Point Molate with the Richmond–San Rafael Bridge and Mt. Tamalpais in background

Cormorants Up There

A colony of double-crested cormorants has been nesting in the lattice work of girders beneath the lower deck of the Richmond–San Rafael Bridge since at least the early 1970s. Some 300 nests have been counted in recent years, as these birds have adapted to urban life. They build nests of sticks, grass, marsh plants, seaweed, feathers, guano, and often also use debris, such as plastic rope and packing tape. To study the birds, biologists dress up like Caltrans workers: they put on helmets, suspension belts, and orange vests.

The cormorants begin to arrive here in mid-March, and most settle beneath the north side of the

Cormorants nesting in bridge girders

bridge. To feed their chicks, they commute to mainland bays and estuaries and forage in fresh and brackish water. Their diet in the bay is not well known, but they may feed on the migrating toadfish (see p. 205), which mates noisily and produces young just when the cormorant chicks are most hungry.

RICHMOND–SAN RAFAEL BRIDGE

Construction of this double-decker bridge began in 1952, partly encouraged by two major ferry strikes that had seriously disrupted bay transportation. Four years later, the 5.5-mile-long bridge opened to much fanfare while sealing the fate of the nearby ferry terminal at Castro Point. It is now a vital link between Marin County and East Bay cities. Some 64,000 cars cross it daily.

CASTRO POINT

This is the site of the former Richmond–San Rafael Ferry Terminal, which operated four ferries between here and Point San Quentin from 1915 until the Richmond–San Rafael Bridge opened in September 1956. You could ride the key system trolley (streetcars that served East Bay cities from Richmond to Oakland) to the ferry terminal from much of the East Bay. After the ferry service ended, the pier was converted to the Red Rock Marina and Fishing Resort. This was a productive fishing area until it closed in the late 1970s.

POINT MOLATE BEACH PARK

This shoreline park has seen better days. Located off Western Drive, the park occupies the site of a former Chinese fishing village and offers a sweeping view of the Richmond–San Rafael Bridge and the San Rafael area across the water, with Mt. Tamalpais in the backdrop. Richmond closed the park when soil and water remediation work began at the former Point Molate Naval Fuel Depot, but the park has remained closed due to a lack of city resources. A lonely beach and unused picnic tables and barbecue pits still sit here. The city is looking for alternative resources to reopen the park. Meanwhile, the East Bay Regional Park District has a long-range vision of a regional park at Point Molate that would include Point Molate Beach Park.

POINT MOLATE U.S. NAVAL FUEL DEPOT

In 1942, the U.S. Navy purchased 400 acres along the Richmond

Point Molate Beach Park

shoreline, including the old Winehaven property, and created a fuel depot. The depot was closed in 1998, and Richmond is considering what to do with this land. Although you can drive through this area to Point San Pablo Yacht Harbor, there is not much to do here except to appreciate the unique views of the bay.

POINT SAN PABLO AND SARDINES

The tip of Point San Pablo is now the site of Richmond Municipal Terminal No. 4. The cove to the northeast was the home port for some 100 sardine boats during the 1940s, until the fishery collapsed.

During the height of the season, purse seiners often delivered over 10,000 tons of sardines here in a 24-hour period. The fish were processed onshore for the production of fish meal and fish oil.

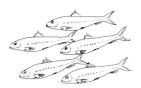

CHEVRON U.S.A.

Chevron (formerly Standard Oil of California) is a major physical and economic presence in Richmond. Initial construction of Chevron's refinery began here in 1901, and the facility has since grown to cover 2,900 acres. This refinery's statistics are best understood in a summarized form. (One barrel of oil = 42 U.S. gallons.)

Number of Oil Storage Tanks: 500
Total Oil Storage Capacity: 15 million barrels
Largest Tank: 750,000 barrels
Miles of Pipelines: Over 5,000
Length of Chevron Long Wharf: 1 mile
Tanker Traffic: 550/year (average)
Barge Traffic: 900/year (average)
Employees in Richmond: 1,500

Richmond–San Rafael ferries, 1952

Red Rock, Molate, Castro Rocks, Rancho San Pablo, and Contra Costa

The desolate-looking island rising some 170 feet off the Richmond shoreline immediately south of the Richmond–San Rafael Bridge is Red Rock. An abundance of iron oxides gives it a brick-red hue. To the Spanish it was Moleta, named for the similarly shaped grinding stone. (This name was later misspelled *Molate* and applied to several shoreline sites in the early 19th century.) For a time, it was also known as Golden Rock, owing to tales of hidden pirate treasure. Red Rock is the exact location where the boundaries of three counties meet: Contra Costa, Marin, and San Francisco. The name Contra Costa is Spanish, meaning "opposite coast"—that is, across the bay from the San Francisco Presidio.

Closer to shore, Castro Rocks are named after Joaquin I. Castro, whose father, Francisco, was granted Rancho San Pablo by the Mexican government in 1823. Rancho

Red Rock with Mt. Tamalpais in the background

San Pablo once encompassed most of the territory from Albany to Point Pinole and inland to the El Sobrante area. If the tide is low and you drive carefully, you can glance at the harbor seals using this low-lying cluster of rocks as a haul-out.

Wine in Richmond?

Between 1908 and 1919, one of the world's largest wineries—Winehaven—stood on the land now occupied by the closed Navy fuel depot. The winery maintained its own school, hotel, post office, and steam-generating plant. The California Wine Association built Winehaven here because of the area's access to shipping lanes and rail service. California grapes were brought to Winehaven from 40 different growing regions stretching from Yolo and Napa counties south to San Bernardino County.

Until 1919, when Prohibition shut it down, Winehaven produced 67 types of wine, brandy, and champagne. Its annual production averaged 12 million gallons. Some 25,000 tons of grapes could be processed in one crushing, 4 miles of passages linked 3,000 aging vats, and 15 million bottles of wine were kept in storage. About 500,000 gallons of wine were shipped by sea or rail monthly for destinations around the globe. Forty ships sailed annually for New York alone, and Winehaven's bulk tanker ships carried 300 barrels of wine daily to San Francisco.

After the winery was forced to close, alcohol was illegally leaving the facility, so federal authorities knocked the bungs out of the storage vats and some 240,000 gallons of wine flowed into the bay. Legend has it that local fishermen scooped marinated fish off the surface of nearby waters the next day. The principal winery buildings and employee housing—now national historic buildings—still stand. The brick main building resembles a medieval castle, with turrets and parapets.

Wine label, 1899

Winehaven, 1907

Winehaven's bottling room, 1920

EAST AND WEST
BROTHER ISLANDS

East and West Brother islands are near the tip of Point San Pablo and directly southeast of The Sisters, islands off Point San Pedro in Marin County. These two points, and their sibling islands, mark the entrance to San Pablo Bay.

The lighthouse on East Brother was built in 1873–74 and is one of 17 lighthouses erected in the region. Only three remain: East Brother's, the South Hampton Lighthouse on Tinsley Island in the Delta, and the Carquinez Lighthouse (see p. 152). East Brother's is the oldest lighthouse still working. The station was staffed until 1969, when the light and fog signals were automated and the buildings were boarded up. That same year, the station was listed on the National Register of Historic Places. In 1979, a nonprofit organization was formed to preserve the station. It eventually

Point San Pablo Yacht Harbor

East and West Brother Islands

obtained a lease to the island and began a restoration program. Today, the buildings have been completely restored, and the organization operates a bed-and-breakfast getaway here (proceeds help pay for maintenance costs).

As Bay Area explorer and writer Margot Patterson Doss notes, East Brother's ugly relative, West Brother Island, is as "bare as a basking whale," even though it once supported enough grass to provide pasture for the lightkeeper's goat. Today, its guano-covered crown is frequented by gulls, cormorants, and other seabirds.

POINT SAN PABLO
YACHT HARBOR

Roaming the western breakwater of this isolated harbor, you may feel transported back in time, and far from the heavily urbanized Bay Area. Behind you are grassy hills; bayward the entire San Pablo Bay lies still and blue. Marking the end of the winding, 4-mile Western Drive, this sleepy harbor is home to a few houseboats, some two dozen pleasure boats, a scattering of commercial and sportfishing boats, and a wealth of human characters, including former whalers.

Rock Watch

Look for road cuts as you wind along Western Drive. What you see are Franciscan Complex rocks, primarily thin layers of graywacke, a type of sandstone. Graywacke is the most common rock in the Franciscan Complex, which also includes chert, pillow basalt, serpentine, and metamorphic rocks. In the East Bay, you'll find Franciscan rocks west of the Hayward Fault. East of the fault, you'll see younger sandstone and chert and more recent volcanic rocks. (For more on bay geology, see p. 98.)

Franciscan rock formation

Wildcat Marsh and West County Landfill in the foreground with Point San Pablo and Mt. Tamalpais in the background

The harbor's principal buildings are the San Pablo Bay Sportsmen Club, the harbor master's office, and a building that housed the now-closed Gallery Cafe. The western breakwater was built by sinking an abandoned fleet of steam schooners and then filling the boats with dirt.

Whaling

Whalers sailed into San Francisco Bay as early as the 1820s, seeking supplies and rest. By the mid-19th century, whale hunters called frequently on San Francisco while following gray whales migrating to the Bering Sea and Arctic Ocean for the summer and to Baja California for the winter. Many whaling stations sprang up along the California shoreline. After the transcontinental railroad reached the Bay Area in 1869, many whalers chose San Francisco as a home port to speed the transport of their products—principally whale oil and bone—to East Coast markets. By the late 19th century, San Francisco was the world's largest whaling port. The whaling industry collapsed just before World War I, as petroleum replaced whale oil and spring steel replaced whale bone. The whaling station at Point San Pablo, now reduced to a burned-out building west of Point San Pablo Yacht Harbor, was active until 1971, when it was closed by federal order after the United States banned whaling. It was the last active whaling station in the United States.

Humpback whale

WILDCAT MARSH

At Wildcat Marsh, you can see a living marsh in the midst of a heavily industrialized landscape. Contra Costa County and the U.S. Army Corps of Engineers had plans to control floods by building a concrete-lined channel on the creek that feeds into the marsh—Wildcat Creek—where it flowed through the communities of San Pablo and Richmond. This channel would have dumped sediment into the marsh, turning it into upland. Activists and resource agencies had a different vision: a natural, sinuous, tree-lined waterway through the heart of a low-income urban area. Both visions would guard against flooding; the latter was far more appealing and eventually won favor. Chevron voluntarily restored Wildcat Marsh, following a plan prepared by the State Coastal Conservancy.

Where the creek enters the marsh, a berm was constructed to keep out storm water and direct most of the sediment into the bay, where it disperses.

Today, Wildcat Creek is just beginning to develop into the envisioned verdant passageway through an otherwise bleak urban landscape. The East Bay Regional Park District has completed the first phase of the Wildcat Creek Trail and has plans to extend the trail from the observation platform atop the berm overlooking vibrant Wildcat Marsh all the way up to Wildcat Canyon in the East Bay hills. Parking for the marsh and creek trail is located off the west side of Richmond Parkway at Wildcat Creek between Gertrude and Pittsburg avenues. As you walk west on the trail from Richmond Parkway to the observation platform, look to the left. That's the modified creek channel. Near the platform, you can see two ponds in the marsh. Canada geese often rest nearby. The pickleweed here is habitat for the endangered salt marsh har-

Point Pinole Pier

vest mouse, and the endangered California clapper rail forages in the cordgrass along marsh channels. From the platform, you'll

West County Landfill with views of Mt. Tamalpais

notice the Chevron refinery to the southwest. You can continue north along the Bay Trail next to the West Contra Costa County Sanitary District's treatment plant and then to the almost 3 miles of gravel trail that loops around the closed West County Sanitary Landfill. From this Landfill Loop Trail, you'll have amazing views of Mt. Tamalpais and terns, shorebirds, and other waterfowl in San Pablo Creek Marsh and Wildcat Marsh.

POINT PINOLE REGIONAL SHORELINE

The sweeping grasslands and stately eucalyptus groves of Point Pinole Regional Shoreline would be spectacular anywhere in the Bay Area, but here, along this stretch of industrial bayshore (which some locals call the "oil coast"), the tranquility and recreation opportunities of this park are especially welcome. This is one of the largest waterfront parks in the entire Bay Area, with some 2,315 acres on the Point Pinole Peninsula and adjacent marshlands. From the parking lot (where you pay a

Giant Powder Company

After several deadly explosions at its San Francisco and Berkeley factories in the late 19th century, the United States' first producer of dynamite—the Giant Powder Company—moved to Point Pinole's isolated peninsula in 1892. The company town of Giant grew rapidly, drawing on the large Croatian community of nearby Sobrante. Giant's products were used internationally for mining, dam building, and other large construction jobs. Although it's hard to detect evidence of Giant's plant in the park today, the company produced explosives here until 1960.

Point Pinole

fee on weekends and holidays), visitors must cross the Paul J. Badger Bridge to enter the main park. Stop on the overpass for a few minutes and you might see a cargo or Amtrak train rumble by directly beneath you. Move into the park, beyond a playground and picnic area, and you'll find over 12 miles of trails crisscrossing the peninsula, weaving through meadows and stands of eucalyptus that shelter monarch butterflies and varied birds. Although most of the grasses here are introduced species, as are the eucalyptus, you can also find native bunchgrass. A paved trail, just under 1.5 miles long, leads across Point Pinole to the park's sturdy fishing pier. A shuttle also runs between the parking area and the popular, 1,250-foot-long pier. (Call ahead for the shuttle schedule and fee.) The pier was built next to the re-mains of a wharf where explosives

were transported from the turn of the 20th century until 1960. Now anglers catch flounder, perch, striped bass, sturgeon, jacksmelt, and kingfish, to name but a few species. The view from the pier is spectacular. Bayward, the vista takes in five counties; inland, the bluffs of Point Pinole rise above the rocky beach and the bay to your right, and to your left the

Whittell Marsh covers the park's shoreline.

GETTING AROUND 🚶🚶

To reach Western Drive and Point Molate Beach Park from Point Richmond, use city streets and Interstate 580. Western Drive is the last exit off Interstate 580, heading west, before the Richmond–San Rafael Bridge. From

Point Pinole Regional Shoreline

Western Drive, just north of Interstate 580, there's a hidden trail lined by fences that leads underneath the bridge to the south side of Interstate 580, where there's a bench that overlooks the Chevron Long Wharf and Red Rock. Western Drive continues for 4 miles, ending at Point San Pablo Yacht Harbor. To reach Wildcat Marsh from Interstate 580, take Castro Street and proceed to Richmond Parkway. To get to Point Pinole Regional Shoreline, use city streets.

Because some of Richmond's inland districts have had problems with street crime, be sensible when venturing away from the shoreline.

INFORMATION

Public Transit
Call 511 or visit 511.org.

Transit & Trails
www.transitandtrails.org

AC Transit
www.actransit.org
510-891-4700

East Bay Regional Park District
www.ebparks.org
888-327-2757

East Brother Light Station
www.ebls.org
510-233-2385

Point San Pablo Yacht Harbor
www.pspyh.com
510-233-3224

Richmond Parks and Landscaping Division
www.ci.richmond.ca.us
510-231-3004

Legend

— **Bay Trail** (off street)
Shared-use paved or gravel paths

— **Bay Trail** (on street)
Bike lanes and sidewalks

— **Unimproved Bay Trail** (off street)
Narrow path and/or rough surface

— **Unimproved Bay Trail** (on street)
No bike lanes and/or no sidewalks

--- **Planned Bay Trail**
Future route – not developed

— **Other Trails**
Paved or gravel paths connecting
to Bay Trail

--- **Planned Other Trail**
Future connection to Bay Trail
– not developed

⚓ Boating/Marina

Ⓟ Parking

🐟 Fishing Pier

0 .5 mile 1 mile
0 1 km

N

2011

San Pablo
Bay
National
Wildlife
Refuge

Knight
Island

South Slough

Dutchman Slough

Hwy 37

Napa River

Sears
Point
Bridge

Marine World Pkwy

White Slough

Sacramento

Sonoma Blvd

Redwood St

Kimberly
Park

Severe

Mini

Meadows

Donner Pass

Tobin

Daniels

Terrace
Park

Wilson

River
Park

Mare Island Causeway

Vallejo
Marina

Marina
Vista
Memorial
Park

Municipal
Dock

Ferry

Maine

Broadway

Vallejo

Curtola Pkwy

Mare
Island

Mare Island Strait

Wilson/
Lake
Dalwigk
Park

Lemon

Sonoma Blvd

5th St

Derr

Porter

Hwy 29

Seaport

San
Pablo
Bay

Carquinez Strait

Carquinez
Park

California
Maritime
Academy

Vallejo/Baylink Ferry

Vallejo/Baylink Ferry

Davis
Point

San
Pablo
Bay
Regional
Trail

San Pablo

Vista Del Rio

San Pablo

Downie

Pom

Way

Crockett

Lone
Tree
Point

2nd St

Garretson

Parker Ave

Pacific

California

4th St

7th St

Hawthorne

Hwy 80

Rodeo

Willow

Linus
Pauling

Alfred Nobel

Refugio Creek

Railroad

Pinole
Bayfront
Park &
Treatment
Plant

San
Pablo
Bay
Regional
Park

Pinole
Shores
Regional
Park

Point
Wilson

Proposed
trail
follows
railroad
tracks

Lettia

Montalvin
Park

Heather

Rachel

San Pablo

Tara Hills

Pinole Shores Dr

Piñon

Pinole Creek

Ternent

Hercules

Hercules

San Pablo

Fernandez
Park

John Muir Pkwy

Bayberry

Sycamore

Refugio
Valley
Park

Refugio Valley

Refugio
Valley
Park

Crockett
Hills
Regional
Park

Hwy 4

Hilltop
Lake
Park

Lakeside

Atlas

Blume

Hilltop Mall

Appian Way

Pinole Valley Rd

Pinole

Hwy 80

PINOLE SHORES REGIONAL PARK TO SAN PABLO BAY REGIONAL TRAIL

Most people who pass this stretch of shoreline while traveling on Interstate 80 see it as one continuous oil refinery zone, with the vast ConocoPhillips complex in Rodeo and a few smaller refineries to the immediate north. If you get off the freeway, however, you can visit five shoreline parks, large stretches of preserved marshland, and shoreline bluffs overlooking the entire San Pablo Bay.

Pinole Shores Regional Park

Pinole Bayfront Park

PINOLE SHORES REGIONAL PARK

At the end of Pinole Shores Drive, a small parking lot marks the entrance to Pinole Shores Regional Park. A paved trail leaves the parking area and leads a half mile to the northeast. Several turnouts with benches are good perches for gazing out across San Pablo Bay (which the Spanish called "Circular Bay") and looking down the cliff face at trains rumbling by on the shoreline tracks. To the southwest, a paved trail slices across grassy slopes for a mile, past Point Wilson. It runs between the shoreline railroad tracks and a neighborhood just upslope. Pinole Shores Regional Park eventually will be linked with Point Pinole Regional Shoreline to the southwest and with San Pablo Bay Regional Park to the northeast.

PINOLE BAYFRONT PARK AND SAN PABLO BAY REGIONAL PARK

The beautiful picnic area of Pinole Bayfront Park overlooks extensive mud flats and patches of fine marsh grasses visited by shorebirds. A trail (paved, then gravel) follows the shoreline for several hundred yards and works its way around the front of the city of Pinole's sewage treatment plant. A small boat ramp (for hand-launched craft only) is to the northeast of the plant, on the shore of Pinole Creek. See p. 7 for information about the Bay Area Water Trail. You can cross Pinole Creek on a footbridge (alongside the railroad tracks) and follow a dirt path into San Pablo Bay Regional Park, which is undeveloped except for a small segment of paved trail near the intersection of Santa Fe and Railroad, opposite

the small neighborhood park. Eventually, shoreline explorers will be able to wander unimpeded between San Pablo Bay Regional Park and Point Pinole Regional Shoreline—a stretch of some 5 miles.

Pinole

The name Pinole originates from *pinolli*, the Aztec word for toasted and ground seeds. As the Spanish moved north through Mexico and then California, they changed the word to *pinole* and used it to describe a variety of flours and seed cakes. In 1775, some local inhabitants offered *pinole* to José de Cañizares (first sailing master of the frigate *San Carlos* under Lieutenant Juan Manuel de Ayala) near today's city of Pinole, and the name has become permanently linked with the location.

Fernandez Park

Lone Tree Point

PINOLE CREEK AND FERNANDEZ PARK

A tram once ran along Pinole Creek, bringing produce and livestock from creekside farms and ranches to the wharf that jutted out into the bay where Pinole Bayfront Park is today. A paved path follows the old tram route from the Bay Trail for half a mile along the tree-lined creek, ending near Pinole Valley Road. As the path nears San Pablo Avenue (about a quarter mile from bay shoreline), it passes Fernandez Park, with playgrounds, picnic areas, baseball and basketball areas, and a large lawn with shade trees.

RODEO AND LONE TREE POINT

During California's Spanish era, cattle were rounded up from nearby hills and led to the shoreline at the point where the town of Rodeo is today. They were herded onto boats and taken to Vallejo for further fattening. Raucous rodeos are said to have taken place here during roundups. After California became a state and the railroad arrived, roundups and cattle shipments ceased. Today, a couple of aged marinas provide a place to stroll and evoke a time when a lucky fisherman could reel in hun-

Hercules and the Historic Company Town

For nearly one hundred years, Hercules was known mainly for its production of dynamite, black powder, TNT, and intermediate chemicals. Explosive manufacturing ceased completely in 1964, and by the late 1970s, industrial activity had ended. A general plan adopted in 1972 led to the creation of today's suburban city. A few buildings still survive from the Hercules company town and plant. While the Bay Trail is not continuous through Hercules, there are two short sections of the trail in the city. The southern segment of Bay Trail in Hercules is over a half mile long and is a part of the San Pablo Bay Regional Park. You can access it from San Pablo Avenue by taking either the Pinole Creek Trail or by taking Hercules Avenue to Santa Fe Avenue. On the way, you'll come across the small historic residential district, where workers once lived in company-owned homes, located southeast of Railroad Avenue and Santa Fe Avenue. Continuing up the hill along Railroad Avenue, you can see the former Masonic Hall and a Craftsman bungalow that has been repurposed as a restaurant. Atop the hill are the 19th-century clubhouse and a sturdy brick plant office. On the northern edge of town, the other section of Bay Trail in Hercules is a part of Shoreline Park and is about a half mile long. Next to the trail, there are large lawn areas, picnic tables, and benches. There's also an overlook where you can sit on a bench and watch the bay and passing ferries. Farther east from the trail is a larger lawn area with a playground and restrooms at its eastern edge. Hercules and the East Bay Regional Park District are working to finish the Bay Trail in Hercules and close the gap between the two trail segments in the future.

Hercules Explosives Company buildings, including historic clubhouse

Rodeo Marina

dreds of fish in a single day here. This area provides a quiet break and a bit of isolation in this mostly industrial landscape on the border of one of the Bay Area's few remaining working-class towns. From the edge of the marinas, you can survey San Pablo Bay and the immense ConocoPhillips refinery to the northeast. A few restaurants provide hearty meals. To the immediate southwest of the marinas, a lone eucalyptus stands on a grassy bluff overlooking a small beach. This is Lone Tree Point, a small regional park. From the gravel parking lot at the intersection of San Pablo Avenue and Rodeo Avenue, you can hike the quarter-mile loop trail out to Lone Tree Point, where you can sit on a bench and enjoy views of San Pablo Bay. The park also has several picnic tables and a rustic restroom.

The Oil Coast

Oil has had a strong presence along this Contra Costa County shoreline since 1896, when Union Oil built the Bay Area's first oil refinery in Rodeo. Six petroleum refining and storage facilities now occupy over 8,000 shoreline acres in the northeast bay (one is in Solano County), constituting the Bay Area's largest waterfront industry. The ConocoPhillips facility alone covers more than 1,000 acres in Rodeo. Its refinery operates around the clock, employs 650 people, processes some 100,000 barrels of crude a day, and makes products ranging from jet fuel to food-grade waxes. Half of its output is gasoline. In Martinez, the Shell Oil refinery processes 165,000 barrels of crude daily. For better or for worse, our society depends on oil and its byproducts. But oil also continues to be a major polluter of Contra Costa County's shoreline and the entire San Francisco Bay. Petroleum and chemicals used in oil's processing enter the water and air through routine refinery waste discharges and some accidental spills. Selenium from refineries processing lower-grade crude oil between Richmond and Benicia threatens bay ecosystems and the health of people who eat fish. This may be the most serious preventable toxics problem in the bay today, according to some scientists. In addition, motorists who dump used automotive oil in the gutter or on the ground contribute a significant amount of pollution. When it rains, this oil washes down storm drains and creeks into the bay. (See p. 188 to learn how you can help to prevent this type of contamination.)

San Pablo Bay Regional Trail

SAN PABLO BAY REGIONAL TRAIL

Some 3 miles northeast of Rodeo, on the bay side of San Pablo Avenue, is the San Pablo Bay Regional Trail. It consists of several miles of dirt paths winding through some 25 hilly acres, offering sweeping views of San Pablo Bay; turkey vultures and red-tailed hawks search the grassy slopes for meals. The sole access point to this trail is difficult to find. It's on the turn of San Pablo Avenue, at the top of a hill, across from Vista Del Rio Road. Parking here is limited; only two cars can park off-road at the access point. There is no other parking nearby.

The Salt Wedge

Bay waters are a mix of Pacific Ocean saltwater and freshwater from numerous rivers—principally, the Sacramento, San Joaquin, and Napa rivers. The salt-to-fresh transition is gradual between the Golden Gate and the Sacramento/San Joaquin Delta. Saltwater is denser than freshwater, so it "wedges" underneath incoming fresh water, forming a mixing zone that moves up and down the bay's estuary several miles daily, depending on the tides and freshwater flow. This migrating mixing zone is highly productive. The shallow waters of the Suisun and San Pablo bays nourish phytoplankton (small plants that float in the water) and zooplankton (small floating animals), which in turn feed numerous aquatic species. Because of freshwater diversions by federal and state water projects, the salt wedge has shifted upstream. Around 1900, so much freshwater flowed down through the Carquinez Strait that residents of Crockett drew their drinking water directly from the strait. Today, freshwater has retreated to the confines of Suisun Bay, some 6 to 8 miles to the east. Not only has this damaged phytoplankton and zooplankton—and therefore fish populations—but also such freshwater marsh plants as tule and bulrush have retreated upstream, while salt-tolerant cordgrass has moved in. A range of species adapted to freshwater has been displaced from historic habitats. To say that water issues are complicated could qualify as the understatement of the century. Industry, agriculture, fish and wildlife protection agencies, municipalities, and environmental groups have claims on the freshwater that naturally flows into the delta and bay. While these interests compete, the salt wedge continues to migrate upstream, spreading damage to the bay/delta's farms, as well as to its fish, wildlife, and plants.

THE CARQUINEZ STRAIT—CROCKETT TO MARTINEZ

Thousands of years ago, during a much wetter climatic period, water carved its way through the mountains here at the confluence of the Sacramento and San Joaquin rivers. These two great rivers drain almost the entire western Sierra Nevada and the interior slopes of the coastal mountains. Much of their flow is now diverted and captured for various uses, but they continue to feed freshwater to San Francisco Bay through the maze of rivers, creeks, and sloughs of the

Carquinez Strait

Sacramento/San Joaquin Delta. This freshwater is essential to the health of the bay. It mixes with saltwater as it passes through the Carquinez Strait into San Francisco Bay. Six miles long, the strait is no more than half a mile wide at several points and as deep as 122 feet near Dillon Point. It is a transition zone and a meeting place ecologically, sociologically, and economically. The Karkin people who lived along the shoreline, harvesting its natural bounty, greeted some of the first European explorers here in the 18th century. Later, industry and commerce flourished as transportation via water, cart, and rail converged here. Now the old towns along the strait are attractive to people and businesses seeking to get away from congestion and other problems faced by metropolitan centers on the bay. This is a great shoreline area to explore, and it's surprisingly little known by Bay Area residents.

First Encounters

In 1775, Father Vicente Santa María (chaplain of the frigate *San Carlos* under the command of Lieutenant Juan Manuel de Ayala) and several sailors approached a Karkin village in the *San Carlos*'s longboat. The priest's report provides a glimpse into the past and a feeling for the distant meeting of two cultures that profoundly influenced the Bay Area's history and environment:

"Our men made a landing, and when they had done so the Indian chief addressed a long speech to them. He would not permit them to sit on the bare earth; some Indians were at once sent by the chief to bring some mats cleanly and carefully woven from rushes, simple ground coverings on which the Spaniards might lie at ease. Meanwhile a supper was brought them; right away came atoles [porridge], pinoles [seed cakes], and cooked fishes, refreshments that quieted their pangs of hunger and tickled their palates too. The pinoles were made from a seed that left me with a taste like that of toasted hazelnuts. Two kinds of atole were supplied at this meal, one lead-colored and the other very white, which one might think to have been made from acorns. Both were well flavored and in no way disagreeable to a palate little accustomed to atoles. The fishes were of a kind so special that besides having not one bone they were most deliciously tasty, of very considerable size, and ornamented all the way round them by six strips of little shells [sturgeon have shell-like dorsal plates]. The Indians did not content themselves with feasting our men, on that day when they met together, but, when the longboat left, gave more of those fishes and we had the enjoyment of them for several days."

Crockett and the Carquinez Bridge, which is actually two bridges

CROCKETT

Crockett is a great walking town, and a stroll in its downtown neighborhoods will bring you past historic buildings, antique shops, parks, and restaurants. In the Crockett Historical Society and Museum on Loring Street, items from the town's past are on display, and friendly volunteers answer questions. One of the more unusual exhibits is a mounted sturgeon, the largest recorded in California. It weighed 468 pounds when it was caught in San Pablo Bay in 1992. (In the Black Sea, a related species of sturgeon can weigh up to 2,500 pounds!) Under the southwestern foot of the Carquinez Bridge is the Crockett Marina and Dowrelio Pier (off Dowrelio Drive). Here you might land a flounder, sturgeon, shad, salmon, steelhead, or striped bass. (This is a private pier, so a fishing license is required.) The marina offers boating, a seafood restaurant, and great views of the bridge, the opening of the strait, and—across the water—the California Maritime Academy. The town of Crockett is named after Joseph B. Crockett, who owned 1,800 acres here in the 1860s with his partner, Thomas Edwards. Edwards's first house, built in 1867, stands on Loring Street, across the street from the Crockett Historical Society and Museum and is now referred to as The Old Homestead. It can be argued that when the Carquinez Bridge was completed in 1927, Crockett was bypassed by both traffic and time. In 1958, another three-lane bridge was erected alongside the original structure (Carquinez Bridge is really the Carquinez Bridges). In 2003, the older of the two bridges

Bicyclist riding on the Zampa Bridge path

Carquinez Etymology

Carquinez Strait and Suisun Bay were first described by Europeans during the Lieutenant Pedro Fages overland expedition of 1772. The Spanish named the strait Boca del Puerto Dulce—Mouth of the Freshwater Port. The present name is derived from the earlier local inhabitants, the Karkin. The spelling *Karquines* was commonly used on documents until the early 19th century.

Carquinez Strait Regional Shoreline

Port Costa

was replaced with a new suspension bridge that was named the Alfred Zampa Memorial Bridge after a local ironworker who helped build the 1927 bridge. Together,

Western bluebird

the Zampa Bridge and the 1958 bridge are still known collectively as the Carquinez Bridge. Today, some 100,000 drivers skirt Crockett daily via this bridge.

CARQUINEZ STRAIT REGIONAL SHORELINE

The 1,294-acre Carquinez Strait Regional Shoreline encompasses several pieces of land stretching from eastern Crockett to Martinez. Nearly 14 miles of dirt trails

wind through coastal scrub and grasslands, past bay laurels, buckeyes, and through oak woodlands. Common resident wildlife species include the western meadowlark, western bluebird, American goldfinch, golden eagle, gray fox, mule deer, and raccoons (listen for their songs; look for their tracks). The shoreline's bluffs rise 750 feet to summits and ridges with sweeping views. Look for tugboats pushing barges up the strait, directing large ships, or moving from one

Grain and Sugar

When the Central Pacific Railroad (later known as the Southern Pacific) arrived at the strait via Martinez in 1879, this shoreline became a major shipping center for California agricultural products. Large sailing vessels, river steamboats, scow schooners, and rail cars met here to transfer grains, particularly wheat. By 1884, grain wharves extended almost continuously along some 4 miles of the strait, from Crockett to Port Costa, as California's prized wheat fetched top prices on England's Grain Exchange. Many of the old wharf pilings can still be seen. During the 1880s, the grain facilities at Port Costa—which could service over a dozen transport ships at once—stored some 70,000 tons of grain in specially equipped warehouses. It wasn't unusual for dozens of ships to be anchored here waiting to load up with hardy California wheat before heading around Cape Horn en route to European markets. As transcontinental rail service improved, grain was more frequently sent to Eastern ports via rail cars to shorten the delivery time to Europe. In 1893, the international wheat market collapsed,

Advertisement from the 1930s

and during the ensuing decade the grain wharves were gradually abandoned. Port Costa continued as an important ferry terminal for rail cars, but the great warehouses and associated businesses fell into disrepair. Crockett's Starr Flour Mill converted to a beet sugar refinery, and in 1906 C&H Sugar (short for California & Hawaii) bought out the beet refinery and opened its own operation, using sugarcane. It is now the world's largest sugarcane refinery.

Refurbished Port Costa School

Martinez Marina and Martinez Regional Shoreline

job to another. From Franklin Ridge (in the eastern part of this shoreline park), you can see Mt. Tamalpais to the west and Mt. Diablo to the east. To reach the western part of the park, use the Bull Valley Staging Area; for the eastern part, use the Carquinez Strait East Staging Area.

PORT COSTA

This quiet small town was a focus of the world grain trade a century ago (see p. 146). The original downtown—a large block of multistory buildings fronting the Carquinez Strait—now offers a variety of shops and restaurants. Typical of the buildings here is the McNeer warehouse, which once stored wheat, hay, and potatoes and now houses several different businesses. Built in 1886 as "the first fireproof building in Contra Costa County," this structure survived devastating fires in 1889,

The *Solano*

1909, 1924, and 1941 and earthquakes in 1892 and 1906.

The town is now separated from its waterfront by fencing and railroad tracks. In the 19th century, however, Port Costa was a major ferry terminal and a critical rail link to Benicia and all points eastward. Among the ferries stopping here was the *Solano*, built in 1879 and touted as a "wonder of the age." It was longer than a football field and had four sets of tracks on deck, which enabled it to carry two complete passenger trains at once. It plied the waters of the strait until 1930, when the Southern Pacific Company completed the steel span connecting Martinez and Benicia.

MARTINEZ REGIONAL SHORELINE

In 1974, the city of Martinez teamed up with the East Bay Regional Park District to transform a seldom-used 350-acre waterfront property into a park that has become wildly popular. The marshland was protected, and what was once industrial fill became picnic grounds and athletic facilities for soccer, bocce ball, and baseball. The baseball complex is named for Joe DiMaggio, a Martinez native. Three miles of dirt and paved trails wind through the park; they also lead toward the Martinez Marina and public pier. The pier

The Mothball Fleet

After World War II, more than 300 military ships were anchored in neat rows just east of Benicia. In the ensuing decades, the Mothball Fleet (as most folks call it) has shrunk in size to a few dozen ships. A few are being maintained in case of military emergencies; the rest are gradually being scrapped and should be completely removed from the bay by 2017.

Mothball Fleet

was built from the remains of the bay's last automobile ferry slip, which closed in 1962, when the Benicia-Martinez Bridge opened. Anglers here hook striped bass, flounder, and sturgeon. Pier visitors can look east toward the Shell Oil refinery, and west down the strait toward the Carquinez Strait Regional Shoreline. In the town of Martinez, Rankin Park (off Talbart Street) features a large playground and picnic area.

JOHN MUIR HISTORIC SITE AND THE MARTINEZ ADOBE

The most famous structure in Martinez is the home of John Muir, the visionary explorer and naturalist who is revered in the West, both for his wilderness conservation work and for his writing. Muir was the chief advocate for the establishment of Yosemite National Park in

John Muir House

"I only went out for a walk and finally concluded to stay out till sundown, for going out, I found, was really going in."

JOHN MUIR, 1913

1890 and played a key role in the creation of several other national parks. From 1890 until his death in 1914, he lived and worked here when he was not climbing mountains, crossing glaciers, and exploring great forests. The John Muir home is now an 8.8-acre National Historic Site (near the intersection of Alhambra Avenue and Highway 4). Both the mansion and the Vicente Martinez Adobe, a two-story adobe ranch house built in 1849, are open to the public.

GETTING AROUND

To reach Pinole Shores Regional Park from Point Pinole Regional Shoreline, follow San Pablo Ave northeast to Pinole Shores Drive, which winds through a housing complex to the park. To continue on to Pinole Bayfront Park and San Pablo Bay Regional Park, return to San Pablo Avenue and continue northeast to Tennent Avenue, then turn bayward to the end of Tennent. A quarter mile northeast of Pinole Bayfront Park, the almost 1.5-mile trail up Pinole Creek stretches from the Bay Trail to the west side of Interstate 80.

To reach Shoreline Park in Hercules, continue northeast on San Pablo Avenue and take Victoria Crescent and then Victoria Park through the Victoria-by-the-Bay development until you reach Tug Boat Lane. In Rodeo, take Pacific Avenue to reach the marinas and Lone Tree Point. Turn right onto San Pablo Avenue from Pacific to reach the parking lot for Lone Tree Point near the intersection with Rodeo Avenue. The entryway to the trail on the Zampa Bridge is on the northwest corner of where San Pablo Avenue turns into Pomona Street and intersects with Merchant Street.

Through Crockett, the route follows city streets—Dowrelio,

Striped Bass—Troubled "New Natives"

In 1879, one of the first rail cars to arrive in Martinez from the East Coast carried 132 live young striped bass, which were released into the Carquinez Strait. Three years later, 300 more were shipped in and released. The West Coast's entire striped bass population evolved from these introductions. That's right, this popular game fish is not a true native, but what some biologists call a "new native," an introduced species that has been here long enough to become established. Of California's 30 or so freshwater game fish, less than a fourth are native or endemic species. Stripers (as aficionados call them) can grow to 4 feet in length, weigh 90 pounds, and live for over 20 years. Most pier catches, however, weigh less than 5 pounds. These bass are anadromous; they spend part of their lives in freshwater, and part in saltwater. Each winter, they migrate from the open ocean near the Golden Gate, and from salty bay waters, into the brackish delta. They spawn the following April or May, and then return to saltwater. Today, stripers are in trouble in the bay. State biologists believe legal stripers (over 18 inches) numbered just under 2 million in the early 1970s. But now, because of pollution and freshwater diversions in the delta by federal and state water projects, the population of legal stripers hovers around 800,000. Present efforts to save the striped bass include complicated diversion pump screens (which critics say don't work), costly hatchery programs, and high-stakes water politics.

Striped bass

Chinook Salmon, The Royal Native

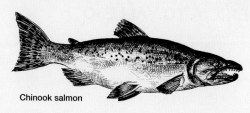

Chinook salmon

Before streams and rivers were dammed and their flows diverted for varied human uses, hundreds of thousands of chinook salmon would arrive through the Golden Gate annually and pass through the Carquinez Strait en route to their spawning grounds. As recently as 1969, some 117,000 winter-run chinook made the journey. By the mid-1980s, however, only 2,000 returned from the ocean, and in 1991 a mere 191 were counted. The Sacramento River winter-run chinook salmon is now listed as a federal threatened and state endangered species. The only salmon species to enter San Francisco Bay, the adult chinook averages 20 pounds, with a length of 2 feet. The salmon's life cycle takes it from freshwater to saltwater and back again to the same stream to spawn. Four times a year—in fall, late fall, winter, and spring—different races of chinook enter the bay and try to reach their ancient spawning grounds in the Sacramento and San Joaquin river systems. But this has been ever more difficult because of freshwater diversion, destruction of spawning sites, dams that block passage, and pumps and fish screens. The winter-run salmon, unable to pass Shasta and Keswick dams, have been forced to spawn south of them, where high water temperatures in early summer often kill eggs and young.

Though the winter-run salmon have suffered most disastrously, other runs have also declined precipitously. Diversion pumps for the Central Valley Project and the State Water Project (located in the delta), combined with some 1,800 agricultural diversion pumps, capture and kill millions of eggs, larvae, juveniles, and some adults. Fish screens that have been installed to keep fish out of the pumps become barriers that kill or damage many juveniles making their way downstream. Survivors are trucked downstream past the pumps, but this transport also takes a toll. The California Department of Fish and Game is trying to mitigate the losses by various means, including improved fish screens and the release of hatchery fish. But these amazing salmon migrations can only be expected to survive if adequate freshwater inflow into the bay and delta is secured and the spawning habitat is protected.

Loring, Rolph, Winslow—to Carquinez Scenic Drive. It then continues on Carquinez Scenic Drive, through the Carquinez Strait Regional Shoreline, to Port Costa. Just above Port Costa, the route divides. The first branch continues on Carquinez Scenic Drive to Martinez, but don't try to drive: the middle portion of Scenic Drive is indefinitely closed to motor vehicles but accessible to bikers and hikers. This first branch continues through Martinez on Talbert and Escobar streets, then goes northeast on Marina Vista to Interstate 680 and the Benicia-Martinez Bridge. The second branch—popular with bicyclists—follows the rural inland route from Carquinez Scenic Drive to McEwen Road, crosses under Highway 4, and then joins Franklin Canyon Road, moving east and parallel to Highway 4. It then connects with Alhambra Avenue and moves north toward the strait and Martinez, to connect with Marina Vista and the first route. The trail on the Benicia-Martinez Bridge can be accessed from Mococo Road off Marina Vista.

INFORMATION

Public Transit
Call 511 or visit 511.org

Transit & Trails
www.transitandtrails.org

AC Transit
www.actransit.org
510-891-4700

Crockett Historical Society and Museum
www.crockettmuseum.org
510-787-2178

East Bay Regional Park District
www.ebparks.org
888-327-2757

Hercules Historic Clubhouse
www.herculeshistory.org

Hercules Parks and Recreation Department
www.ci.hercules.ca.us
510-799-8291

John Muir National Historic Site
www.nps.gov/jomu
925-228-8860

Martinez Recreation Department
www.cityofmartinez.org
925-372-3510

Pinole Recreation Department
www.ci.pinole.ca.us
/recreation
510-724-9062

BENICIA TO VALLEJO

The northern expanse of the Carquinez Strait, the mouth of the Napa River, is an open landscape facing steep wooded hills on the strait's southern shores. Rolling grasslands ease down to shoreline parks and public areas that offer a variety of recreational activities. The Bay Trail route briefly dovetails with the Bay Area Ridge Trail here (see "Carquinez Strait Scenic Loop Trail" on p. 153), and together they traverse an area enduring both rapid population growth and industrial and military cutbacks. This area also has significance in California history.

Benicia waterfront

Benicia State Capitol

Inside the Benicia State Capitol

> "On crossing from Martinez a great change comes over the landscape. There are open groves, beautiful trees, and cool shade; here, not a tree to break the wind or to invite rest in its shade. Yet the land is fertile, and rich fields of grain lie on every side."
>
> WILLIAM H. BREWER, 1862

BENICIA

Benicia was established in 1846 by Mexican General Mariano Vallejo (see p. 168) and a young U.S. lieutenant, Robert Semple. They named it for the general's wife and hoped to see it grow into a port city to rival San Francisco, 27 miles to the southwest. At first Benicia's prospects looked good. It became an important shipping point, the center of wooden ship-building for the Pacific Coast, the home to the Pacific Mail Steamship Company, and the site of the Benicia Arsenal. In 1853, it even became the state capital. But San Francisco kept growing, the capital was moved to Sacramento, some key industries shut down, and history bypassed Benicia. Ironically, much of Benicia's charm today exists only because its grand expectations came to naught. It offers tranquility and historic character within easy driving distance from dense urban areas. The old State House, at the corner of 1st and West G streets, is a state historic park. The Benicia Arsenal, at the end of Military East, has been successfully converted to civilian use. Many of the arsenal's 19th-century buildings house artists' studios and businesses. The Benicia refinery is also on arsenal property. On 1st Street, along the waterfront, old brothels and taverns have been refurbished as restaurants and antique shops. Where ships were built and launched, people now picnic, fly kites, and exercise by the water.

9th Street Park in Benicia, offering a Bay Area rarity: a sandy beach   Benicia Marina

SHORELINE PARKS

West of Point Benicia are waterfront homes, several street-end parks, and two large waterfront parks. Some 3 miles long, the Bay Trail route here is relatively well marked between the point and the Benicia State Recreation Area. Popular 9th Street Park, at the shoreward end of West 9th Street in an old neighborhood, has a small pier and a shoreline where anglers hook striped bass, salmon, and flounder. It also contains a lawn, playground, and picnic areas. Matthew Turner Shipyard Park, at the end of West 12th Street, is a California registered historic landmark. This 6-acre waterfront park features picnic areas, a lawn, and a great view of Carquinez Strait Regional Shoreline.

BENICIA MARINA AND PIER

From the Benicia Marina's eastern end at 5th Street, a 1-mile trail (pavement, fine gravel, and dirt) swoops around berths and the Benicia Yacht Club, then continues to the tip of Point Benicia and the public pier at the foot of 1st Street. From the pier (known for its catches of sturgeon, salmon, flounder, and striped bass), you have a panorama of the Carquinez

Bridge to the west, Carquinez Strait Regional Shoreline across the water, and Mt. Diablo rising from the distant landscape to the east. The sprawling Shell Oil refinery in Martinez occupies the foreground. In earlier years, travelers en route from the East Coast to San Francisco arrived at the Southern Pacific Railroad Station that still stands at the foot of 1st Street, next to a wooden building that housed the Jorgenson Saloon. The train ferry carried the travelers from here to Port Costa, where they trans-

Shipyards

Benicia's shipbuilding history dates from 1849, when independent craftsmen labored on the shores here. In 1850, the Bay Area's first major ship repair plant, the Pacific Mail Steamship Company, started operations in town. In 1882, Matthew Turner relocated his San Francisco shipyard to Benicia. Turner became known as North America's most productive shipbuilder. He and his workmen constructed 228 vessels, and 169 of them were launched in Benicia. The shipyard closed in 1903, and a park was built on its site and named in Turner's honor. At low tide, some old pilings and platforms protrude offshore.

ferred to another train and then yet another ferry, which delivered them to their destination.

BENICIA STATE RECREATION AREA

A walk across the 438 acres of the Benicia State Recreation Area offers a sense of the shoreline as it was in the time of the Karkin people. Grassy hills slope down to Southampton Bay, giving way to stands of willows and cattails along freshwater channels; farther out, a rich variety of marsh plants thrive. Large numbers of resident and migratory shorebirds frequent this embayment, along with mockingbirds, red-winged blackbirds, and several species of sparrows and finches, as well as the ubiquitous European starling. Open space and natural rhythms prevail here. A paved trail, with a parcourse, leaves the eastern parking lot (off Military West) and then turns into a paved trail/road at the main entrance (state park road, with a fee). From the main entrance, you can hike or drive out to the Dillon Point parking lot, passing two wooded picnic areas en route. The distance between the eastern parking lot and the Dillon Point parking lot is nearly 1.5 miles. (Dogs must be on leash.) To

Benicia State Recreation Area

Glen Cove Marina

reach the point—an especially good fishing area for sturgeon, striped bass, king salmon, and flounder—walk down to the shoreline from the parking lot and follow the gravel trail for a quarter mile. About half a mile before you arrive at the Dillon Point parking lot, the Bay Trail route veers west off the paved trail/road and leads to Glen Cove Waterfront Park on a dirt path.

GLEN COVE

To the immediate west of Southampton Bay, beyond Dillon Point and within Vallejo's city limits, is Glen Cove. The Glen Cove Waterfront Park is a 15-acre waterfront open space hosting both the Bay and Ridge Trails along the shoreline (natural-surface trails)

Carquinez Lighthouse

and through the site. The site has significant Native American history that can be discovered through the interpretive signage on-site. The Glen Cove Marina is actually located in Elliot Cove, due west at the end of Glen Cove Marina Road; from here, you can take in the view from a bench atop a small breakwater. Across

the strait, the C&H factory and the town of Crockett dominate the foreground. On the ridgeline above town, rows of brightly colored homes stand in contrast to the muted tones of Crockett's older homes below. Another big draw to the Glen Cove Marina is the Carquinez Lighthouse. It stood just off the mouth of the Napa River, guiding ships from 1910 to 1957, when it was decommissioned. Shortly thereafter it was sold and barged to its present location. It now houses the Glen Cove Marina harbor master's office.

CALIFORNIA MARITIME ACADEMY

The California Maritime Academy, founded in 1929 as the Califor-

Benicia-Martinez Bridge

Actually two separate spans—one northbound and one south—this bridge is 6,215 feet long, hangs nearly 140 feet above the water, and carries over 17 million vehicles a year. The addition of the second, northbound span in 2007 allowed the southbound span to be retrofitted to include a 12-foot bicycle-pedestrian pathway in 2009, thus completing a key gap in both the Bay Trail and Ridge Trail systems and marking an important step in the formation of the Carquinez Strait Scenic Loop Trail effort. The opening of this bridge on September 16, 1962, ended automobile ferry service on the bay; the car ferry between Martinez and Benicia ceased to run.

Benicia-Martinez Bridge path on opening day, 2009

Shoreline path at the California Maritime Academy

Georgia Street in Vallejo, 1887

nia State Nautical School, wraps around Morrow Cove to the west of Semple Point. All U.S. merchant ships are required to have aboard a licensed officer trained in maritime regulations. This training is provided here. The academy's shoreline—highlighted by a row of stately palm trees—has a section of public shore, about a quarter mile long, with a grassy picnic area. Expansive views of

San Pablo Bay and the Carquinez Bridge are unavoidable. The academy's 7,000-ton training ship, the *Golden Bear*, is open for group tours. Contact the academy for further information.

VALLEJO

This city, founded by Mariano Guadalupe Vallejo in 1850, served as the state capital from 1851 to 1852. Today Vallejo is a city of

some 117,000 people and home to commuters to Oakland, San Francisco, other Bay Area cities, and Sacramento.

VALLEJO'S SHORELINE PARKS

The city has extensive water frontage along Carquinez Strait. Several city parks offer sites for relaxation or exercise as you move toward Vallejo's true waterfront, on the

Bay Area Ridge Trail

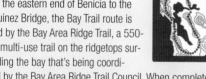

From the eastern end of Benicia to the Carquinez Bridge, the Bay Trail route is joined by the Bay Area Ridge Trail, a 550-mile, multi-use trail on the ridgetops surrounding the bay that's being coordinated by the Bay Area Ridge Trail Council. When completed, this trail will connect over 110 parks and open spaces in nine counties and will be linked with the Bay Trail in numerous places. The two concentric trails will eventually allow hardy souls to circumnavigate the bay on two routes: along the shore, and over the peaks. Over 330 miles of the Ridge Trail are already in use.

Interpretive panels at the Carquinez Bridge overlook

The Carquinez Strait Scenic Loop Trail

In 2008, the Bay Trail and the Ridge Trail began a collaboration to complete the Carquinez Strait Scenic Loop Trail, a 50-mile loop around the Carquinez Strait between the Alfred P. Zampa Memorial Bridge (Carquinez Bridge) and the George Miller Jr. Memorial Bridge (Benicia-Martinez Bridge). The route hugs the shoreline to the north in Solano County, and to the south the alignment splits with the shoreline Bay Trail, offering sights and sounds along the water, and the

higher Ridge Trail providing bird's eye views of the Strait and surrounding landscape. The Carquinez loop is a work in progress, but great trails and open spaces are ready to explore today, including the Carquinez Overlook Trail, Benicia State Recreation Area, Glen Cove Nature Area, Benicia Marina, Martinez Regional Shoreline, Carquinez Strait Regional Shoreline, Hulet Hornbeck Trail, Mt. Wanda, Pinole Watershed, Fernandez Ranch, and Crockett Hills Regional Park. Multi-use paths exist on both the Carquinez and Benicia-Martinez bridges.

Napa River. Carquinez Park, off Sonoma Boulevard, is split in two by a city block but has large lawns and playing fields. Wilson/Lake Dalwigk Park (between 5th Street and Curtola Parkway) features several miles of hard-surface trails, as well as playgrounds and a body of water that would be more appropriately named Marsh Dalwigk than Lake Dalwigk. Between the small boat launching ramp at Maryland Street and the Vallejo Pier—a stretch of some 3 miles—you'll find a promenade, parkland, and marina. Moving up the path en route to the Vallejo/San Francisco Ferry terminal, you'll pass sculptures that incorporate maritime paraphernalia such as anchors and warped propellers. Anglers can drop a hook and line over the railing along the promenade. The train ferry to San Francisco ran from this waterfront from the 1890s to the 1920s, car-

Sears Point Bridge (Highway 37) as seen from the Vallejo Bay Trail

rying passengers, cattle, and merchandise. Opposite today's ferry terminal, across Mare Island Way, is Marina Vista Memorial Park. A winding parcourse follows a paved path past a playground, picnic areas, lawns, and a mounted torpedo. Vallejo Transit serves this

entire area, with connections to BART. Moving farther upstream brings you past the Vallejo Municipal Dock, the Vallejo Yacht Club, and spacious Vallejo Marina. From the northern corner of the marina, you can follow a path underneath the Mare Island Causeway to River

Mare Island

When José de Cañizares first saw this island in 1775, he named it *Isla Plana*, or Flat Island. Some 150 years later, as General Vallejo was crossing the Napa River, he lost some horses to the swift current and apparently thought that one of his favorite mares was among them. Later he learned that the mare had swum to the island. He allowed the horse to live out her natural life here, the story goes, and the island became known as Mare Island. Mare Island, however, is best known for its military history, which began in 1854 with the establishment of the naval shipyard here. During the 1860s, the Russian government arranged for its North Pacific fleet to be serviced at Mare Island because Russia lacked dry docks at its own bases. During World

Mare Island Waterfront, 1940

Welders at the Mare Island Naval Shipyard, 1943

War II, 100,000 workers labored around the clock to launch over 400 ships here. More recently, Mare Island Naval Shipyard serviced several nuclear submarines. The base was closed in 1996, and access is severely restricted. To find out more, visit the Vallejo Naval and Historical Museum, at the corner of Marin and Capital streets in Vallejo. The museum offers group tours to Mare Island and can occasionally accommodate individuals.

Park, with 55 acres of grassland, brush, and shoreline marshes. The park is crisscrossed by gravel trails and dotted with comfortable benches.

GETTING AROUND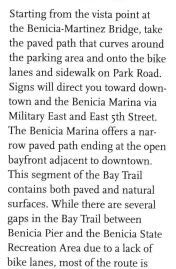

Starting from the vista point at the Benicia-Martinez Bridge, take the paved path that curves around the parking area and onto the bike lanes and sidewalk on Park Road. Signs will direct you toward downtown and the Benicia Marina via Military East and East 5th Street. The Benicia Marina offers a narrow paved path ending at the open bayfront adjacent to downtown. This segment of the Bay Trail contains both paved and natural surfaces. While there are several gaps in the Bay Trail between Benicia Pier and the Benicia State Recreation Area due to a lack of bike lanes, most of the route is along pleasant, wide streets. From

1st, turn left on F, right on 2nd, left on H, right on 3rd, and left on I Street. After several more blocks, you'll be deposited at 9th Street Park, where a narrow paved path moves along the waterfront. Upon exiting the park, turn left on K Street for a few more blocks until you reach the multi-use path at Benicia State Recreation Area. This beautiful paved waterfront path will take you past the ranger's kiosk and into the park.

At the botanical garden, a dirt path heads up and over the hill toward the Glen Cove Waterfront Park. In the future, the trail will connect the Waterfront Park to the Glen Cove Marina at Elliot Cove to the north, but for now exit the park on Whitesides, then turn left on South Regatta and left on Glen Cove Parkway to reach the Glen Cove Marina Bay Trail spur. From here, a steep dirt trail with stairs will preclude all cyclists but the fit

mountain biker willing to "hike-a-bike" on this dead-end spur trail. To connect to the Carquinez Bridge, cyclists must use the city's bike network. The future Vallejo Bluff Trail will connect Glen Cove Parkway to the Carquinez Bridge.

To reach the Vallejo ferry, head north on Sonoma Boulevard (Highway 29) and bear left on Curtola Parkway and onto the waterfront path. Near the Highway 37 entrance on Wilson Avenue, the trail disappears for a short while, but stick with this route—the White Slough Trail awaits after you take the overpass heading east. Look for the trail entrance on the left as the overpass touches down. The White Slough Trail ends at Highway 29, where a future trail will head north into Napa. For now, exercise caution while riding or walking on any roadway without bike lanes or sidewalks.

INFORMATION

Public Transit
Call 511 or visit 511.org.

Transit & Trails
www.transitandtrails.org

Solano County Transit (SolTrans)
Benicia Transit:
707-746-4300, www
.ci.benicia.ca.us/transit
Vallejo Transit:
707-648-4666, www
.vallejotransit.com

Bay Area Ridge Trail Council
www.ridgetrail.org
415-561-2595

Benicia Capitol State Historic Park and Benicia State Recreation Area
www.parks.ca.gov
707-745-3385

Benicia Parks & Community Services Department
www.ci.benicia.ca.us
707-746-4285

California Maritime Academy
www.csum.edu
707-654-1000

Glen Cove Marina
www.glencovemarina.net
707-552-3236

Greater Vallejo Recreation District
www.gvrd.org
707-648-4600

Vallejo Naval and Historical Museum
www.vallejomuseum.org
707-643-0077

ALIENS IN THE BAY

"We are seeing one of the great historical convulsions in the world's fauna and flora."

CHARLES S. ELTON, 1958

Like people who live in the Bay Area, many of the aquatic species in San Francisco Bay have come from elsewhere within the past 150 years. Almost none of the 7.1 million human beings who live in the nine Bay Area counties today have roots in this land that go back more than 200 years, and, according to the 2009 American Community Survey, only 49.7 percent are native Californians. Likewise with the bay's water species. An estimated 150 to 200 marine and brackish-water invertebrates, fish, and algae are nonnatives: they have been brought here, either deliberately or accidentally, and have adapted to local conditions. Though nobody will hazard even an educated guess as to how many plants and animals live in the bay—from sturgeon and striped bass to microscopic plankton—in

Striped bass

some parts of the bay all the species are nonnative, according to specialists in aquatic animal invasions. The presence of these aliens (also known as exotic or introduced species) has increased the bay's biodiversity, but often at the expense of native populations.

Throughout the world, people are moving across time zones and crumbling borders at an ever-accelerating rate, and they are taking other life forms with them, either accidentally or deliberately. Myriad organisms are spreading into new environments, vastly changing plant and animal communities. "This worldwide process, gathering momentum every year, is gradually breaking down the distribution that species had even a hundred years ago," the eminent British ecologist Charles S. Elton wrote in his pioneering work, *The Ecology of Invasions by Animals and Plants*, published in 1958. Perhaps nowhere is this mingling of species from different regions—and the frequent conflict among them—more visible than in California, particularly in San Francisco Bay.

Alien organisms began arriving in large numbers in 1848, when thousands of ships brought men from many ports in search of gold in the Sierra foothills. The hulls of the Gold Rush ships carried stowaways: barnacles, worms, and other aquatic animals and plants. In addition, eastern oysters and at least 29 species of fish have been imported and released into rivers and the bay for sport and commerce. With each crate of oysters, many other alien species arrived.

Lately, it's become evident that it's hazardous to move organisms around as though they were pieces on a game board, without regard to life's interconnections. Now wildlife management agencies are expending enormous effort trying to preserve what is left of some natives. (See p. 76 for the story of the alien red fox and the California clapper rail.) But the mixing continues. New species keep arriving—in the ballast water of ships, in people's luggage, and in many other ways that are hard to control. An alien species that succeeds in adapting to a new habitat can wreak havoc on a native ecosystem. Typically, such a species can tolerate greater environmental fluctuations than native species can. Many thriving alien species flourish around natural and human-caused disturbances, and these abound in the bay. Far from the predators that kept their populations in balance in their native habitat, some of these species become invasive when their population explodes.

Asian clams

The Asian clam *Potamocorbula amuresis* is native to Asia's east coast and one of San Francisco Bay's most common alien invaders. First detected in 1986, it reached concentrations of up to 1,500 per square meter in Suisun Bay within a short time, consuming amazing amounts of food and dominating habitat that would otherwise serve native species. Before long, it was the most abundant invertebrate species in Suisun and San Pablo bays and had changed the food chain in the upper estuary.

To keep aquatic alien species out of the bay is extremely difficult. Boats offer them many travel opportunities. Federal and state laws have been passed to reduce invasions, but even with perfect compliance, introductions can still occur. You can help native species by never releasing live bait fish or other aquatic species—pet fish, turtles, salamanders, and frogs—into the bay or nearby streams, ponds, and reservoirs. Boaters should clean, drain, and dry their boats and equipment when moving from one body of water to another.

Many animals and plants released into the bay do not survive, and some find their niche within the ecosystem without causing trouble. Some are benign, or even outstandingly valuable. A prime example is the striped bass, which was introduced into the bay and delta in 1879 and is now a prized sport fish and a focus of conservation programs (see p. 148).

As scientists struggle to under-stand the species that have already invaded the bay, they worry about what might be coming next. Of special concern is the European zebra mussel (*Dreissena polymorpha*) and its relative, the quagga mussel (*D. rostriformis bugensis*). The zebra mussel was first seen in Lake Erie in 1983, and the quagga was first found there in 1989. Both species probably arrived through the Saint Lawrence Seaway in the ballast water of ships, and now both mussels clog freshwater pipes, obstruct boat plumbing, and attach to structures in the Great Lakes and many other water systems throughout the United States. It may only be a matter of time before one or both arrive in the fresher reaches of the bay. Already, dead zebra mussels have turned up on boats being transported overland to California, and live zebra mussels have been found in one California reservoir.

The quagga mussel has colonized many reservoirs in the Colorado River system, including reservoirs in Southern California that have been fed with Colorado River water. Mussel infestations can be quite destructive to infrastructure and ecosystems, and costly to mitigate. A University of California study estimated that the cost to remove invasive species clogging the pipes and screens of power plants and other water-consuming facilities on the U.S. Great Lakes alone is a half billion dollars per year.

The effect of transferring aquatic organisms is often not understood until it's too late to control. Therefore, it's wise to be as careful as possible in order to slow down the "great historical convulsion in the world's fauna and flora" that Elton began to describe more than 50 years ago.

Here's a sampler of undesirable aliens in the bay—species that have not found a comfortable niche within the ecosystem but, rather, have overwhelmed and displaced native species' populations:

The Atlantic green crab, which arrived on this continent from Europe some decades ago, is a small species that eats just about anything—including the invasive Asian clam. Very prolific, it's more tolerant of environmental fluctuations than native crab species. This crab apparently made its way here from the East Coast.

The shipworm *Teredo navalis* uses its shell to tunnel into wood. It appeared here early last century and was soon causing serious damage to ships and wooden structures, even weakening ferry slips and pier warehouses to the point where they collapsed into the bay. Its destructive abilities were so great, and its spread so rapid, that efforts to control it led to one of the earliest studies of a bay species. Today, shipworms are kept in check by chemical treatment of lumber and hulls.

Shipworm *Teredo navalis*

Invasive spartina was introduced to the bay in the early 1970s as part of a salt marsh restoration project in Hayward. It adapted extremely well—too well. Soon *Spartina alterniflora* and its hybrids were outcompeting native cordgrass and spreading quickly to mud flats, where native cordgrass does not grow, and converting these ecologically rich areas into relatively barren cordgrass islands. An interagency project is actively working to eliminate alien cordgrass species from the bay.

Spartina alterniflora x foliosa

GUIDE TO SHIPS AND BOATS

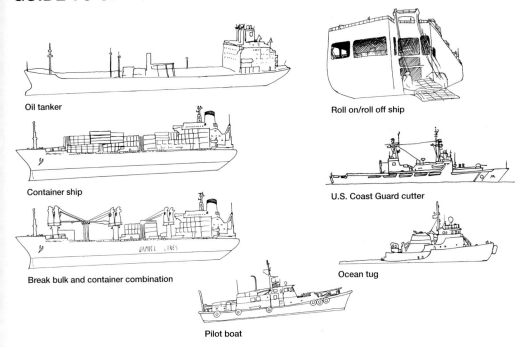

Oil tanker

Roll on/roll off ship

Container ship

U.S. Coast Guard cutter

Break bulk and container combination

Ocean tug

Pilot boat

Oil tanker
Tankers bring crude oil to refineries along the Carquinez Strait, in Hercules, Martinez, and Richmond. Sometimes several tankers are anchored south of the Bay Bridge, near the Alameda Naval Air Station. After the oil is refined, petroleum products are transported to further destinations by barge, ship, or truck.

Container ship
This type of cargo ship carries intermodal containers designed to be transferred mechanically between ships and trucks or trains. The containers are 8 feet wide, 9.5 feet high, and either 20 or 40 feet long. They are moved by huge gantry cranes that stand on the shore. The largest (Post-Panamax class) container ships are more than three football fields long (almost 1,000 feet) and 16 containers wide—too big for the Panama Canal.

Break bulk and container combination
This ship has its own gantry cranes aboard to move cargo between the shore and the ship's hold. The containers it also carries are moved by shore cranes.

Roll on/roll off ship
"Ro/Ro" ships are built to transport large vehicles. On the bay they look like giant boxes. In this ground-level view the stern ramp is down, ready for vehicles to be driven aboard or ashore.

U.S. Coast Guard cutter
The primary mission of the high-endurance, high-speed cutters is maritime law enforcement. They patrol to ensure that U.S. fishing rights are protected and to interdict illegal drug shipments. They also undertake search and rescue missions.

Ocean tug
Tugs such as this one pull barges up and down the coast and in the bay. They also assist larger container ships and tankers with docking in the bay.

Whale boat
You may notice sturdy 26-foot-long whale boats, with eight rowers each, practicing along the San Francisco waterfront and in the Oakland Estuary. The modern era of whale-boat racing as a sport began in 1934, but it goes back to the 19th century, when there were always seamen around and they had access to boats. Whale boats were used not only by whalers but on many other ships and at shoreline life-saving stations. The whale boats today are built to historical specifications. They weigh more than 2,000 pounds.

Pilot boat
This boat is used to assist arriving and departing ships. It carries the pilot, who is familiar with local waters, to and from cargo ships entering and leaving the bay.

Four-person shell
Crew teams often practice and race light-weight shells on the Oakland Estuary and other calm bay waters.

Dragon boat
This is a wooden, hand-built boat powered by a team of 20. Dragon boats originated in southern China and are steadily gaining popularity nationwide and in the Bay Area in particular.

Kayak
A kayak is a small human-powered boat that traditionally has a covered deck and one or more cockpits, each seating one paddler who strokes a double-bladed paddle.

Canoe
A canoe is a small and narrow human-powered boat, pointed at both bow and stern and open on top.

PARK HOURS
7 AM - 8 PM

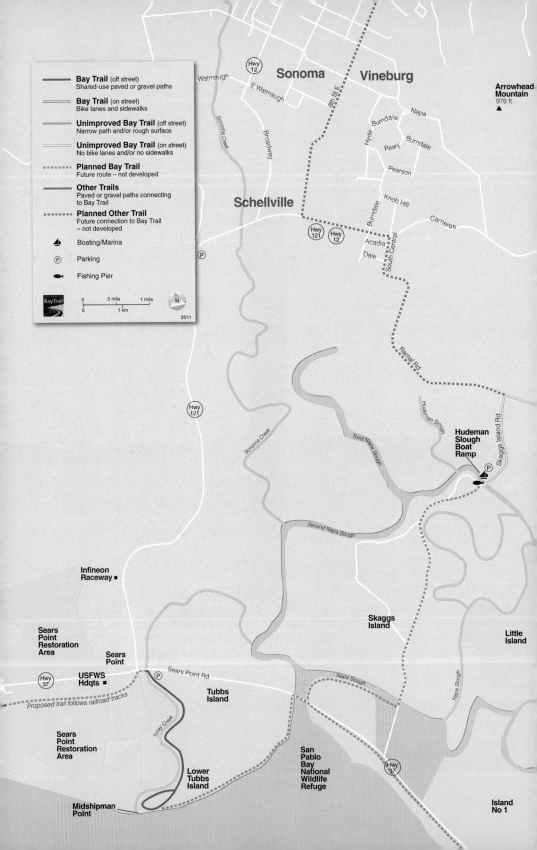

Bay Trail (off street)
Shared-use paved or gravel paths

Bay Trail (on street)
Bike lanes and sidewalks

Unimproved Bay Trail (off street)
Narrow path and/or rough surface

Unimproved Bay Trail (on street)
No bike lanes and/or no sidewalks

Planned Bay Trail
Future route – not developed

Other Trails
Paved or gravel paths connecting
to Bay Trail

Planned Other Trail
Future connection to Bay Trail
– not developed

⛵ Boating/Marina

Ⓟ Parking

🐟 Fishing Pier

Bay Trail

0   .5 mile   1 mile
0   1 km

N

2011

Watmaugh

Hwy 12

Sonoma   **Vineburg**

E Watmaugh

Sonoma Creek

Broadway

6th St E

Napa

Burndale

Hyde

Burndale

Peary   Pearson

Arrowhead
Mountain
976 ft

Schellville

Knob Hill

Burndale

Carneros

Hwy 121   Hwy 12

Acadia

Dale

South Central

Ⓟ

Ramal Rd

Hwy 121

Sonoma Creek

Third Napa Slough

Hudeman Slough

Skaggs Island Rd

**Hudeman
Slough
Boat
Ramp**

Ⓟ
⛵

Second Napa Slough

**Infineon
Raceway** ■

**Skaggs
Island**

**Little
Island**

**Sears
Point
Restoration
Area**

**Sears
Point**

Hwy 37

**USFWS
Hdqts** ■

Ⓟ   Sears Point Rd

**Tubbs
Island**

Tolay Creek

Napa Slough

Napa Slough

Proposed trail follows railroad tracks

**Sears
Point
Restoration
Area**

**Lower
Tubbs
Island**

**San
Pablo
Bay
National
Wildlife
Refuge**

Hwy 37

**Midshipman
Point**

**Island
No 1**

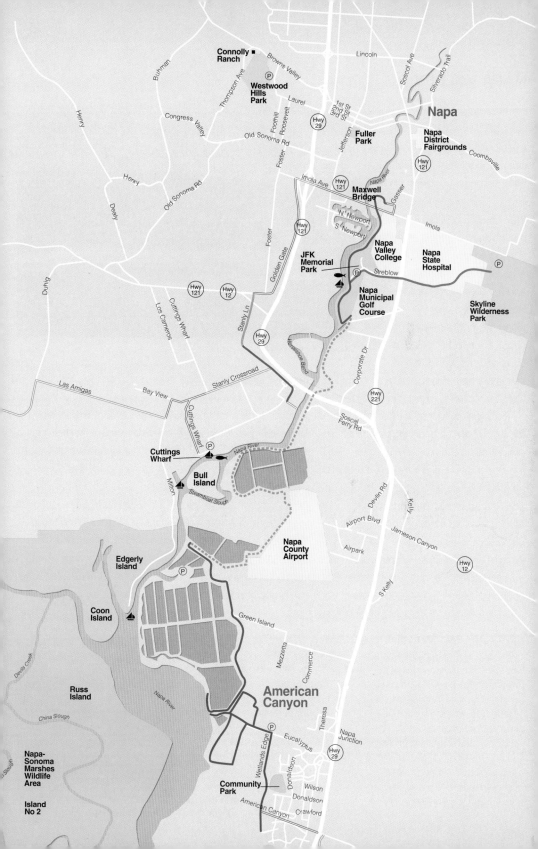

NAPA VALLEY

Mention Napa, and most people think of California wine. This is the most famous of California's wine-producing regions, and it attracts roughly 5 million visitors a year. Most come to sample the fruits of viticulture in their many varieties and to enjoy the manicured landscape, chateau-style wineries, fine restaurants, and the area's Old World feel. But there is far more to discover along this northern reach of bayshore. Bountiful populations of birds and other wildlife find

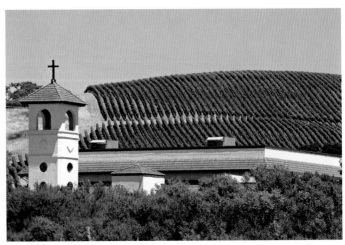

Napa Valley vineyards

sanctuary here. Tranquil hills and shaded waterways invite exploration by bike and on foot. You can also fish, soak in a mud bath (in Calistoga), or ride in a hot air balloon.

Rolling hills rise to the east of Napa Valley, while to the west, the Mayacamas Mountains separate the valley from neighboring Sonoma Valley. About 30 miles long, the Napa Valley widens from slightly over a mile in the north to about 6 miles in breadth south of the city of Napa. The Napa River flows off the slopes of Mt. Saint Helena through the city and into the bay. In the last century, scow schooners and steamboats navigated all the way to the Third Street Bridge in downtown Napa. Like Petaluma and Sacramento, Napa has recently undergone a riverfront renaissance. Multi-use trails flank each side of the river, and a gourmet ghetto is growing in the new riverfront buildings. Most towns in the Napa Valley sprang up in the late 1840s to house and feed miners en route to the gold fields in the Sierra foothills or the quicksilver (mercury) mines on Mt. Saint Helena and in Lake County. Early agriculture mainly yielded fruit, grain, and cattle. Since the 1850s, however, wine has ruled the landscape and the economy. More than 45,000 acres of vineyards produce about 9 percent of California's wine grapes.

NORTH BAY SALT PONDS

At the edge of the Napa River and San Pablo Bay, 9,850 acres of a former salt farm were acquired by the state in 1994, to be managed as a wildlife preserve by the Department of Fish and Game. Many species of shorebirds, waterfowl, and other waterbirds feed in the interconnected salt ponds and tidal marsh. See "Wetland Restoration Around the Bay" on p. 170.

JOHN F. KENNEDY MEMORIAL PARK

Just south of downtown Napa, along the Napa River off Highway 221, is John F. Kennedy Memorial Park. As you wander the park's 340 acres, over grasslands and beneath magnificent oaks, you may sense you're far from the bay or a river. This is especially true during the dry summer months. But just climb to the top of the

Kennedy Park in Napa

Downtown Napa: a riverfront renaissance

levee on the Bay/River trail on the park's western edge, and the Napa River will be rushing past your feet en route to the bay. The park's picnic area, playground, soccer and baseball fields, boat launch,

Hot Air Balloon Rides

Just after sunrise on clear mornings, up to 20 colorful balloons launch from several locations between Yountville and Saint Helena and ascend over the vineyards. Flights last about an hour, and the view of the valley is magnificent. Call the Napa Visitors Bureau for more information.

Hot air balloons in the Napa Valley

and adjacent Napa Municipal Golf Course are guarded by raucous bands of acorn woodpeckers. Egrets and herons can be found on the river's edge. Dogs may be off leash, but they must be under voice command.

NAPA

When Padre José Altimira entered the Napa Valley in 1823, he came across several thousand Indians living in villages scattered along the valley floor. Pioneers soon followed, the indigenous peoples were displaced, and by 1848 the city of Napa was founded. During the next decade, Napa flourished as cattle ranches, sawmills, orchards, grain fields, and small wine growers shared the fertile valley. The Napa riverfront was a busy place throughout the rest of the century, and San Franciscans frequently took the three-hour steamboat trip up the Napa River

for business and pleasure. Hot springs in the area were a major tourist attraction. Calistoga continues as a popular resort, featuring mud baths.

The city of Napa is bypassed by

Napa Valley Vine Trail

The Napa Valley Vine Trail Coalition is a grassroots nonprofit with a vision to build a walking/biking trail system connecting the entire Napa Valley. The coalition is working to design, fund, construct, and maintain 44 safe and scenic miles of level, paved, family-friendly, free-access trail stretching from the Vallejo ferry to Calistoga. The Bay Trail and the Vine Trail planners have been collaborating on many important segments of trail in Solano and Napa counties.

Fishing at Cuttings Wharf

Stanly Lane

major highways, and therefore often missed by visitors. Slow down and pull over. Not only do some 77,000 people live here (more than half the county's population), but the town is also rich in history, packed with excellent restaurants, and graced with shady parks and quiet side streets. Historic walking tours of Napa and other cities in the valley are offered by the nonprofit Napa County Landmarks.

SKYLINE WILDERNESS PARK

To the east of John F. Kennedy Park, one can access the 850 rugged acres of Skyline Wilderness Park via a dirt trail beginning at the intersection of Highway 221 and Streblow Drive. Most of the topography here is steep, but a comfortable picnic area and a gradual 2.5-mile trail to Lake Marie ensure fun for the entire family. A segment of the Ridge Trail moves through this park on the 4.4-mile Skyline Trail (dirt).

CUTTINGS WHARF

As you stand on the small public dock at Cuttings Wharf, cattails and tule reed texture the shores of the Napa River; the scent off the fresh water conjures up images of glistening trout, leisurely canoe rides through crystalline waters, and long cool drinks. Yet you're only about 10 miles from the bayshore as the crow flies. It was the abundant freshwater of the Napa River that attracted Francis Cutting to this very spot in 1893 to expand his San Francisco–based fruit-packing business into fruit growing. From the original wharf here, steamboats hauled fruit from Cutting's orchards and neighboring orchards to Bay Area canneries. Cutting's operations ended in 1909, and the wharf was acquired by Napa County and eventually opened to the public.

GETTING AROUND

The Bay Trail in Napa has made tremendous strides in recent years. While an alignment from the Solano/Napa county line to existing Bay Trail at Wetlands Edge in American Canyon is still under development, you can get off Highway 29 at American Canyon Road and head west until you reach the Wetlands Edge Trail. The trail currently ends approximately a quarter mile to the south, but continues uninterrupted for several miles to the north. A staging area with parking, restrooms, and a water fountain can be found at the intersection of Eucalyptus and Wetlands Edge Road. From here north to the current end of the trail near the Napa County Airport, most of the paths are gravel.

Head west on Eucalyptus toward the Napa River. Keep straight to complete the Landfill Loop Trail, or turn north for the Napa

Intrepid Anglers

If you ever drive on Highway 37 in autumn, you may see crowds of fishermen along the highway's northern shoulder between the Napa Slough and the Napa River. These determined anglers often endure chilling fog and blasting winds in their quest for the striped bass that congregate in the shallow waters of the former salt farm's "Island No. 1" (inundated year-round). To stop or start your car along the highway is extremely dangerous, so don't. To find out more about striped bass and fishing in this area, contact the California Department of Fish and Game, whose office is in Yountville.

Has Anyone Ever Walked or Biked the Whole Bay Trail?

Yes and yes! In 2009, Corinne DeBra decided she'd walk the entire bay. Starting in Mountain View, Corinne followed the Bay Trail up the peninsula to San Francisco; across the Golden Gate Bridge; through Marin, Sonoma, and Napa; across Carquinez Strait; and down through the East Bay to the South Bay. Corinne

What Corinne saw walking the Bay Trail

walked the Bay Trail one section at a time and took photographs along the way for her Walking San Francisco Bay website, where she chronicled her adventures and wildlife sightings.

Bob biking the Bay Trail

In the winter of 2010, Pat Koren and Bob Siegel rode around the entire San Francisco Bay over a five-day period. They overnighted in hotels and on friends' couches, discovered little-known gems of public art, got caught in the rain, and found amazing beauty, both urban and rural, on their sojourn. They were occasionally joined by both Bay Trail and Bay Area Ridge Trail staff. Both Corinne DeBra and Pat Koren have graciously provided photographs from their journey throughout this guide.

Northern California Wine Country

The Napa and Sonoma valleys, and much of the land to the north and west, are internationally famous for their wine. Because this region's cool, wet winters, fog-influenced summers, and fertile soils uniquely favor wine grape production, wineries have been here for over a century. California has more than 500,000 acres of vineyards and produces some 450 million gallons of wine annually at more than 1,000 wineries. Almost half of those wineries and more than 100,000 acres of the vineyards are in Napa and Sonoma valleys.

The first vineyard was planted in Napa County in 1838. By the 1870s, many more were established. Meanwhile, near the Russian River in Sonoma and Mendocino counties, Italian immigrants were developing another region. Lately, vineyards have been expanding in Mendocino County, to the north, where many pear, prune, and walnut orchards have been cut down to make room for grapes.

Wine grapes were introduced in the Sonoma Valley at Mission San Francisco Solano, founded in 1823 by Franciscan monks. Agoston Haraszthy, a Hungarian immigrant who founded Buena Vista Winery in 1857, is credited with the amazing expansion of wine varieties in northern California. In 1861, he brought from Europe some 100,000 cuttings from 300 different varieties of wine grapes.

Northern California wine country

River Trail. A bridge over a slough brings you onto the California Department of Fish and Game's Napa Plant Site levee (referenced on p. 170 under "Wetland Restoration Around the Bay"). Have your bird book and binoculars in hand for this stretch. The trail currently ends at the railroad tracks on Green Island Road. The Bay Trail Project is working with the California Department of Fish and Game and Napa County to connect the trail to the Napa County Airport and Napa Sanitation District properties to the north.

To continue north from here, head east on Green Island Road back to Highway 29 North. Go west on Streblow to Kennedy Park and pick up the River/Bay Trail to the Maxwell Bridge on Imola. Cross the river to the west, then head south on Golden Gate Drive to Stanly Lane and west on Stanly Crossroad to Cuttings Wharf; from there, take the spur down to the river for a snack and a rest. Come back up Cuttings Wharf Road and head west on Las Amigas to the Sonoma County border.

River Boats

California's numerous rivers were an early, and natural, transportation network. Steamboats began running on the Sacramento and San Joaquin rivers during the Gold Rush in 1849, linking foreign ports and San Francisco with California's vast interior. Trips up the shallow Napa and Petaluma rivers—and far up the Sacramento River to Red Bluff, and on the San Joaquin River into Fresno County—were accomplished with smaller steamboats with as little as 15 inches of draft. The first steamboats came from the East Coast via the Strait of Magellan under their own power, or they were dismantled and transported on sailing ships. By 1851, 28 steamboats plied the Sacramento and San Joaquin rivers, ushering in the glory years for California steamboats. Luxurious boats such as the *New World*, *Chrysopo-*

The steamboat *Capital*, built in 1866

lis, and *Capital* (277 feet long) offered fast and comfortable passage between San Francisco and Sacramento. However, by the late 1920s, most of the steamboats were gone, casualties of the more competitive railroad and automobile. The last working survivor of the more than 300 California steamboats was the *Petaluma*, which transported goods for the ranches of Sonoma County until 1950.

INFORMATION

Public Transit
Call 511 or visit 511.org.

Transit & Trails
www.transitandtrails.org

Napa Valley Transit (VINE)
www.nctpa.net
707-259-2800

California Department of Fish and Game
www.dfg.ca.gov
707-944-5500

Napa Chamber of Commerce
www.napachamber.com
707-226-7455

Napa County Landmarks
www.napacountyland marks.org
707-255-1836

Napa County Land Trust
www.napalandtrust.org
707-252-3270

Napa Parks and Recreation Services Department
www.cityofnapa.org
707-257-9529

Napa Valley Vine Trail
www.vinetrail.org

Napa Valley Visitors Bureau
www.napavalley.org
707-226-5813

SONOMA VALLEY

If you want wine country charm with a pinch more history and a dash less crowds, then Sonoma might be the place to go. There are probably more state historic parks in a 20-mile radius from downtown Sonoma than anywhere else in California. And as in Napa, you can ride in a balloon here; call the Sonoma Visitors Bureau for information. The Sonoma Valley is some 17 miles long and 7 miles wide, and the town of Sonoma is situated about mid-valley. The Maya-camas Mountains separate the

Rural roads of the North Bay

valley from Napa to the east, and to the west, the Sonoma Mountains help temper the cool winds off the Pacific. About 14,000 acres of the valley floor are dedicated to wine grapes. The connector trail into Sonoma is currently incomplete and is located on narrow rural roadways.

INFINEON RACEWAY

This race track—one of the largest in the western United States—was first opened in 1968 on 800 acres of former grazing land just north of Highway 37 off of Highway 121. Since its opening, scores of local and national racing, drag car, and motorcycle events have taken place here, and the race-way's popularity has soared. Not all people who drive north on Highway 121 have wine on their minds!

HUDEMAN SLOUGH BOAT RAMP

To get a true feel for the wide open, windswept expanses of the North Bay, venture down Skaggs Island Road through the hay fields to Hudeman Slough boat ramp. Winds blasting off San Pablo Bay race across this country with no more than grass-covered levees to slow them down. They even toss about the turkey vultures and white-tailed kites soaring over

General Mariano Guadalupe Vallejo

General Vallejo

Mariano Guadalupe Vallejo was one of California's most important citizens of the 19th century. Born in Monterey in 1807, when Spain still controlled the region, he rose quickly through the Spanish military ranks and survived the 1822 transition to Mexican rule to become *Comandante General* of Alta California for Mexico in 1835. Despite a minor setback during the 1846 Bear Flag Revolt (p. 168), he continued his political career as a U.S. citizen after California became part of the United States in 1850. Although Vallejo played a key role in the founding of Benicia and Vallejo (he owned the land), he lived most of his life in Sonoma, where he helped to raise his 13 children. In 1834, he was deeded the Rancho Petaluma, one of the earliest and largest land grants in northern California, encompassing some 45,000 acres. As commander general, he was in charge of protecting the settlement and Mexico's northern frontier. But he found ample time to pursue personal interests and amass a fortune in land and livestock. His troops "gathered" laborers by raiding Indian settlements and tracked down "infidels" who fled the missions.

Hudeman Slough boat ramp

the fields, as well as the terns and egrets working the sloughs and watery byways. Also to be found among the sloughs are the intrepid captains of human-powered boats—kayaks, canoes, etc.—who are likely to have miles of curving waterways to themselves.

SAN PABLO BAY NATIONAL WILDLIFE REFUGE

Open bay waters, tidal wetlands, and mud flats between northern Mare Island and the vicinity of the Petaluma River mouth have been preserved as the 16,500-acre San Pablo Bay National Wildlife Refuge, most of which is offshore. The few accessible parts of the refuge are difficult to reach, but they offer a dramatic feel for the bayshore primeval. Hundreds of acres of tidelands and marsh along the shore here provide habitat for

the endangered salt marsh harvest mouse and many other species. More canvasback ducks and scaup feed on these tidal areas during the winter than anywhere else on the Pacific Coast. Hundreds of thousands of migrating shorebirds rest and feed on mud flats throughout the refuge, and harbor seals

find shelter on countless muddy shoals.

The most accessible portion of the refuge is Lower Tubbs Island (off Highway 37 near Tolay Creek, east of Sears Point and Highway 121). It is some 3 miles to the island, and another 1.5 miles to Midshipman Point, all on a levee-top

The Bear Flag Revolt

Sonoma's central plaza is the birthplace of the California Republic. On June 14, 1846, a small group of pioneers (also called "brigands" and "American highwaymen") rode into the town, "captured" Mexican *Comandante General* Mariano Vallejo, and declared independence from Mexico. Vallejo, ever the astute tactician and politician—and known to favor U.S. annexation, despite his official position—surrendered cordially after serving brandy to his captors. Later, the "revolutionaries" moved to the central plaza and replaced the Mexican flag with a handmade "Bear Flag," a version of which remains the state flag today. (When the handmade flag was first hoisted, according to reports, a perplexed crowd of *Californianos* thought the bear was a pig!) After Vallejo returned from a two-month detention at Fort Sutter in Sacramento, he was one of the few *Californianos* who went on to become an important California politician. He is buried in the cemetery overlooking the town.

San Pablo Bay National Wildlife Refuge

dirt trail. Jack rabbits and pheasants dash across the trail as you move from hay fields to marshland. San Pablo Bay and the entire North Bay command the horizon. The terrain is flat, exposed, and windblown. This is a landscape of extremes, and somehow nature seems intensified here. Winds are not cool, they're freezing; the sun does not warm, it pinkens your brow in an instant; and yet, you can be chilled in summer and overheated in winter. Shorebirds don't trickle through your view here, they explode across the sky in gray-brown clouds united by the communal energy unique to migrants. Waterfowl and pheasant hunting is permitted in designated areas of the refuge. (See p. 50–51 for more information about hunting along the shoreline). Dogs are not allowed.

GETTING AROUND 🚶🚶

While much of the Bay Trail route in this area currently follows roadways, some levee-top segments exist, and others are under development for future use. From Napa, the route moves into Sonoma via Ramal Road, through Skaggs Island (currently inaccessible) and onto levees south of Highway 37 (inaccessible). The Tubbs Island/Tolay Creek trail at San Pablo Bay National Wildlife Refuge can only be accessed from eastbound Highway 37. Access to the 2.5-mile Sonoma Baylands Bay Trail is from Port Sonoma Marin. Parking is located immediately off Highway 37 near the marina entrance sign. A planned future route into Sonoma County will parallel Highway 37 from Vallejo.

INFORMATION

Public Transit
Call 511 or visit 511.org.

Transit & Trails
www.transitandtrails.org

Golden Gate Transit
www.goldengate.org
415-455-2000

Sonoma County Transit
www.sctransit.com
707-576-7433

San Pablo Bay National Wildlife Refuge
www.fws.gov/sfbayrefuges
707-769-4200

Sears Point International Raceway
www.infineonraceway.com
800-870-RACE

Sonoma Chamber of Commerce
www.sonomachamber.org
707-996-1033

Sonoma State Historic Park
www.parks.ca.gov
707-938-9560

Sonoma Visitors Bureau
www.sonomavalley.com
707-996-1090

WETLAND RESTORATION AROUND THE BAY

The Bay Area is prized for its beauty and is one of America's great estuaries. Amid a population of 7 million people (and growing), hundreds of species of fish and wildlife abound in the streams, rivers, wetlands, and watersheds that surround this iconic body of water. Over the years, urbanization and the transformation of open spaces to more intensive land uses have contributed to the marginalization of the region's native species and their habitats—wetlands in particular.

A 1961 U.S. Army Corps of Engineers map showing the likely configuration of the bay in 2020 was an important wake-up call.

The map indicated that the bay would be little more than a river, based on the fact that about 4 square miles of bay were being filled each year. Filling in the bay began to be regulated by the state in the late 1960s (see p. 8 for a discussion of the San Francisco Bay Conservation and Development Commission). Since then, many local, state, and federal laws have been enacted and programs have been established to better protect, manage, and restore the area's natural resources.

By the mid 1990s, public and agency sentiment was ripe for the announcement of a major wetland restoration effort. Save the

Bay spearheaded a campaign to restore 100,000 acres of marshes, wetlands, and sloughs around San Francisco Bay with the goals of restoring and enhancing a mix of wetland habitats and providing wildlife-oriented public access and recreation. In many areas such as Napa, the East Bay, and the South Bay, the restoration projects will provide the added benefit of flood management.

The Bay Trail Project's mission complements the wildlife-oriented public access and recreation goals associated with the restoration projects. Where noted, the following wetland restoration projects include segments of the Bay Trail.

    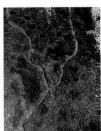

April 2008   September 2009   May 2010   October 2010   June 2011

Unique kite photography captures salt pond restoration progress from 2008 to 2011.

NAPA SONOMA MARSH

- 13,000 acres on the north shore of San Pablo Bay

NAPA PLANT SITE

- 1,400 acres 1 mile north of American Canyon
- 3 miles of existing levee-top Bay Trail

HAMILTON/BEL MARIN KEYS

- 2,600 acres in Novato
- 2.6 miles of future levee-top Bay Trail (2013)

SEARS POINT

- 2,300 acres between Port Sonoma Marin and Infineon Raceway
- 2.5 miles of future levee-top Bay Trail (2014)

SONOMA BAYLANDS

- 320 acres near Port Sonoma Marin
- 1.5 miles of existing levee-top Bay Trail

SOUTH BAY SALT PONDS

- 15,100 acres of former salt ponds in the South Bay
- Over 20 miles of future levee-top Bay Trail

View of Sonoma Baylands and Sears Point Restoration Area

Wetland restoration in progress at Hamilton Field in Novato

"San Francisco Bay is now the center of the most ambitious environmental restoration effort ever undertaken in any urban area in the world."

SAVING THE BAY

Petaluma/Novato

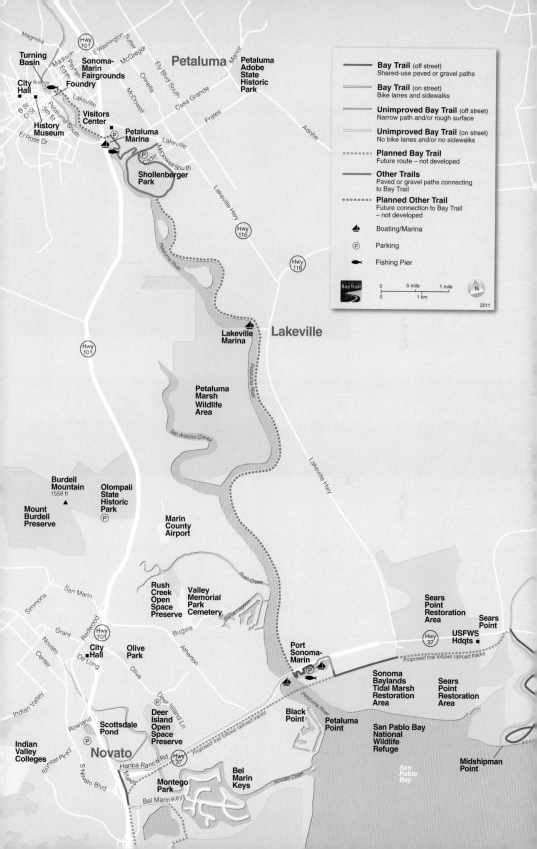

Turning
Basin

City
Hall

History
Museum

El Rose Dr

Magnolia

Hwy
101

E Washington

Sutter

McGregor

Madison
Payran
Edith

Bodega

B St
D St
5th St
Petaluma South

Sonoma-
Marin
Fairgrounds
Foundry

Lakeville

Visitors
Center

Petaluma
Marina

Shollenberger
Park

McDowell South

Cader

McDowell

Crinella

Ely Blvd South

Casa Grande

Frates

Lakeville

Petaluma

Manor

Petaluma
Adobe
State
Historic
Park

Adobe

Lakeville Hwy

Hwy
116

Hwy
116

Petaluma River

Hwy
101

Lakeville
Marina

Lakeville

Petaluma
Marsh
Wildlife
Area

Petaluma River

San Antonio Creek

Lakeville Hwy

Burdell
Mountain
1558 ft

Mount
Burdell
Preserve

Olompali
State
Historic
Park

Marin
County
Airport

Rush Creek

Sears
Point
Restoration
Area

Sears
Point

USFWS
Hdqts

San Marin

Simmons

Grant

Redwood

Hwy
101

San Marin

Novato

Center

Indian Valley

Rush
Creek
Open
Space
Preserve

Valley
Memorial
Park
Cemetery

Bugeia

Atherton

Bahia Lagoon

Port
Sonoma-
Marin

Proposed trail follows railroad tracks

Hwy
37

Sonoma
Baylands
Tidal Marsh
Restoration
Area

Sears
Point
Restoration
Area

City
Hall

De Long

Olive
Park

Olive

Deer Island Ln

Deer
Island
Open
Space
Preserve

Proposed trail follows railroad tracks

Black
Point

Petaluma River

Petaluma
Point

San Pablo Bay
National
Wildlife
Refuge

Midshipman
Point

Indian
Valley
Colleges

Rowland

Scottsdale
Pond

Sunset Pkwy

S Novato Blvd

Marsh

Hanna Ranch Rd

Novato

Hwy
37

Montego
Park

Bel Marin Keys

Bel
Marin
Keys

Novato Creek

San
Pablo
Bay

PETALUMA/NOVATO

Stretching along this shoreline and north along the Petaluma River is a flat and fertile region of marshes and diked baylands that sustains dairy and poultry farms, related industry, and a growing human population in Petaluma, Novato, and along the Highway 101 corridor. This is a gentle, welcoming landscape, perfect for leisurely bicycle rides and hikes. You can also sail, row, or paddle on the Petaluma River and its countless sloughs.

Petaluma River from Black Point

Hayfields being restored as marsh habitat for wildlife

SONOMA BAYLANDS TIDAL MARSH RESTORATION AREA

On the north shore of San Pablo Bay, near the mouth of the Petaluma River, you can study a pioneering attempt to resolve an environmental dilemma. A tidal marsh was reconstructed here, with the use of clean dredged material from the Port of Oakland. The port had been losing Pacific container trade to other ports, due in part to a lack of deep water channels. Dredging had become difficult as fishermen and environmental groups protested plans for dumping material into the bay or the ocean, and no suitable sites on land were available. Here, however, nearly 3 million cubic yards

of clean silt were put to beneficial use in a project to restore 322 acres of diked baylands to salt marsh for the endangered salt marsh harvest mouse, the endangered California clapper rail, migratory shorebirds, and other wildlife. The dredged material was used to raise the elevation of a hayfield, a former marsh that had subsided after it was diked off. This jump-started the natural restoration process. After the elevation was raised, the tide sculpted new channels and recreated the marsh. The largest single marsh restoration effort at the time in California, this project shows how economic growth and jobs can be created by a cost-effective project that provides environmental benefits. The State Coastal

Conservancy and the Sonoma Land Trust launched the Sonoma Baylands project, with broad public and government support.

PETALUMA: THE RIVER AND THE CITY

Petaluma is at the head of the Petaluma River, which is actually not a river but a 14-mile-long tidal slough that was once surrounded by a large saltwater marsh teeming with birds, a breeding ground for crab, sturgeon, shellfish, and other marine life. Herds of elk and deer roamed the valley and wooded hills beyond. After the discovery of gold in the Sierra foothills in 1848, hunters flocked here for game to feed Gold Rush crowds. They set up camps by the

Black Point boat launch

fresco dining, and lots of strolling people. Like the Bay Trail, the Petaluma River Trail is a work in progress. This connector to the Bay Trail will eventually stretch 12 miles from downtown Petaluma to Port Sonoma Marin.

SHOLLENBERGER PARK

This 165-acre park was named after Richard Shollenberger, a Petaluma Park Department chief. Several hundred people visit daily for dog-walking, jogging, or just enjoying nature—especially the many species of birds that can be seen here (herons, egrets, ducks, cormorants, etc.). The park features a 2-mile circular trail and a 1-mile trail through Alman Marsh to the Petaluma Marina.

PORT SONOMA MARIN AND BLACK POINT PUBLIC BOAT RAMP

Many drivers don't realize Port Sonoma Marin exists as they zip over the mouth of the Petaluma River on Highway 37. If you slow down and turn toward the bay on the east side of the bridge, however, you'll find a popular marina and windsurfing site. A half-mile trail (rough pavement) will take you around the marina and to a quiet fishing spot at the river's mouth (the end of the frontage road). The Sonoma Baylands Bay Trail can also be accessed from here by heading toward the bay on the paved road near the marina entrance sign. Park and use the trail to the side of the vehicle gate. From the tables by the river, you can look upstream, as well as across the river toward houses with long, catwalk-like piers at Black Point. On the river's west side, below the Highway 37 bridge, the Black Point Public Boat Ramp

river, where Petaluma later developed. Later, disillusioned miners came here to settle as farmers and ranchers.

By the 1850s, the Petaluma River was one of the busiest waterways in California. On a typical day, scow schooners and sailboats would crowd the turning basin. They were met here by overland stage and freight lines—first horse-drawn wagons, then trains—that linked Petaluma with Santa Rosa, Healdsburg, Tomales, and Sonoma. Lumber, grains, hay, and

milk products would be taken on board; other goods were unloaded for distribution throughout the region. The first steamboat came up the river in 1852; the last made the journey in 1950. Some ship captains who came to know the beautiful valley returned to live here in retirement.

Like many cities, Petaluma has recently undergone a "river renaissance." A town that once turned its back on its riverfront now embraces it with walkways, promenades, seating, landscaping, al

Petaluma's Washington Street, ca. 1900

Acorn woodpecker

Deer Island Open Space Preserve

offers good access to the water, as well as picnic areas and fishing opportunities. Road access is via Harbor Drive off Highway 37.

PETALUMA MARSH WILDLIFE AREA

About midway downriver, between downtown Petaluma and Port

Sonoma Marin, the Department of Fish and Game's 2,000-acre Petaluma Marsh Wildlife Area encompasses Petaluma River's western shore. Although it is only accessible by water until the Petaluma River Trail is complete, it is well worth exploring. If you can manage to sail or paddle into the small sloughs here, you'll get a

duck's-level perspective. Seasonal hunting is permitted throughout the marsh, so call the Department of Fish and Game office in Yountville for season dates. This office monitors San Francisco Bay's wildlife and game resources and administers large tracts of state-owned wildlife habitat.

DEER ISLAND OPEN SPACE PRESERVE

The 135 acres of oak savanna in the Novato Creek floodplain, known as Deer Island, are owned and operated by the Marin County Parks and Open Space District. The preserve is immediately north of Highway 37 and open all year. (Park on Deer Island Lane off Olive Avenue and look for a green preserve sign by an old homestead.) A dirt trail, some 2 miles long, ambles across this preserve and affords visitors 360-degree views. Hikers may be serenaded by the ratcheting of acorn woodpeckers while gazing out over inundated marshland and flocks of waterfowl. Dogs are permitted off leash, but must be under voice command. Bikes are not allowed.

Bicycle Coalitions

Bay Area bicycle coalitions are an important partner to the San Francisco Bay Trail. With their in-depth knowledge of local conditions, broad membership base, and connections to local decision makers, they have helped move the Bay Trail forward in immeasurable ways throughout our history.

Rush Creek Open Space Preserve

Clo, the Udderly Amazing Cow

Highway travelers throughout the North Bay enjoy billboards featuring Clo the Cow, the cartoon mascot and official spokescow for Clover Stornetta Farms. Clo the Cow has adorned milk cartons since the 1960s and has been seen on billboards for decades, dishing up puns and one liners, always attired to match the theme of the ad. Among the favorites:

- Tip Clo Through Your Two Lips
- Clo's Encounters of the Curd Kind
- Splendor in the Glass
- Clo's Line
- Moooey Bueno
- Supreme Quart
- Claude Mooonet

SCOTTSDALE POND

Immediately off Highway 101 and Rowland Avenue is a favorite spot for bird-watchers, dog owners, and walkers: Scottsdale Pond. Although a de facto undeveloped park, it is technically a flood control basin that drains to Novato Creek. The pond itself covers some 7 acres and is ringed with cattails and brush. It's surrounded by an equal amount of open space crisscrossed by informal paths and dog runs. Both resident and migrant birds feed along the pond's edge and bathe in its freshwater.

RUSH CREEK OPEN SPACE PRESERVE

This 36-acre preserve, north of Valley Memorial Park Cemetery, is a valuable marshland habitat in the Petaluma River floodplain. Together with the 194 adjoining acres held by the Department of Fish and Game, the Rush Creek Preserve helps ensure that resident and migratory waterfowl can find shelter and food. The area also serves as a winter flood basin

for Novato. The Rush Creek Preserve is surrounded by private oak woodlands, but you can reach it by parking on Bugeia Lane (off Atherton Avenue) and walking along the cemetery's western boundary. Look for a metal livestock gate and entrance (no sign) by a prominent row of eucalyptus trees. Follow the eucalyptus for a half mile to the preserve. A 1-mile section of fire road cuts across this preserve. Dogs are permitted off leash, but must be under voice command. Bikes are not allowed.

THE MARIN MUSEUM OF THE AMERICAN INDIAN

Excellent exhibits of Miwok crafts and domestic items—including rabbit-skin clothing, arrowheads, and tools—make up this museum. The collection of Native American baskets from around the state is small but exquisite. A small store sells books and Native American crafts. Outside, some native plants grow in a modest garden, including canyon sage and matilja poppy. The museum is in Novato's Miwok Park (off

Marin County Parks

Since 1972, this public agency has helped preserve and protect over 12,000 acres in Marin County. The district itself manages some 9,000 acres of open space across 25 preserves and is a key reason that over 50% of the land in Marin County is permanently protected open space. The Marin County Parks and Open Space District offers ranger-led hikes and activities, as well as volunteer opportunities.

Novato Boulevard). Admission is free, but donations are gladly accepted.

NOVATO HISTORY MUSEUM

Housed in a restored 1850s Victorian (off DeLong Avenue at Reichert Avenue), the Novato History Museum is a quaint collection of antique dolls, miniature trains, and a variety of everyday 19th-century items. It also features an exhibit on nearby Hamilton Air Force Base. Admission is free, but donations are accepted.

GETTING AROUND

From Sonoma, the Bay Trail route predominantly follows levees through this area; however, only about 2.5 miles of gravel levee-top trail at Sonoma Baylands and 5 miles at the Tubbs Island/Tolay Loop are currently open for hiking or biking. An additional 2.5 miles associated with the Sears Point Restoration Project will begin construction in the near future.

The future route will wind through Skaggs Island, cross Highway 37 onto the Vallejo Sanitation District levee, and connect with the U.S. Fish & Wildlife Service's existing Tubbs Island Loop Trail. Heading west on Sears Point Restoration levees, the trail will then hook into the Sonoma Baylands levee and deposit riders and hikers at Port Sonoma Marin. There is currently no safe crossing of the Petaluma River into Marin County, and the Bay Trail alignment currently parallels Highway 37, with no bicycle or pedestrian facilities. As of this printing, the best walking and riding in this area can be accessed by parking at the reserved "public shore" parking spaces just off Highway 37 at Port Sonoma Marin and walking down to the levee path at Sonoma Baylands. Access to the Tubbs Island Loop Trail is only possible from the eastbound direction of Highway 37. About a half mile after Infineon Raceway at the intersection of Highways 37 and 121, prepare to turn right into a small gravel parking lot managed by the California Department of Fish and Game. Note that hunting does occur on these lands. Please check postings or the Fish and Game website for current information.

INFORMATION

Public Transit
Call 511 or visit 511.org.

Transit & Trails
www.transitandtrails.org

Golden Gate Transit
www.goldengate.org
415-455-2000

Sonoma County Transit
www.sctransit.com
707-576-7433

California Department of Fish and Game
www.dfg.ca.gov
707-944-5500

Marin County Parks
www.co.marin.ca.us
415-499-6387

Marin Museum of the American Indian
www.marinindian.com
415-897-4064

North Bay Rowing Club
www.northbayrowing.org
707-769-2003

Novato History Museum
www.cityofnovato.org
415-897-4320

Novato Parks, Recreation, and Community Services Department
www.ci.novato.ca.us
415-899-8200

Petaluma Parks & Recreation Department
www.cityofpetaluma.net
707-778-4380

Port Sonoma Marin
707-778-8055

Legend

Bay Trail (off street)
Shared-use paved or gravel paths

Bay Trail (on street)
Bike lanes and sidewalks

Unimproved Bay Trail (off street)
Narrow path and/or rough surface

Unimproved Bay Trail (on street)
No bike lanes and/or no sidewalks

Planned Bay Trail
Future route – not developed

Other Trails
Paved or gravel paths connecting
to Bay Trail

⛵ Boating/Marina

Ⓟ Parking

🐟 Fishing Pier

BayTrail

0   .5 mile   1 mile
0   1 km

N

2011

Novato

Proposed trail follows railroad tracks

Hwy 37

Hanna Ranch Rd

Marsh

Bel Marin Keys

Novato Creek

Montego Park

S Novato Blvd

Bel Marin Keys

Bel Marin Keys Restoration Area

Hwy 101

Ignacio Blvd

Pacheco Pond

Alameda Del Prado

Ignacio

Trail Section Opening 2013

Loma Verde Open Space Preserve

Reservoir Hill

Hamilton Pkwy

Palm

Oakwood

Hangar

Caliente Real

Hamilton Wetland Restoration Area

State Access

Main Gate

Nave Dr

Bolling

Pacheco Valle Open Space Preserve

Trail Section Opening 2013

Hwy 101

Marinwood Open Space

Lucas Valley Rd

Miller Creek

St Vincent's

Las Gallinas Valley Sanitary District

Marinwood Park

Proposed trail follows railroad tracks

Terra Linda

Deer Valley

North Ave

John F. McInnis Park

Santa Venetia Marsh Open Space Preserve

Terra Linda

Redwood Highway

Smith Ranch Rd

Sleepy Hollow Divide

Manuel Freitas Pkwy

Santa Margarita Island Open Space Preserve

Yosemite

McInnis

Vendola

Meadow

La Pasada

Sunny Oaks

Las Gallinas Creek

Bayhills

Back Ranch Meadows

Buckeye Point

N San Pedro Rd

Weber Point

Rat Rock

Open Space Preserve

Civic Center Dr

Marin County Civic Center

N San Pedro Rd

Civic Center Lagoon Park

Santa Venetia

China Camp State Park

China Camp Village

San Pedro Mountain Open Space Preserve

Nike Site

Villa

Biscayne

McNears Beach

San Rafael

Red Hill

Hwy 101

Boyd Park

Grand

Locust

Harry A. Barbier Memorial Park

Riviera

San Pedro Hill

Point San Pedro

Lagoon

Cantera Way

Sir Francis Drake

4th St

3rd St

2nd St

Tamalpais

Dominican College

Highland

Lagoon

D St

A St

Mission

Margarita

Point San Pedro Rd

Terwilliger Nature Education Center

Lindaro

Grand

Beach Park

Harbor

Canal

Pickleweed Park

College of Marin

College

Wolfe Grade

Andersen Dr

Kerner

Catalina

Schoen Park

West Marin Island

Creekside Park

Bellam

Lagoon

East Marin Island

San Rafael Bay

Hamilton Park

Magnolia

Sir Francis Drake

Eliseo

Bon Air Landing

Cora Madera Creek

Niven Park

Greenbrae

Remillard Park

Shoreline Park

Piper Park

Doherty

Hwy 580

Hwy 101

Ferry

E Francisco

Shoreline

Pelican Way

Kerner

HAMILTON FIELD TO SANTA VENETIA

North Marin County's winding shoreline once sheltered and sustained many Indian villages. Today, its expansive marshlands, stretching from Novato Creek through Hamilton Field to Gallinas Creek, offer excellent bird-watching and countless recreational activities. Parks are scattered along this shoreline, but are particularly numerous in the Gallinas Creek area.

Reservoir Hill trail at Hamilton

The skate park at John F. McInnis Park

HAMILTON FIELD

Hamilton Field was named in memory of Lt. Lloyd A. Hamilton, a pilot in World War I. It was dedicated as a military airfield in 1935, declared surplus in 1969, and deactivated in 1976. As mentioned in "Wetland Restoration Around the Bay Area" (p. 170), 650 acres are currently being reclaimed as marshland wildlife habitat. As part of this project, 2.6 miles of new Bay Trail will be constructed. Some segments are open today, and the transformation of the old airfield can be observed from the trail. The levee trail is a gravel surface.

Lt. Lloyd A. Hamilton

LAS GALLINAS WILDLIFE PONDS

South of Hamilton Field are the Las Gallinas Valley Sanitary District Wastewater Reclamation Project Wildlife Ponds. People don't normally associate sewage plants with wildlife, but Las Gallinas is a bird-watcher's paradise. At the entrance, behind the sewage plant on Smith Ranch Road, you'll find a kiosk that lists the 187 bird species seen here, including white pelicans, barn swallows, Canada geese, and numerous shorebirds. In 1985, 385 acres of marsh, water

White pelican

treatment storage ponds, and irrigated pasture were incorporated into a wildlife area. About 3.5 miles of public trails wind through the area. Las Gallinas is just one of several marshes on the bay that have been either restored or created with treated wastewater. Others are in Palo Alto, Richmond, Martinez, and Hayward.

JOHN F. McINNIS PARK

John F. McInnis Park includes 441 acres on the northern shore of Gallinas Creek, just off Smith Ranch Road and Highway 101. It offers piers for hand-launched craft, such as kayaks and canoes, (see p. 7 for information about the Bay Area Water Trail) and also has tennis courts, baseball diamonds, a golf course, a driving range, miniature golf, soccer fields, a state-of-the-art skate park, and a restaurant. A 2.5-mile trail (mostly dirt) loops around this county park to the bay's shore.

Duck Blinds in the Bay

When waterfowl were more numerous on the bay and duck hunting was more popular, elevated duck blinds dotted the nearshore. Not owned by anyone in particular, the wooden blinds were used on a first-come basis by generations of hunters. Most have been removed or have fallen down, but a few remain, particularly in the North Bay and the San Pablo National Wildlife Refuge. Look bayward from China Camp, McInnis Park, or Hamilton Field, and you'll see a few weathered blinds rising above the bay on rotting pilings.

Santa Venetia Marsh Open Space Preserve

The sports facilities can be reserved by calling the Marin County Parks Department.

SANTA MARGARITA ISLAND OPEN SPACE PRESERVE

Santa Margarita Island Open Space Preserve is a small, beautiful island

Marsh wildflowers

on the south fork of Gallinas Creek (at the end of Meadow Drive off San Pedro Road). A wide paved bridge, the only access, is a good spot to watch the tide work through the surrounding marsh. A half-mile rough dirt path encircles the island, with several small trails leading to an oak-covered rocky summit. Warning: Look out for large poison oak bushes; they are so big they don't look like poison oak!

SANTA VENETIA MARSH OPEN SPACE PRESERVE

The Santa Venetia Marsh Open Space Preserve is dominated by

stands of tough-skinned pickleweed, although bright yellow patches of brass buttons can be seen March through December. A dirt path circles the marsh for just over a mile, with no less than nine access points from the nearby community of Santa Venetia.

GETTING AROUND

While much of the shoreline from the Marin County line at the Petaluma River to Hamilton Field is currently inaccessible, short segments of the Bay Trail are usable under the intersection of Highways 101 and 37, as well as along Bel Marin Keys Boulevard to the

Frank Lloyd Wright

With its skylights, interior fountains, and tropical plants, the Marin Civic Center building—the last major project of architect Frank Lloyd Wright—is a structure the county takes pride in. It stands amid rolling green space, behind a lagoon circled by a trail and populated by ducks and geese. Docents lead tours of the building every Wednesday at 10:30 a.m., which leave from the second-floor café, Room 233. The cost is $5 per person, and reservations aren't required. Groups of ten or more can arrange a private docent tour by calling the Visitor Services Office at 415-499-7009.

Marin Civic Center

edge of Hamilton Field. To access the Bay Trail at Hamilton Field, head to the Reservoir Hill trailhead off Hamilton Parkway near Palm. This 0.75-mile trail leads up and over an oak-studded hill and down to the 1.3-mile Hamilton levee trail, which separates residences from the ongoing marsh restoration. The Hamilton levee trail does not currently connect to the Bay Trail at Las Gallinas.

To reach the parking lot at Las Gallinas Valley Wastewater Treatment Plant, use streets. The McInnis Park Bay Trail segment can be accessed from this point, approximately 100 yards south of the parking lot. The Bay Trail route continues south on Redwood Highway Frontage Road to the Civic Center, then moves onto North San Pedro Road to China Camp State Park. The route divides at Back Ranch Meadows' entrance. One arm continues on North San Pedro Road to McNears Beach; the other follows a dirt trail, merging with the paved road just north of McNears Beach.

Parallel Pelicans

Both white and brown pelicans frequent the bay. Both fly in flocks with heads pulled back on their shoulders, have similar outlines, and feed principally on fish. Aside from their differences in color, other features aid in their identification.

White pelican
The larger of the two species, the white pelican has a 9-foot wingspan and nests in the interior of the western United States. While present year-round, white pelicans are a more common sight in the bay from summer through winter, when large numbers can be seen circling high above the water. These birds are almost completely white, except for black primary feathers and a yellow bill. White pelicans swim on the surface of the water and scoop up fish, often in cooperative fishing groups.

California brown pelican
The brown pelican, with a 7-foot wingspan, nests off California's southern coast and in Mexico during the summer. During the non-nesting season, it's often seen flying in formation inches above the surface of bay waters. This dusk-colored bird with a white or yellowish head plunges beak-first into the water in search of fish. The brown pelican was driven to near extinction by the pesticide DDT in the late 1950s and 1960s. Recently removed from the federal endangered species list, the species has rebounded.

The Bike Commuter

Steven Plunkett lives in San Anselmo and works in Alameda. Like a growing number of folks wanting to leave the car at home, Steven commutes by bicycle five days a week. He rides 20 miles from Marin to San Francisco and then takes the ferry or BART into Alameda. Once a multi-use path is added to the Richmond–San Rafael Bridge or is completed on the San Francisco–Oakland Bay Bridge, Steven will be able to make the journey on pedal power alone. While you may not be ready for 40 miles a day in rain, wind, or fog, you can at least whet your appetite on a Bike to Work Day (the second Thursday in May)—it may be habit-forming!

Bike commuter Steven Plunkett travels from San Rafael to Alameda by bike.

Shrimp

San Francisco Bay shrimp, which once supported this and numerous other fishing villages on the bay, are now collected exclusively for sturgeon bait. The shrimp spawn in the depths of the bay in winter and spring, and the young migrate to shallow waters at the bay's edge in spring and early summer to avoid predators and to grow. Once mature, the shrimp return to the bay's deep channels in fall and winter.

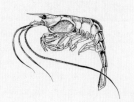

POINT SAN PEDRO TO SAN RAFAEL CREEK

The oak-studded peninsula separating San Pablo Bay from San Rafael Bay, known today as Point San Pedro, is largely undeveloped thanks to the creation of China Camp State Park and McNears Beach County Park. Numerous city parks offer welcome breaks in the midst of residential areas along the shores of San Rafael Creek.

China Camp Pier

CHINA CAMP STATE PARK

China Camp State Park's 1,500 acres include much of Point San Pedro and encompass miles of shoreline, salt marshes, grasslands, coastal scrub, valleys shaded by oak and bay trees, and grassy ridgelines that afford unparalleled views of San Pablo Bay. Numerous day-use areas are scattered throughout the park. There are 30 walk-in campsites (for a fee) at Back Ranch Meadows. Sixteen miles of trails wind past marshes, through woodlands, and along ridges. China Camp is popular with mountain bikers. See the trail map in the historic village. (Be prepared to pay a parking fee.)

CHINA CAMP HISTORIC AREA

Once a Chinese fishing and shrimping village, China Camp Historic Area is now reduced to a few weathered buildings and one excellent museum. In 1870, 76 men—aged 12 to 62—lived in the China Camp region. Their families followed. By 1880, 469 people in villages at Point San Pedro exported a million pounds of dried shrimp to China annually. Beginning in 1882, exclusion laws severely restricted Chinese immigration and denied Chinese residents the right to become citizens and own property. By the early 1900s, this legislation and outright hatred slowly brought an end to the Chinese villages (although there was a brief revival here in the 1930s). At China Camp, only the Quong family remained, and thanks to their perseverance, we have a taste of what life used to be like here. To-

China Camp Village

Chinese settlement at Point San Pedro, ca. 1888

Sunrise at McNears Beach

"I begin to work when the sun rises; I rest when the sun sets. I dig a well for my drinking water; I plow the field to provide my food. Powerful as the emperors are, what has that power to do with me?"

CHINESE FOLK SONG

day, the beach where shrimp boats once unloaded is a popular site for launching kayaks and is an official Water Trail site. The historic old store is next to the beach, still open on weekends. Nearby are the ranger's quarters.

McNEARS BEACH

This 52-acre park is named for John McNear, who manufactured bricks at Point San Pedro in the 1880s. McNears Beach is often bathed in sunlight when other portions of Marin are fogbound. With its large lawn, public pool, snack bar, pier, and mile-long beach, this park is a popular destination (but there's a fee to enter). A line of stately palm trees was planted when this was a private resort. Sturgeon, striped bass, and kingfish are caught seasonally off the large concrete pier. Just offshore are some rocky islands called the Sisters, covered by cormorants and guano. Rat Rock can be seen toward China Camp State Park. Views of the Richmond refineries and San Pablo Bay define the horizon. The tip of Point San Pedro (outside the park) is an active rock quarry.

PICKLEWEED AND SCHOEN PARKS

Pickleweed Park is a 25-acre expanse of marsh, with a grass field and several boardwalks, on the southern shores of San Rafael Creek. A 2-mile dirt trail with a

Pickleweed Park

parcourse circles this park. A Children's Center and the Pickleweed Park Community Center are in front of the park on Canal Street. A community garden next to the park overflows with flowers and vegetables year-round. A few yards east on Canal is the miniature Schoen Park, with a children's play area and lawn.

SHORELINE PARK

Shoreline Park, which begins at Schoen Park and winds south along the bay's edge, offers parcourse stations (continued from Pickleweed Park) and spectacular views of West and East Marin is-

Terwilliger Nature Education Center

The Terwilliger Nature Education Center at Wildcare in San Rafael offers classes, exhibits, and nature outings for children aged 3 to 7. Teaching techniques developed by Mrs. Terwilliger ("Mrs. T" to her many fans) invite children to explore the natural world while they learn about environmental issues and ecology.

185

Art on the Bay Trail

From the whimsical to the classical, new public art is continually popping up on the Bay Trail.

Sculpture of a painter in Emeryville

Trailside memorial to founding Bay Trail board member Bill Bliss

Sheet-metal sheep in Napa

Whimsical Bay Trail art in Benicia

Carquinez Drive rocket monsters

Statues on the Bay Trail

Cupid's Span, San Francisco waterfront

Great Egrets, Snowy Egrets, and Black-Crowned Night Herons

Great egrets

Great egrets are all-white with large yellow bills and black legs and feet. Standing over 3 feet tall, adults grow long plumes on the backs of their necks during breeding season. A slow, methodical hunter, the great egret stands perfectly still in shallow water, looking for fish to grab with a quick jab.

Snowy egrets

About 2 feet tall and snowy white, snowys have slender black bills, black legs, and bright yellow feet that look like slippers. They walk briskly in shallow waters, stirring up food with their feet, and repeatedly jab at the water. At the turn of the 20th century, graceful head plumes made egrets targets of plume hunters, who decimated their populations. Protection has since increased their numbers.

Black-crowned night herons

With their stocky, 2-foot-tall bodies and short necks and legs, these herons resemble stout old men in formal attire. Breeding adults have black heads and backs and wispy, white head plumes. The young are brown. Although nocturnal, these herons can be seen roosting in trees and tall grass near marshes during the day. When disturbed, they emit a single loud *quok*.

Shoreline Park, San Rafael

San Rafael. To reach Pickleweed, Schoen, and Shoreline parks, farther south, take Bellam Boulevard. Shoreline Park's paved trail becomes dirt for a short stretch, then returns to pavement, and continues south along the shoreline to the Marin Rod & Gun Club by the Richmond–San Rafael Bridge and San Quentin State Prison. The club, bridge, and prison are inaccessible to the public.

lands. The trail here is wheelchair-accessible for the first 0.1 mile. From the South Pond trailhead off Grange Avenue, 0.7 miles are wheelchair-accessible.

THE MARIN ISLANDS

The Marin Islands National Wildlife Sanctuary and State Ecological Reserve, established in 1992, takes in West and East Marin islands and surrounding tidelands. These two small islands, off-limits to humans, support one of the

most important heron and egret colonies in Northern California. If you bring binoculars in spring, you might see great egrets, snowy egrets, and black-crowned night herons building nests, caring for their young, and feeding. Good viewing areas are Shoreline Park and the Loch Lomond Marina on the north side of San Rafael Creek.

GETTING AROUND

From McNears Beach, the Bay Trail moves onto Point San Pedro Road and heads southwest into

INFORMATION

Public Transit
Call 511 or visit 511.org.

Transit & Trails
www.transitandtrails
.org

Golden Gate Transit
www.goldengate
transit.org
415-455-2000

**China Camp
State Park**
www.parks.ca.gov
415-456-0766

**Marin Civic
Center Tours**
www.co.marin.ca.us
415-499-7009

**Marin County
Parks and
Open Space
District**
www.co.marin
.ca.us
415-499-6387

**Terwilliger Nature
Education Center**
www.wildcare
bayarea.org
415-456-7283

HOW TO CARE FOR THE BAY

There are many simple but important ways you can help to protect the bay and its shoreline for your own and future generations' enjoyment.

STORM DRAIN POLLUTION

During storms, rainwater moves over the surface of the ground and soaks into the soil. In most places, the soil is a natural filter that cleans water before it reaches creeks and bays. But in much of the San Francisco Bay Area, there are so many buildings, parking lots, and streets that rainwater can't soak into the ground. Instead, it flows downhill across pavement and concrete until it enters a storm drain and pours into your local waterway *without* being cleaned. Along the way, the water picks up oil and pollution from the streets. (See p. 78 about the DUST Marsh.) This

Coastal cleanup day

Storm drain stencil

runoff also carries wastes that people pour directly into their gutters and local storm drains. Did you know that just one can of motor oil can contaminate up to 250,000 gallons of water? In San Francisco Bay, and across the United States, it is estimated that half of all water pollution comes from storm drains. *It is pollution that is preventable.*

WHAT CAN YOU DO?

Neighborhood storm drain projects and recycling programs abound in

the Bay Area. By participating in these programs you will not only be helping to improve the nearest stretch of shoreline, you will help the entire bay. To find out how to prevent storm drain pollution, contact your city's Public Works Department. Ask what you can do in your neighborhood to prevent this form of pollution.

WHAT TO DO WITH WASTES

Disposing of products commonly referred to as "household hazardous wastes" directly into your trash or recycling containers not only harms the Bay, it is illegal and unsafe. Used motor oil, antifreeze, pesticides, herbicides, oil-based paints, gasoline, paint thinner, and turpentine should be poured into separate, sturdy, sealed containers. Do not mix such wastes. Tape the caps on, label with a permanent ink marker, and ask your city's recycling program where you can drop them off, or have someone pick them up. Excess or old latex paint that has been completely air dried in its can, can be discarded in the trash. Other items that require

careful handling include batteries, electronic devices such as computers and cell phones, mercury thermometers, medicines, and fluorescent lights.

All counties and some cities have household hazardous waste facilities where you can drop off these products. Many have useful information on their websites on less toxic alternatives to common household cleansers and pesticides. Visit www.savesfbay.org/household-toxics-disposal for links to local and other programs.

Water that is contaminated by chemicals also needs proper handling. Chlorinated water from swimming pools and hot tubs should be allowed to stand for two weeks before draining, without adding additional chlorine. Chlorine will completely evaporate from pool and tub water within two weeks. Pour clean-up water (followed by a good rinse of tap water) down sinks that lead to wastewater plants. Don't pour clean-up water down storm drains.

If you see what you think is harmful waste going down a storm drain, entering a creek, or being dumped along a shoreline, report it to one of the agencies or organizations listed on p. 215. How can you recognize such waste? Oil leaves sheen on water, as does gasoline. Antifreeze produces milky or bright green water. Excessive silt muddies the water. Its presence may indicate illegal shoreline activity. Most soaps and detergents create suds.

LOSS OF WETLANDS AND SHORELINE WILDLIFE HABITAT

Since 1850, 85 percent of the bay's wetlands have been destroyed, either buried under landfill or diked off and dried out. The destruction of shoreline habitats threatens the health of the bay and the survival of resident and migratory wildlife.

WHAT CAN YOU DO?

Join one of the organizations fighting to save the bay and its near-shore habitats (see the References/Resources section). Volunteer for education and clean-up projects. Follow local planning issues that have an impact on the shoreline. Contact your city, county, state, and federal representatives when bay and shoreline issues come up. If you think you see illegal filling along the shoreline, report it to one of the agencies or organizations listed in the References/Resources section.

ALIEN SPECIES

Alien species introduced into San Francisco Bay harm natives by dominating habitats and competing for resources (p. 156). Never

Feral cat

dump live bait fish or other foreign aquatic species—pet fish, turtles, salamanders, frogs—into the bay or nearby creeks, streams, ponds, or reservoirs. Never feed feral cats or release cats into the wild—even if they are sterilized. Feral cat colonies are now doing more damage to wildlife and wildlife habitat than even the red fox (p. 76), according to wildlife biologists. Keep your dog on leash or under voice control when visiting shorelines. Don't allow dogs to run through marshes or sprint down beaches chasing shorebirds. It may be good exercise for your canine, but shorebirds need a chance to rest and feed peacefully. There are ever fewer places where shorebirds can do so. Dogs can also damage marsh species and habitat.

If your home is on the bay, plant and cultivate your garden to prevent soil from washing into the bay. Consider planting natives and avoid invasive alien species, such as broom, pampas grass, ice plant, and eucalyptus. Once established, native plants are both beautiful and beneficial, and most require minimal attention and watering. Many water saving plants popular with nurseries are actually aliens; they may conserve water, but they are more likely than natives to die with the first cold snap. To find out about natives appropriate for your yard, visit your local nursery and ask if it carries native plants. Another source for information and free literature regarding drought tolerant plants, most of which are natives, is your water company's customer service department.

The East Bay Municipal Utility District sells an excellent book,

Replanting native species

Plants and Landscapes for Summer-Dry Climates.

Bay Friendly Landscaping and Gardening provides resources and information to help residents make environmentally friendly choices about landscaping and gardening to protect the watersheds of San Francisco Bay. Resources such as *Bay-Friendly Gardening Guide* and *Bay-Friendly Landscape Guidelines: Sustainable Practices for the Landscape Professional* are available at www.stopwaste.org. The California Native Plant Society will also gladly answer your questions. Contact them via their website at www.cnps.org.

ADOPT-A-BEACH

The California Coastal Commission's Adopt-A-Beach program has volunteer groups cleaning up beaches, marshes, and shorelines year-round. During Coastweeks in September, a massive cleanup operation takes place. Join the crowds on a shoreline near you. To find out more about these activities, call 1-800-COAST-4U (1-800-262-7848).

Separately, the steps above may not seem very influential. But together, and with time, the individual actions of many inhabitants of the San Francisco Bay Area can make a powerful difference in the state of the bay, the health of its plant and animal species, and the well-being of the shoreline environments.

South Marin

LARKSPUR AND CORTE MADERA

These two cities are closely linked to the bay via Corte Madera Creek and the Corte Madera Channel. The creek's shorelines are graced by numerous popular parks. Corte Madera State Ecological Reserve is a model for marshland restoration, despite the fact that little of the original shoreline remains.

Larkspur ferry

Statue of Sir Francis Drake at Remillard Park

LARKSPUR FERRY

The ferry between Larkspur and San Francisco's Ferry Building runs daily except on some major holidays. Kiosks and posters throughout the building are full of historical information and details on local sights and activities, including the Bay Trail. A pedestrian overpass from the terminal crosses Sir Francis Drake Boulevard and leads to the Larkspur Landing Shopping Center and the Cal Park Hill Tunnel.

CAL PARK HILL TUNNEL

Crossing Larkspur Landing Circle from the shopping center to the movie theater brings you to the Cal Park Hill Tunnel, which was originally constructed in 1884 for trains hauling lumber and freight and, later, passengers. It was sealed shut in 1978 after a series of fires and structural collapses. Reopened in 2010 after more than a decade of work by local advocates and Marin County, today it's

Cal Park Hill Tunnel

Remillard Park

Bon Air Landing Park

a thoroughfare for bicyclists and pedestrians between Larkspur and San Rafael.

PIPER PARK

Larkspur's Piper Park, built on 30 acres of fill, has baseball diamonds, picnic grounds, soccer fields, a parcourse, and numerous pines and willows. A 0.75-mile dirt trail circles the park on the edge of marshland and Corte Madera Creek. A small pier for hand-launched craft is on the creek. An organic community garden, fenced dog run, restrooms, and ample parking round out Piper Park.

REMILLARD PARK

Remillard Park is on Sir Francis Drake Boulevard East, between the huge metal statue of Sir Francis Drake (some believe he landed here) and the windsurfing pullout. Observation platforms and interpretive signs help you view the wildlife around two small ponds. Benches on the bayshore offer a nice view of the Corte Madera State Ecological Reserve, the Larkspur Ferry Terminal, and Mt. Tamalpais in the distance. Across the street is the renovated Remillard Brickyard, a state historic

landmark. Between 1891 and 1915, this brickyard produced 500,000 bricks a year. After the 1906 earthquake, much of San Francisco was rebuilt with Remillard bricks. The windsurfing spot next to the park is enormously popular.

CORTE MADERA CREEKSIDE PARKS

The north shore of Corte Madera Creek is green with parks. Niven Park has a large grass area that extends to the creek and a scattering of benches. Bon Air Landing Park features benches, a small grass area, and a pier for hand-launched craft. Hamilton Park offers a nice view of the creek, a grass area, and benches, with ample parking throughout. Creekside Park overlooks the waterway and a small restored marsh that was once a U.S. Army Corps of Engineers dump site for dredged material from the creek. A boardwalk and observation deck provide good bird-watching opportunities. Gravel paths wind around the children's play area and an information kiosk. A multi-use trail, with parcourses, extends from Creekside Park to the College of Marin. A dirt path starts across the creek from the park and also leads to the college. The Marin Rowing Association

maintains a facility on the shores of Corte Madera Creek and offers lessons for beginners.

CORTE MADERA STATE ECOLOGICAL RESERVE

In the 1950s, 225 acres of salt marsh in Corte Madera were diked and slated for development. After 20 years—and no development— the desiccated wasteland became an outdoor laboratory for testing salt marsh restoration procedures. Dredgings from the construction of the Larkspur Ferry Terminal were used to reconstruct the marsh. In 1976, dikes were breached to allow

Pickleweed

193

tidal waters to return. Pickleweed appeared quickly and was soon flourishing. Cordgrass followed, along with a healthy showing of shorebirds and other marsh plants and animals. Further experiments have increased biological diversity. Today, 125 acres of healthy salt marsh habitat survive as the Corte Madera State Ecological Reserve—a fantastic location for bird-watching (look for the red-tailed hawks on the electrical towers). With binoculars, you may also spot harbor seals resting on isolated shores. The reserve is accessible from the front-age road (Old Redwood Highway) and San Clemente Drive. You'll also find good access and parking off Channel Drive, which runs off Harbor Drive and Yolo Street. A gravel parking lot lies at the end of Industrial Way. Some 4 miles of dirt trails (many on the old levees) wind through the marsh.

SAN QUENTIN STATE PRISON MUSEUM

An 1880s staff residence and inmate post office now serve as a unique museum. San Quentin Prison has been in operation

San Quentin shackles

since 1854, when it began as a ship tied to the shore in this location. Historical photographs, documents, and artifacts make up the bulk of the museum's holdings. Drive to the prison's East Gate and tell the guard you are visiting the museum. Hours fluctuate, so call ahead. A donation is requested. The town of San Quentin, just outside the East Gate, has a small public shore accessible from a path through a eucalyptus grove off Main Street.

INFORMATION

Public Transit
Call 511 or visit 511.org.

Transit & Trails
www.transitandtrails.org

Blue and Gold Fleet
www.blueandgoldfleet.com
415-705-8200

Golden Gate Transit
www.goldengatetransit.org
415-455-2000

Larkspur Ferry
www.goldengateferry.org
415-455-2000

Muir Woods Shuttle
www.goldengatetransit.org
415-455-2000

Marin Rowing Association
www.marinrowing.org
415-461-1431

San Quentin Museum
415-454-5000

GETTING AROUND 🏃

From Point San Quentin, the Bay Trail route moves northwest on Sir Francis Drake Boulevard East toward Remillard Park, the Larkspur Ferry Terminal, and the Corte Madera Channel. The Bay Trail winds under Highway 101 on a boardwalk, turns north near the Marin Rowing Association, and hooks onto a pathway adjacent to the freeway heading south. The Bay Trail route continues on a pedestrian overcrossing at Rich Street and heads south on the Redwood Highway Frontage Road, where the trail borders Shorebird Marsh. A left turn on San Clemente near the shopping center takes you toward Paradise Drive and the Tiburon Peninsula. Portions of this segment have minimal bicycle and pedestrian facilities.

TIBURON PENINSULA

The Tiburon Peninsula boasts some 17 miles of shoreline, a rich history, and a unique name. Punta de Tiburon is Spanish for "Shark Point." Whether an active shark fishery or frequent shark sightings lie behind the name is uncertain. Today's community began in 1884, when a small waterfront settlement formed around a spur of the San Francisco and Northwestern Pacific Railroad.

Tiburon Bay Trail

Paradise Beach Park

Ring Mountain

PARADISE BEACH COUNTY PARK

Paradise Beach Park offers 19 acres of beautiful landscaping, generous facilities, and views of the Richmond–San Rafael Bridge, the Larkspur ferry, oil tankers, and San Quentin Prison. A large concrete pier, perfect for fishing and crabbing, juts out from a narrow beach. (The park charges an admission fee.)

RING MOUNTAIN

The Tiburon Peninsula's lower portions are wrapped in oaks, bay trees, and exotic grasses, while at higher elevations unique serpentine soils nurture some of the state's rarest plant species. The peninsula's serpentine cap is the Nature Conservancy's 400-acre preserve, Ring Mountain (park on Paradise Drive just east of Westward Drive; look for the small sign and hike uphill). Common native plants are joined here by uncom-

Richmond–San Rafael Bridge

Paradise Beach Park is the best place in the entire bay region for viewing the silvery Richmond–San Rafael Bridge, formally the John F. McCarthy Memorial Bridge. Opened September 1, 1956, it is 5.5 miles long, with major spans stretching 1,070 feet over dual shipping channels, 185 feet above the water. Some 60,000 vehicles cross its two decks daily.

Marin dwarf flax

Indian paintbrush

Serpentine reedgrass

Downtown Tiburon

mon and endangered companions: Marin dwarf flax, serpentine reedgrass, the Tiburon Indian paintbrush, and the Tiburon mariposa lily. Many of these plants survive only within the boundaries of this preserve.

TIBURON COVE

About 3 miles east of downtown Tiburon, on meandering Paradise Drive, is a quiet stretch of shoreline where coastal Miwok people lived before successive waves of foreigners arrived. Like most California Native Americans, they were either killed or expelled. Their home was given away as a Mexican land grant and eventually sold off and developed. In 1877, a large codfish plant was estab-

lished nearby to dry fish hauled here from the Okhotsk and Bering seas. In 1904, the Navy purchased the shoreline for a coaling station. In 1930, the tract was leased to the state of California for a nautical training school, and in 1940, the Navy converted it into a submarine net depot (reactivated during the Korean War). In 1961, the federal government established the Tiburon Marine Laboratory, which preceded the current National Marine Fisheries Service. The buildings here are now occupied by the Romberg Tiburon Centers, a complex that includes public and private organizations. A 0.7-mile loop trail, which begins in some beautiful oaks and bays across the street from the center, leads into the 24-acre Tiburon Uplands Nature Preserve.

Picnic on Tiburon Ridge

DOWNTOWN TIBURON

Tiburon's Main Street is lined with small shops and restaurants, including several with al fresco bayside seating. The Angel Island ferry and the San Francisco ferries dock off Main Street, at separate piers. The old quarter of Main Street is a scant block long, ending at the Corinthian Yacht Club and a parking lot (which charges a

Tiburon Gallows

At the corner of Mar West Street and Tiburon Boulevard, a pile of gigantic metal wheels hints at Tiburon's railroading past. They were part of the pier for the Northwestern Pacific Railroad, which was built in 1884. Freight cars were rolled on and off barges that plied coastal waters between San Francisco and the Redwood Empire to the north. A mechanism called a "gallows frame" raised and lowered the ramp between the barge and pier to adjust to the changing tides. The wheels were part of the gallows frame. The railroad ceased operating in 1967, and the pier was dismantled in 1974.

Angel Island

and can be accommodated on ferries. There's a fee for the ferry or for docking a boat.

ELEPHANT ROCK

Tiburon's Elephant Rock is "dedicated to all girls and boys under 16 years of age who love to fish." A short walkway leads to a small pier built atop Elephant Rock where you can drop a line or crab nets. (Even older people are welcome.)

LYFORD TOWER

Lyford Tower, a nationally registered historic site, was built about 1889 for Dr. Benjamin F. Lyford as the gateway to his planned utopian community, Hygeia (named for the Goddess of Health). Park by Shoreline Park and walk the short distance.

GETTING AROUND

The Bay Trail route follows Paradise Drive to Trestle Glen Boulevard, where the Trail splits and Trestle Glen Boulevard cuts over to Richardson Bay. To continue on the Paradise Drive segment, you must use the road shoulder and pass downtown Tiburon, where Paradise Drive turns into Tiburon Boulevard. Bike lanes and sidewalks turn into a shoreline path at Mar West Street, across from the police station and Town Hall. Here a spectacular multi-use path showcases the vision of what the Bay Trail is meant to be. The narrow, winding two-lane Paradise Drive is popular with bicyclists, but hiking is not advised.

---

fee). Public parking is available on street or at the paid lot across the street. Shoreline Park begins just off Main Street at Tiburon Boulevard, where benches, grass strips, walking areas, and unimpeded views of San Francisco and Angel Island abound.

ANGEL ISLAND STATE PARK

This 758-acre island has served many purposes in the past 200 years. Juan Manuel de Ayala set anchor in 1775 in what is now called Ayala Cove and named the island Isla de los Ángeles. His men exchanged gifts with the Miwoks. (Several Miwok middens remain on the island.) In 1839, Mexico gave the island to Antonio Maria Osio as a land grant. The U.S. military took over in the mid-1800s and expelled him. The oldest surviving building on the island is a mule barn built in 1863 at Camp Reynolds, a recruit depot during the Civil War and the "Indian Wars." From 1898 through World War II, the island was the site of one of the world's largest military induction centers. From 1910 until 1940, an estimated 175,000 Asians were detained at Point Simpton waiting for permission to live and work in the United States. Over a million immigrants of all nationalities passed through this "Ellis Island of the West."

Today Angel Island State Park offers expansive vistas of the bay and nearshore communities. Two trails lead to 781-foot Mt. Livermore, a former Nike missile site. Another trail, about 5 miles long, circles the island. At Ayala Cove are the ranger's office, visitor center, historic buildings, and many picnic areas. There are excellent interpretive signs throughout. The ferries from San Francisco, Tiburon, and Vallejo dock in front of the snack bar and bathrooms. Campsites are available by reservation for a fee. No dogs, skateboards, or skating are allowed on the island. Bicycles are welcome

INFORMATION

Public Transit
Call 511 or visit 511.org.

Transit & Trails
www.transitandtrails.org

Angel Island/Tiburon Ferry
www.angelislandferry.com
415-435-2131

Angel Island State Park
www.parks.ca.gov
415-435-5390

Ring Mountain
www.maringov.org
415-499-6387

RICHARDSON BAY

Some 911 acres of shoreline and bay waters in the city of Tiburon form the Audubon Society's Richardson Bay Sanctuary, which combines

Captain William Richardson

with the 55-acre Richardson Bay Park to make up 1.5 miles of preserved shoreline. The bay was named after Captain William Richardson, who was given the 19,000-acre Mexican land grant Saucelito in 1838.

Richardson Bay

RICHARDSON BAY AUDUBON CENTER

The sanctuary, established by the Audubon Society in 1957, encompasses one of the few remaining unaltered bay wetlands. About 80 species of waterbirds feed and rest here during fall migration, and you can also see many resident threatened wildlife species, including harbor seals, brown pelicans, and

Lyford House

great and snowy egrets. The sanctuary also includes grasslands, woodlands, coastal sage scrub, and a freshwater pond. The Audubon Society's Education Center and bookstore are on Greenwood Beach Road. An excellent half-mile nature trail begins at the center. Sanctuary waters, closed to boats October through April, are patrolled by volunteers to prevent disturbance of migrating waterbirds.

The striking yellow Victorian on sanctuary ground is the Lyford House. It was constructed on Strawberry Point, across Richardson Bay, in the late 1870s and was the center of Lyford's Eagle Dairy. After Dr. Benjamin Lyford and his wife, Hilarita Reed, died in the early 1900s with no heirs, it stood empty for decades. In 1957, it was donated to Audubon, barged to its present site, and refurbished. The Lyford House may be rented for weddings and other events for a fee.

RICHARDSON BAY PARK

It may be long and thin, but Richardson Bay Park is big on recreation options. A visit on any day will prove the point—runners, hikers, bikers, and rollerbladers use the shoreline path almost continuously. From the junction of Tiburon Boulevard and Trestle Glen Boulevard, where there is ample parking in the former Blackie's Pasture (look for an explanatory plaque in one corner of the lot), you can work out on a parcourse that begins near the parking lot. Look for the marsh by the parking area and the interpretive signs near the water treatment plant. A large grass playing field, McKegney Green, is a great place to relax and take in the views of the Strawberry Peninsula and Sausalito. Dogs must be leashed.

GETTING AROUND

At the corner of Mar West Street and Tiburon Boulevard, the Bay

Waterfowl of Richardson Bay

More than 80 species of migratory waterfowl have been observed in the sanctuary in numbers reaching into the thousands. Six of the more abundant, and therefore easier-to-spot species are described in their winter plumage. During migration, however, various stages of plumage can be seen.

Western grebe
North America's largest grebe has striking black-and-white plumage, an elegant neck line, and stunning red eyes, all of which help identify this strong underwater swimmer. During the winter, these birds can easily be confused with the also-present Clark's grebes.

Bufflehead
An oversized head, steep fore-head, and short bill distinguish the bufflehead, one of the smallest North American ducks. The male is black above and white below, with a large white patch on his head. The female is duller, with a white patch on each side of her head.

Lesser scaup
Two similar-looking species—greater and lesser scaup—visit the sanctuary (the greater, not surprisingly, is a bit bigger). Remember "black at both ends and white in the middle," and you'll know how to identify scaup.

Ruddy duck
A small and compact duck, the male has white cheek pouches and a dull blue bill in winter, with a tail often pointing stiffly skyward. Its small stature and short wings give the ruddy duck a "buzzy" flight pattern. The San Francisco Bay Estuary attracts one of the largest wintering concentrations of this species.

Canvasback
This duck's sloping head profile and the whitish "saddlebag" across its back help identify it. The male has a rusty red head. Canvasbacks are divers and breed from the Arctic to the prairies of North America.

Surf scoter
Informally known as the "skunk duck" (because of the male's black plumage and white head patches), the male scoter sports a wildly colorful bill. Tundra nesters, scoters winter along the Pacific and Atlantic coasts.

Trail route from Paradise Drive moves onto a paved path parallel to Tiburon Boulevard. This piece of the Bay Trail leads to Richardson Bay Park, as well as the Richardson Bay Audubon Center on Greenwood Beach Road. Near the intersection of Greenwood Beach Road and Tiburon Boulevard, an older, narrow section of the Bay Trail weaves along the shoreline near apartments and condominiums. Cross a bridge and you'll come to Strawberry Point School, at the bottom of Harbor Cove Road. Head up Harbor Cove and turn west (left) on Strawberry Drive. The Bay Trail in this location consists of bike lanes and sidewalks.

INFORMATION

Public Transit
Call 511 or visit 511.org.

Transit & Trails
www.transitandtrails.org

Golden Gate Transit
www.goldengatetransit.org
415-455-2000

Richardson Bay Audubon Center
www.tiburonaudubon.org
415-388-2524

STRAWBERRY POINT

Strawberry Point

Between Tiburon and Mill Valley hides unincorporated Strawberry Point. The peninsula leading to Strawberry Point provides grand vistas of the bay. Harbor Cove Dock, off Strawberry Drive, is a great place for hand-launching small craft. From the peninsula along Seminary Drive, you can view landings and takeoffs of the only commercial seaplane operation on the bay. At the northern end of Strawberry Landing (a spit created by fill), a fenced wildlife preserve is one of only several harbor seal haul-out spots in the entire bay. A channel was dug to create an "island" at the tip of the landing, and a fence was erected to protect the reclusive seals from dogs, hikers, and runners. At the other end of the landing is a small grass area for wildlife viewing. There are water-level panoramas of San Francisco, the Bay Bridge, Belvedere, and Tiburon throughout. The Northwestern Pacific Railroad once operated a line from San Rafael along Strawberry Peninsula's eastern shore, crossing Richardson Bay via a trestle to Sausalito. San Francisco passengers transferred to ferries from there.

BRICKYARD AND STRAWBERRY COVE PARKS

At the meeting of Seminary Drive and Great Circle Drive, a children's playground is tucked beneath a grove of shoreline-hugging trees. This is Brickyard Park, and the broken bricks strewn about the shore testify to the name's origin. Farther along Seminary Drive, near the frontage road, is Belloc's Lagoon and small Strawberry Cove Park. The marsh here is an even expanse of cordgrass nestled between De Silva Island (now a peninsula) and the park. A pathway follows Seminary Drive to a small exercise station. Stop on Seminary as it wraps around the cove and train your binoculars on the eucalyptus grove on De Silva Island. In spring, you may see nesting pairs of great blue herons squabbling and caring for young here.

Harbor Seals

Although present in the bay throughout the year, these seals are best seen on shore during the breeding season from March to July. In early summer, the females give birth on land to one pup. Harbor seals can stay underwater up to 20 minutes when they're searching for fish, shellfish, and squid.

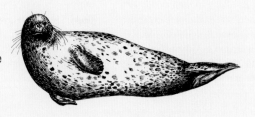

MILL VALLEY

Mill Valley was named after a sawmill built in 1836 by John Thomas Reed on Cascade Creek. Overlooking this community, and every inch of the Bay Trail here, is Mt. Tamalpais.

MT. TAMALPAIS

We will never know what the indigenous Miwok called their sacred mountain. To the Spanish, it was Picacho Prieto—"Dark Peak." Today, it's Mt. Tamalpais. Most of the mountain is open space owned and managed by the Marin Municipal Water District and state and federal agencies. Nearly 200 miles of public trails weave a long tale of human use, including the "crookedest railroad in the world," which ran from Mill Valley to Tamalpais's East Peak from 1896 to 1930. The 2,571-foot summit is a fantastic perch for examining most of the central and northern bay. Numerous trails lead to Tamalpais, including those at the heads of Blithedale and Cascades canyons in Mill Valley, as well as from the Panoramic Highway en route to Stinson Beach.

BAYFRONT PARK AND BOTHIN MARSH

Whether you have two legs or four, want to run, walk, paddle, or just rest, Mill Valley's 14-acre Bayfront Park has something for you. On the western side of the park is a large dog-run area (elsewhere, dogs must be leashed) and a public pier for kayaks and canoes. A parcourse zigzags throughout. Crossing a bridge to the park's east side leads to a

Mt. Tamalpais

baseball diamond, more parcourse stations, soccer fields, and a large children's playground. Next to the park is Bothin Marsh, a 112-acre open space preserve defined by the Bay Trail toward the marsh's southern and western fringe. Four small bridges along the trail rise over creeks and channels—great places to stop and watch for marine life when the tide surges in or

out through these restricted waterways. Shorebirds abound. Dogs must be leashed.

GETTING AROUND

From Strawberry Drive at Harbor Cove Road, the Bay Trail moves around the Strawberry Peninsula on roads. A half-mile paved trail on Strawberry Landing can be reached via Harbor Point Drive.

Bayfront Park

From the corner of Seminary Drive and the Redwood Highway Frontage Road, the trail route crosses under Highway 101 en route to Mill Valley. There is also a public overpass a quarter mile north on the frontage road. A public pier and small-craft launch area are located about 200 yards west of Highway 101 behind an office park. The Bay Trail route weaves past restaurants, more office buildings, and condominiums to Bayfront Park, and the first of several bridges, via Hamilton Drive. The trail route moves down Shelter Bay Drive to the water's edge and some nice benches. At the last footbridge in Bothin Marsh, a Bay Trail/Ridge Trail connector—the Tennessee Valley Trail— leads southwest into Tennessee Valley,

Bothin Marsh

the Marin Headlands, and the Golden Gate National Recreation Area en route to the Bay Area Ridge Trail. The paved Bay Trail route continues south under the Richardson Bay Bridge toward Sausalito.

SAUSALITO WATERFRONT

In just over 2 miles, the Sausalito waterfront offers a wealth of colorful history, sites, sounds, parks, piers, restaurants, and shops. Sausalito's mellifluous name originates from *sausal*, Spanish for "willow grove," which Spanish commander Juan Manuel de Ayala spied on its shores in 1775 and knew to be a sign of freshwater. Much of southern Marin, including Sausalito, was later included in Rancho

Sausalito shoreline

Saucelito, a Mexican land grant deeded to Englishman William Richardson. Over the past 150 years, this stretch of bayshore has been used by Azorian whalers, brothels, railroads, gambling houses, massive shipyards, artist colonies, luxurious estates, and rickety houseboats. Today's explorer will find a bounty of parks and spectacular views. Except for Swede's Beach, the entire waterfront is wheelchair-accessible to varying degrees.

FLOTSAM AND JETSAM

Gate 6 Road, off the northern tip of Bridgeway (Sausalito's main drag), leads to Kappas Harbor and a small loop of public shore. Venture out onto the spit of land, find the bench, and take in the views or study contrasting lifestyles: to one side of the spit are Sausalito's famous houseboats; on the other side, pricey yachts and sailboats glisten in their berths. Hidden among Sausalito's numerous parks and walkways off Bridgeway are public shores and docks that require some searching to find. They are all great places to observe boats and maritime businesses. Flynn's Landing, for example, is a public dock stretching between Sausalito Point and Johnson Street. The end of Johnson Street also has a small

unnamed public shore consisting of a dock and a few benches overlooking Pelican Harbor. On the bay side of Turney Street, another public pier with benches wraps around a restaurant and continues to Locust Street and another viewing spot.

NORTHSIDE COMMONS

With a nice grass area, benches, and a small marsh on its northern shore, Shoreline Park is also home to sailing clubs that offer sailing lessons and rentals. See p. 7 for information about the Bay Area Water Trail.) Marinship Park has three public tennis courts, with night lights, and a large grass field. At Schoonmaker Point, you can launch a kayak, spread a picnic, or

just rest. A beautiful beach (no dogs allowed) grades into the bay. A lifeguard is on duty seasonally. If you drive, don't be deterred by a "Permit Parking Only" sign. Smaller letters say public parking is available in green areas, and there are plenty of those. A large lawn surrounded by weeping willows, with a refurbished gazebo, is the centerpiece of the 10-acre Carl Dunphy Park. At a small beach, you can you cool off your feet or watch for migrating shorebirds while children romp in the playground. Just offshore, a narrow gravel bar is a well-used resting spot for egrets and other shorebirds. Parking and restrooms are available. Sausalito's Civic Center, library, and Historical Society are upslope from Dunphy, off Litho and Caledonia streets.

SECRET SOUTHERN BEACHES

Don't blink or you'll miss Tiffany Beach and Park, a few square feet of sand just off Bridgeway. Several benches along the length of Bridgeway invite you to rest and watch. Note the Municipal Pier, good for fishing, watching sea lions, and studying Albert Sybrian's bronze sea lion sculpture 10 feet offshore. Moving south, you can bounce along a public boardwalk. Down a flight of wooden stairs at the bayside end of Valley Street (just off 2nd) hides Swede's Beach. About 200 feet of narrow beachfront offers exceptional views of Angel Island, Belvedere, the East Bay, and a confusion of old pilings.

DOWNTOWN SANCTUARIES

Downtown is always busy, but three small parks offer rest. Gabrielson Memorial Park, just south of the ferry terminal, opens onto the water and is ringed with benches. Plaza Viña del Mar is next to the ferry terminal. It was built in 1904 and honors Sausalito's sister city, Viña del Mar, Chile. Two 14-foot-high elephants sculpted for the

Carl Dunphy Park

1915 Panama-Pacific Exposition stand guard. To stretch your legs and gain perspective, climb the Excelsior Lane steps directly across from the plaza and Bridgeway. Yee Tock Chee Park, named in memory of "Willie" Chee, owner of the Marin Fruit Company for 60 years, is a fascinating work of concrete and pilings tucked in between Bridgeway and the water's edge. Various levels of seating have been created with concrete and wooden platforms. This is a spot where ferries landed in the late 1800s.

RICHARDSON BAY'S FLOATING COMMUNITY

Sausalito's houseboat community started slowly in the 1950s, when artists and writers began arriving along the bayshore. By the 1960s, scores of abandoned vessels had been converted to residential use. Today, two distinct types of residential structures float on Richardson Bay: houseboats and live-aboard boats. Houseboats are of two basic types: boats that are no longer used for navigation and have been converted into homes, and residences built on floating platforms (floating

Marinship Shipyards

A memo dated March 2, 1942, marked the end of the tranquil Sausalito waterfront: "It is necessary in the interests of the national emergency that the maximum number of emergency cargo vessels be completed prior to December 31, 1942." Marinship Shipyards were created to meet that goal, and shipbuilding began that year. More than 26,000 piles were pounded into the bay to create the yards, more than 24,000 feet of new railroad track were put down, and a rich tidal marsh was completely filled. A channel 300 feet wide and more than a mile long was dredged to accommodate oceangoing vessels. During three and a half years of production, 93 ships sailed out of the yards, as some 75,000 people worked around the clock seven days a week. Marin City was constructed to house shipyard workers. The most

Marinship Shipyards, 1944

rapidly built ship ever produced here took 28 days from keel to launching. Today, the site of the shipyards is occupied by Marinship Park and the U.S. Army Corps of Engineers maintenance yard and Bay Model (see p. 205).

Floating homes

Ride a Ferry

The Red and White Fleet ferry leaves the Sausalito terminal and ventures out under the Golden Gate Bridge before looping back to San Francisco's Pier 43½. On its return voyage, it passes by Alcatraz and Angel Island before turning into Sausalito. The commuter ferry operated by the Golden Gate Ferry runs directly between Sausalito and San Francisco's Ferry Building at the foot of Market Street. Bicycles are welcome.

Sausalito ferries

homes). Live-aboards are boats that are used for navigation but also function as the boat owners' homes. Most houseboats and live-aboards are moored at authorized marinas where houseboats are connected to sewers and utilities. However, some houseboats and live-aboards are illegally anchored offshore or moored along the shoreline. Similar but smaller communities are at San Francisco's Mission Creek Harbor, Alameda's Barnhill Marina, and the Berkeley Marina. Richardson Bay's structures shelter fewer artists today than they did in the 1960s, yet this is still a unique community.

BAY MODEL VISITOR CENTER

The U.S. Army Corps of Engineers' Bay Model is a 1.5-acre reproduction of the San Francisco Bay and Sacramento–San Joaquin River Delta system. Built to scale and capable of simulating currents and tidal action, it is used by the Corps to study the bay's ecology and to plan responses to industrial accidents. Exhibits highlight the bay's natural history, geology, wetlands, wildlife, and fishing and boat-building industries.

GETTING AROUND

From Mill Valley's Bothin Marsh, the trail passes under the Richardson Bay Bridge (where there are benches, a bike rack, and parking). East of the bridge, a trail moves around an office complex fringed by marshes. The Bay Trail continues, paved, to Gate 6 Road. From there, a trail leads out to a small peninsula at Kappas Harbor. Shoreline hikers and bikers can continue on bike lanes along Sausalito's main roads for about 3 miles, then follow East Road toward Fort Baker.

Lovesick Toadfish

During July and August 1984, many people were puzzled by some loud and strange nocturnal noises coming from Richardson Bay. Speculations about their source ranged from low-flying B-17s to Russian submarines. In 1985, however, scientists discovered that the weird sounds were the call of the toadfish (*Porichthys notatus*), coming in once again from the Pacific Ocean for the mating season. Toadfish had been common in the bay until the 1960s, when pollution interfered with their migration. Their return in 1984 indicates that Richardson Bay is getting somewhat cleaner and healthier.

INFORMATION

Public Transit
Call 511 or visit 511.org.

Transit & Trails
www.transitandtrails.org

Golden Gate Ferry
www.goldengateferry.org
415-921-5858

Red & White Fleet
www.redandwhite
.com
415-673-2900

Bay Model
www.spn.usace
.army.mil/bmvc
415-332-3871

FORT BAKER

This old military post extends across quiet Horseshoe Bay, tucked under the northern expanse of the Golden Gate Bridge. Its sheltered waterfront and coastal bluffs have been actively used by the military since the 1850s, when the Lime Point Reservation was established to guard the entrance to San Francisco Bay. In 1897, it was renamed Fort Baker after Civil War hero and temporary San

Historic Fort Baker

Franciscan Edward D. Baker. Fort Baker's original military mission diminished after World War I, with the invention of more sophisticated defense systems, but it served through World War II as both a Mine Command Headquarters (San Francisco Bay was spiked with 481 submerged mines by 1945) and an Air Defense Command Headquarters.

Today, the fort is part of the Golden Gate National Recreation Area and a great location to view historic military architecture, visit a gun battery, enjoy the dramatic sights and sounds on the underside of the Golden Gate Bridge, watch massive tanker ships, visit the Bay Area Discovery Museum, and fish off a concrete pier. Renovations completed in 2005 turned some of the historic buildings into an upscale boutique hotel, spa, restaurant, and bar. If you can't afford to stay, pull up a chair on the veranda for a million-dollar view and a slightly less expensive brew!

BAY AREA DISCOVERY MUSEUM

The Discovery Boat, Salt Marsh, Underwater Sea Tunnel, and many other exhibits invite visitors to explore the natural wonders of the bay and nearshore. Other exhibits teach about architecture and design. Classes, tours, and presentations are offered. The museum also contains a small café and gift store.

LIME POINT LIGHTHOUSE

The lighthouse stands at the western tip of Fort Baker on a rocky promontory that is part of the Bay Trail. It was built in 1883 to warn ships away from the Golden Gate's treacherous fog-shrouded shores with a duo of powerful steam whistles. In 1900, Lime Point's keepers mounted a flashing light on the tower. Both warning signals are still used today. Because of lead contamination of the soil from bridge maintenance, some areas near the lighthouse are closed indefinitely to the public.

VISTA POINT

Originally named the Juan Manuel de Ayala Vista Point after the Spanish commander charged with the first official survey of the bay in 1775, this parking area displays an enormous cross-section of a redwood tree from Crescent City marked with important dates in California's history. When the redwood was 50 feet tall, in 1579, Captain Francis Drake sailed to the Point Reyes Peninsula and, some weeks later, to the Farallon Islands. Drake and his crew

Vital Statistics of the Golden Gate Bridge

Work began: January 5, 1933
Bridge opened: May 8, 1937
Length of span: 4,200 feet
Length of suspension bridge: 6,450 feet
Height of towers above water: 746 feet
Depth of piers: 110 feet
Diameter of cables: 36-3/8 inches
Number of wires per cable: 27,572
Total length of wire: 80,000 miles
Weight of bridge: 83,000 tons

"On the entire west coast of the Americas, there is no other estuary like San Francisco Bay. Immense in size, covering over 1,600 square miles, and draining over 40 percent of the land area of California, it is one of the great estuaries of the world."

SAVING THE BAY

Mission Blue Butterfly

Hidden in the bluffs of the Marin Headlands and the chaparral-covered hills of Fort Baker, the mission blue butterfly is making a comeback from near extinction. This tiny endangered species, with sky blue wings that measure about an inch across, lays eggs exclusively on silver lupine plants. Recent efforts to protect its habitat and increase the number of lupine have helped the mission blue rebound. It survives in only four locations in Northern California, so visits to its Fort Baker habitat are limited to ranger-led tours. See the Golden Gate National Parks Conservancy website for information.

Mission blue butterfly: a federally listed endangered species

Sea Floor Rocks

Chert can be seen in the cliffs along the Bay Trail between Golden Gate Bridge and Fort Baker, as well as on Lime Point Trail. This red-brown sedimentary rock is composed of the skeletal remains of microscopic single-celled animals, laid down on the ocean floor millions of years ago. The slow, prodigious movement of Earth's crustal plates forced the Pacific floor under the western edge of the North American continent in a process called subduction, leaving behind contorted samples of chert at this monumental meeting ground. (For more on bay geology, see p. 98)

Hawk-Watching

Between mid-August and early December, from Hawk Hill in the Marin Headlands, Golden Gate Raptor Observatory volunteers monitor the largest concentration of migrating raptors in the Pacific states. Each au-

Northern harrier perched

tumn, 10,000 to 20,000 hawks, eagles, falcons, vultures, kites, harriers, and osprey funnel through the headlands. Nineteen species are seen annually, with the peak numbers coming through between mid-September and early October. View the migration on weekend days in September and October and hear a free, docent-led Hawk Talk. Saturdays and Sundays only, meet on Hawk Hill at noon; heavy fog or rain cancels.

Northern harrier with wings outstretched

stayed 36 days in present-day Marin County repairing his ship, the *Golden Hind*, and stocking provisions. They then set sail for England, arriving some 14 months later, in September 1580. This vantage point has since been renamed the H. Dana Bowers Vista Point, but is most commonly referred to simply as "Vista Point."

GETTING AROUND 🚶🚶

The Bay Trail route follows the shoulder of East Road from Sausalito to Fort Baker—a scenic 2-mile trip with fabulous views of the bay. There are benches and tables along the way. The trail meanders by the fort's shore and in front of the Coast Guard's Station Golden Gate. From the Coast Guard station, one trail leads east toward Point Cavallo. On the edge of Horseshoe Bay, there is a small accessible beach with good exposure at low tides, ample parking, and wheelchair access. The paved trail climbs west to the northern tip of the Golden Gate Bridge and Vista Point. Hikers can connect with the Coastal Trail and the Marin Headlands through a cypress grove west of the bridge. A walkway under the bridge joins Vista Point with the western parking lot. Pedestrians can cross the bridge on the east sidewalk from 5 a.m. to 9 p.m. daily. Bikers can cross at all times, using the west side from 5 a.m. to 9 p.m. on weekends and holidays and 3:30 p.m. to 9 p.m. on weekdays, and the east side at other times.

INFORMATION

Public Transit
Call 511 or visit 511.org.

Transit & Trails
www.transitandtrails.org

Bay Area Discovery Museum
www.baykidsmuseum.org
415-339-3900

Golden Gate National Parks Conservancy
www.parksconservancy.org
415-776-0693

Golden Gate Raptor Observatory
www.ggro.org
415-331-0730

Marin Headlands Visitor Center
www.nps.gov/goga/marin-headlands.htm
415-331-1540

Acknowledgments

More people than can be named gave freely of their time and talents to make this the best guidebook we could produce. The solid foundation and enduring popularity of the original 1995 Coastal Conservancy version have made the preparation of this updated guide a pleasure. Assistance from the original project director and editor, Rasa Gustaitis; encouragement from writer/researcher Jerry Emory; original files, institutional knowledge, and updated cartography by Reineck and Reineck; copyediting and permissions work by Valerie Sinzdak and Amanda Glesmann; the immense talents of Nicole Hayward, book designer, and the unwavering patience of Lindsie Bear and Kate Hoffman at UC Press have made this daunting task manageable.

We are proud of the quality photography and illustrations in this book, and while we owe thanks to innumerable people for their contributions, special gratitude goes to Stephanie Ellis at the San Francisco Bay Bird Observatory (SFBBO) for enthusiastically providing hundreds of spectacular bird photos from a hugely talented pool of members, volunteers, and staff; Wilfred J. Jones for capturing the diverse essence of the Bay Trail in digital format; Corinne DeBra, Pat Koren, Cris Benton, Craig Howell, Will Elder, Ron Horii, Don Weden, Craig Solin, Tom Mikkelsen, Bruce Beyaert, Lewis Stewart, staff at the East Bay Regional Park District, the U.S. Fish & Wildlife Service, and Save the Bay for further photographic and content contributions, and Mimi Osborne, Lee Adair, Gay Reineck, and Helen Muirhead for their beautiful illustrations.

Many people contributed to the first edition in many different ways, and although they did not work on the update, we would like to acknowledge their early role: Brian Weise, Jill Keimach, Ceil Scandone, Ruth Gravanis, Joan Cardellino, Nelia Forest, Karen Rust, David Hayes, Beth Stone, Alan R. Pendleton, Doris Sloan, Phyllis Faber, Elizabeth McClintock, John Inase, Joel Hedgpeth, Michael Herz, Ross Turner, Jon Stark, Paul Wong, John Steiner, Ken Downing, Arthur Okamura, Ray Peterson, Gordon Sherman, Carolyn Rissanen, Bob Walker, Mike Alvarez, James H. Clark, Anthony C. Crouch, Valeurie Friedman, Sam Rosenthal, and Rose Vekony.

Lastly, many thanks to the State Coastal Conservancy for funding this updated guidebook effort, and for the staff support of Sam Schuchat, executive officer; Amy Hutzel, program manager; and Ann Buell, project manager.

References/Resources

SAN FRANCISCO BAY TRAIL INFORMATION

Association of Bay Area Governments
San Francisco Bay Trail Project
510-464-7900
www.baytrail.org

Metropolitan Transportation Commission
Regional Bicycle and Pedestrian Plans
510-817-5700
www.mtc.ca.gov

State Coastal Conservancy
San Francisco Bay Area Conservancy Program
510-286-1015
www.scc.ca.gov

SAN FRANCISCO BAY AREA WATER TRAIL INFORMATION
www.sfbaywatertrail.org

State Coastal Conservancy
San Francisco Bay Area Water Trail Project
510-286-1015
www.scc.ca.gov

Association of Bay Area Governments
San Francisco Bay Area Water Trail Project
510-464-7900
www.abag.ca.gov

Bay Access, Inc.
www.bayaccess.org
415-459-8727

PUBLIC TRANSPORTATION

511
511 is a resource for up-to-date traffic, transit, rideshare, and bicycling throughout the Bay Area. Call 511 or visit www.511.org.

Transit & Trails
Transit & Trails is an interactive website that helps plan trips to parks, open space, and trails using public transit.
www.transitandtrails.org

Buses & trains
Alameda County Transit Authority (AC Transit)
510-891-4700
www.actransit.org

Bay Area Rapid Transit (BART)
510-465-2278
www.bart.gov

Caltrain
800-660-4287
www.caltrain.com

Golden Gate Transit
415-455-2000
www.goldengate.org

Napa Valley Transit (VINE)
707-251-2800
www.nctpa.net

San Francisco Municipal Transportation Agency (MUNI)
415-701-2311
www.sfmta.com

San Mateo County Transit District (SamTrans)
800-660-4287
www.smctd.com

Santa Clara Valley Transportation Authority (VTA)
408-321-2300
www.vta.org

Solano County Transit (SolTrans)
Benicia Transit: 707-746-4300,
www.ci.benicia.ca.us/transit
Vallejo Transit: 707-648-4666,
www.vallejotransit.com

Sonoma County Transit
707-576-7433
www.sctransit.com

Union City Transit
510-471-1411
www.union-city.ca.us

West Contra Costa County Transit (WestCAT)
510-724-7993
www.westcat.org

Caltrans Bay Bridge bicycle shuttle service
Runs during peak commute periods between San Francisco and Oakland. See www.dot.ca.gov/dist4/shuttle.htm for schedules and fares.

Ferry lines
Alameda Harbor Bay Ferry
• Harbor Bay Isle in Alameda–San Francisco Ferry Building
  510-769-5500
  www.eastbayferry.com

Alameda/Oakland Ferry
• Alameda Main Street–Jack London Square, Oakland–San Francisco Ferry Building
• Pier 39 (Fisherman's Wharf)–Angel Island State Park
  510-522-3300
  www.eastbayferry.com

Angel Island-Tiburon Ferry
• Tiburon Ferry Terminal–Angel Island State Park
  415-435-2131
  www.angelislandferry.com

Blue & Gold Fleet
• Angel Island / Tiburon Ferry: San Francisco Ferry Building or Pier 41–Tiburon Ferry Terminal–Angel Island State Park
• Pier 41–Sausalito Ferry Terminal
• Vallejo Baylink Ferry–San Francisco Ferry Building–Vallejo Ferry Terminal
  415-705-8200
  www.blueandgoldfleet.com

Golden Gate Ferry
• San Francisco Ferry Building–Sausalito
• San Francisco Ferry Building–Larkspur
  415-455-2000
  www.goldengateferry.org

Hornblower Alcatraz Ferry
• Pier 33–Alcatraz Island, day and night trips
  415-981-7625
  www.hornblower.com

Red & White Fleet
415-673-2900
www.redandwhite.com

Water Emergency Transportation Authority
415-291-3377
www.watertransit.org

CONSERVATION ORGANIZATIONS & PROGRAMS

Audubon Society

Golden Gate Audubon
510-843-2222
www.goldengateaudubon.org

Marin Audubon
415-924-6057
www.marinaudubon.org

Mt. Diablo Audubon
www.diabloaudubon.com

Napa-Solano Audubon
www.napasolanoaudubon.com

Santa Clara Valley Audubon
408-252-3747
www.scvas.org

Sequoia Audubon
650-529-1454
www.sequoia-audubon.org

Bay Area Open Space Council
510-809-8009
www.openspacecouncil.org
A collaborative of sixty member organizations involved in protecting and stewarding parks, trails, and agricultural lands in the San Francisco Bay Area

Bay Friendly Landscaping and Gardening
510-891-6500
www.stopwaste.org
Provides resources and information to help residents make environmentally friendly choices about landscaping and gardening to protect the watersheds of San Francisco Bay

Bay Institute
415-878-2929
www.bay.org
Protects, restores, and inspires conservation of San Francisco Bay and its watershed

California Department of Fish & Game
916-445-0411
www.dfg.ca.gov
State agency that maintains native fish, wildlife, plant species, and natural communities for their intrinsic and ecological value and their benefits to people

California Native Plant Society
415-447-2677
www.cnps.org
Preserves and protects California native plants and their habitats

California Watchable Wildlife
www.cawatchablewildlife.org
Promotes the value of wildlife viewing to benefit individuals, families, communities, and industries while fostering awareness and support for conservation and protection of wildlife and habitats

Citizens Committee to Complete the Refuge
650-493-5540
www.cccrrefuge.org
Works to save the bay's remaining wetlands by placing them under the protection of the Don Edwards San Francisco Bay National Wildlife Refuge

Don Edwards San Francisco Bay National Wildlife Refuge
510-792-0222
www.fws.gov/desfbay
Federally designated refuge that spans 30,000 acres of open bay, salt pond, salt marsh, mudflat, upland, and vernal pool habitats located throughout south San Francisco Bay

Golden Gate National Parks Conservancy
415-561-3000
www.parksconservancy.org
Preserves the Golden Gate National Parks, enhances the park visitor experience, and builds a community dedicated to conserving the parks for the future

Greenbelt Alliance
510-543-6771
www.greenbelt.org
Protects green space around the urban area and provides guided hikes and bike rides

Lindsay Wildlife Museum
925-935-1978
www.wildlife-museum.org
Natural history and environmental education center in Walnut Creek with more than 50 species of live, non-releasable, native California animals on exhibit

Marine Science Institute
650-364-2760
www.sfbaymsi.org
Offers a discovery voyage for school groups six days a week

Point Reyes Bird Observatory Conservation Science
707-781-2555
www.prbo.org
Bird ecology research, field science training programs, and bird science education programs to advance biodiversity conservation in the west on land and at sea

San Francisco Bay Bird Observatory
408-946-6548
www.sfbbo.org
Guided walks, workshops, special events, and bird-banding demonstrations

San Francisco Bay Conservation and Development Commission (BCDC)
415-352-3600
www.bcdc.ca.gov
A state regulatory agency responsible for the protection and enhancement of San Francisco Bay and expansion of public access to the edge of the shoreline

San Francisco Bay Estuary Partnership
510-622-2304
www.sfestuary.org
A designated National Estuary Program that supports projects and develops policies to protect water quality and restore fish and wildlife habitat in and around the San Francisco Bay Delta Estuary

San Francisco Bay Joint Venture
415-259-0334
www.sfbayjv.org
Brings together public and private agencies, conservation groups, development interests, and others to

restore wetlands and wildlife habitat in San Francisco Bay watersheds and along the Pacific coasts of San Mateo, Marin, and Sonoma counties

San Francisco Bay Regional Water Quality Control Board
510-622-2300
www.swrcb.ca.gov/sanfranciscobay
A regulatory agency responsible for monitoring and maintaining water quality in the Bay Area

Save the Bay
510-463-6850
www.savesfbay.org
A regional organization dedicated to protecting, restoring, and celebrating San Francisco Bay through education and habitat restoration

Sierra Club
San Francisco Bay Chapter
510-848-0800
www.sanfranciscobay.sierraclub.org
A grassroots organization committed to protecting wild places

Urban Creeks Council
510-356-0591
www.urbancreeks.org
Preserves, protects, and maintains the flow of natural streams in urban environments

INTERPRETIVE CENTERS ALONG THE BAY TRAIL

Crissy Field Center
415-561-7690
www.parksconservancy.org

Don Edwards San Francisco Bay National Wildlife Refuge
Visitor Center in Newark
510-792-0222
www.fws.gov/desfbay

Environmental Education Center in Alviso
408-262-5513
www.fws.gov/desfbay

East Bay Regional Park District
888-EBPARKS
www.ebparks.org
Coyote Hills Visitor Center, Tidewater Boating Center, Crab Cove Visitor Center

EcoCenter at Heron's Head Park in San Francisco
415-282-6840
www.lejyouth.org/ecocenter/eco.html

Gulf of the Farallones National Marine Sanctuary Visitor Center
415-561-6625
www.farallones.org/explore

Hayward Shoreline Interpretive Center
510-670-7270
http://www.haywardrec.org/hayshore.html

Lucy Evans Baylands Nature Interpretive Center
650-329-2506
www.cityofpaloalto.org

Marine Mammal Center
415-289-7330
www.marinemammalcenter.org

Richardson Bay Audubon Center and Sanctuary
415-388-2524
www.tiburonaudubon.org

Shorebird Park Nature Center & Adventure Playground, Berkeley
510-981-6720
www.ci.berkeley.ca.us

MUSEUMS ALONG THE SHORELINE

Aquarium of the Bay
415-623-5300
www.aquariumofthebay.org

CuriOdyssey at Coyote Point
650-342-7755
www.curiodyssey.org

Crockett Historical Society & Museum
510-787-2178
www.crockettmuseum.org

Exploratorium
415-561-0360
www.exploratorium.org

San Francisco National Maritime Museum
415-561-6662
www.maritime.org

San Quentin Museum
415-454-5000

Vallejo Naval & Historical Museum
707-643-0077
www.vallejomuseum.org

CAMPING & HOSTELS NEAR THE BAY TRAIL

American Youth Hostels
San Francisco Fisherman's Wharf Hostel, Fort Mason
415-771-7277
sfhostels.com/fishermans-wharf

Marin Headlands Hostel
415-331-2777, norcalhostels.org/marin

California Department of Parks and Recreation
China Camp State Park and Angel Island State Park
800-444-7275
www.reserveamerica.com

East Bay Regional Park District
Coyote Hills Regional Park, group camping only
888-327-2757
www.ebparks.org/activities/camping

Golden Gate National Recreation Area
Kirby Cove and Marin Headlands campsites
415-331-1540
www.recreation.gov

Camping at the Presidio (CAP)
415-561-7695
www.parksconservancy.org/our-work/crissy

Presidio Trust
Rob Hill Campground
www.presidio.gov/experiences

AQUATIC ACTIVITIES & INSTRUCTION

Bair Island Aquatic Center
650-241-8213
www.gobair.org
Rowing and paddling instruction

Bay Access, Inc.
415-459-8727
www.bayaccess.org
Volunteer organization committed to completing the San Francisco Bay Area Water Trail, a network

of launches and landing sites for human-powered boats

Bay Area Sea Kayakers (BASK)
www.bask.org
Sea kayaking club with a large and active membership

Boater's Guide to Harbors & Marinas
415-826-8905
http://californiaboatersguide.com
Guidebook updated annually for San Francisco Bay, Delta, and Outer Coast

Cal Adventures Outdoor Program, UC Berkeley
510-642-6400
www.recsports.berkeley.edu
Instructional sailing, paddleboarding, windsurfing, and sea kayaking classes and various custom designed trips and day programs

Cal Sailing Club, Berkeley
www.cal-sailing.org
Volunteer-run membership organization offering windsurfing and sailing lessons and rentals

California Canoe & Kayak, Oakland
510-893-7833
www.calkayak.com
Sea kayak, whitewater kayak, canoe, and recreational boat lessons and rentals at Jack London Square, Oakland

California Department of Boating & Waterways
916-263-1331
www.dbw.ca.gov
Provides grants for boating facility improvements and resources for boaters

California Dragon Boat Association
www.cdba.org
Youth and adult dragon boat programs and competitions

Cass' Marina, Sausalito
415-332-6789
www.cassmarina.com
Sailing, chartered boats, rentals, and U.S. Sailing certified courses

City Kayak, San Francisco
415-357-1010
www.citykayak.com/
Trips, rentals, and youth camp

Dolphin Swimming & Boating Club, San Francisco
415-441-9329
www.dolphinclub.org
Swimming club for members only

Jack London Aquatic Center
510-238-2196
www.oaklandnet.com/parks/facilities
Boating programs and rentals

Lake Merritt Boating Center, Oakland
510-238-2196
www.oaklandnet.com/parks/facilities
Boating programs and rentals

Marin Rowing Association
415-461-1431
www.marinrowing.org
Sweep and scull instruction

North Bay Rowing Club, Novato
www.northbayrowing.org
Sweep and scull instruction

Oakland Strokes
www.oaklandstrokes.org
Rowing club for East Bay youth

Outdoors Unlimited: UC San Francisco Fitness & Recreation
415-476-1264
www.campuslifeservices.ucsf.edu
Kayaking and windsurfing lessons and rentals

Sailing Education Adventures, Sausalito
415-775-8779
www.sfsailing.org
Sailing and dinghy lessons and trips

San Francisco Bay Area Kiteboarding
www.bayareakiteboarding.com
Kiteboarding organization

San Francisco Board Sailing Association
www.sfba.org
Support network for board sailor members

San Francisco Estuary Partnership
510-622-2304
www.sfestuary.org
Offers a pump-out facility guide and map for boaters

San Francisco Outrigger Canoe Center
www.sfocc.org
Outrigger canoe organization

Sausalito Open Water Rowing Center
415-332-1091
www.owrc.com
Scull instruction and rentals

Sea Trek, Sausalito
415-332-8494
www.seatrek.com
Paddling classes, outings, and rentals

South End Rowing Club, San Francisco
415-776-7372
www.south-end.org
Rowing and swimming club

Spinnaker Sailing
www.spinnaker-sailing.com
Sailing lessons and charters

Stanford Rowing Center & Peninsula Junior Crew
650-576-4634
www.peninsulajuniorcrew.org
Community rowing club for high school students

Tidewater Boating Center, Oakland
1-800-327-2757
www.ebparks.org/parks/mlk
Location of Oakland Strokes and other water-related recreational programs

Tradewinds Sailing School & Club, Richmond Marina
510-232-7999
www.tradewindssailing.com
Sailing outings and lessons

U.S. Coast Guard
Navigation Rules
www.navcen.uscg.gov

Boating Safety Resource Center
www.uscgboating.org

Western Sea Kayakers
www.westernseakayakers.org
Sea kayak club

FISHING

California Department of Fish & Game
831-649-2870 "Ask Marine"
www.dfg.ca.gov/marine
Fishing licenses are not required for non-commercial fishing from public piers and jetties along the California coast, including the bay shoreline. Persons of age 16 and over must be licensed for all other fishing in California.

California Office of Environmental Health Hazard Assessment
916-323-7319
www.oehha.ca.gov/fish/general/sfbaydelta.html
Safe Eating Guidelines are published for consumption of various fish and shellfish species taken from San Francisco Bay waters

EQUESTRIAN INFORMATION

California State Horsemen's Association
559-325-1055
www.californiastatehorsemen.com

Bay Area Barns and Trails
415-383-6283
www.bayareabarnsandtrails.org

Bay Area Equestrian Network
800-943-8883
www.bayequest.info

Bay Area Ridge Trail Council
415-561-2595
www.ridgetrail.org

KITE FLYING

American Kiteflyers Association
609-755-5483
www.aka.kite.org

Bay Area Sport Kite League
www.baskl.org

Berkeley Kitefest at Cesar Chavez Park
510-235-5483
www.highlinekites.com

TO REPORT TROUBLE OR PROBLEMS AROUND THE BAY

To report pollution, oil or hazardous material spills, toxic discharge, dumping:

BayKeeper
415-856-0444
www.baykeeper.org
Pollution in the bay, and local creeks, streams, and sloughs

CALTIP (Californians Turn in Poachers and Polluters)
888-334-2258
www.dfg.ca.gov/marine/protection.asp
Poaching, creek pollution, habitat destruction, fish or bird kills

National Response Center
800-424-8802
Oil or hazardous material spills, 24 hours a day

San Francisco Bay Regional Water Quality Control Board
510-622-5633
www.swrcb.ca.gov/rwqcb2
Spills and water quality problems

U.S. EPA Region 9 (emergency)
888-300-2193
www.epa.gov/region9/cleanup/emergency

Waste Alert Hotline
800-698-6942
Environmental crimes and improper disposal of hazardous materials in California

For information on toxic waste disposal:

California Integrated Waste Management Board Recycling Hotline
916-341-6000

Save the Bay
www.savesfbay.org/household-toxics-disposal

To report suspected illegal shoreline and wetland fill or construction:

San Francisco Bay Conservation and Development Commission
415-352-3600
www.bcdc.ca.gov

To report sick or stranded wildlife:

Lindsay Wildlife Museum
925-935-1978
www.wildlife-museum.org

Marine Mammal Center
415-289-7325
www.marinemammalcenter.org
Report a distressed marine mammal

Wildcare: Terwilliger Nature Education and Wildlife Rehabilitation
415-456-7283
www.wildcarebayarea.org
Report an injured or orphaned wild animal

To report a boat or water-related emergency, call 911

BICYCLING AND WALKING INFORMATION

Bay Area Bicycle Coalition
415-787-2893
www.bayareabikes.org

California Bicycle Coalition
916-446-7558
http://calbike.org/

East Bay Bicycle Coalition
510-845-7433
www.ebbc.org

Marin County Bicycle Coalition
415-456-3469
www.marinbike.org

Metropolitan Transportation Commission
511 Bikemapper
www.bicycling.511.org

Napa County Bicycle Coalition
707-812-1770
www.napabike.org

San Francisco Bicycle Coalition
415-431-2453
www.sfbike.org

Silicon Valley Bicycling Coalition
408-287-7259
www.bikesiliconvalley.org

Sonoma County Bicycle Coalition
707-545-0153
www.bikesonoma.org

Walk Oakland | Bike Oakland
510-269-4034
www.walkoaklandbikeoakland.org

Walk San Francisco
415-431-9255
www.walksf.org

DOG PARKS ALONG THE BAY TRAIL

Bayfront Park, Mill Valley
www.millvalleydogpark.org

Bayside Park, Burlingame
www.burlingame.org

Point Isabel Regional Shoreline, Richmond
www.ebparks.org/parks/pt_isabel

Seal Point Park, San Mateo
www.cityofsanmateo.org

Shoreline at Mountain View Dog Park
www.mountainview.gov

SCIENTIFIC AND TECHNICAL INFORMATION

California Academy of Sciences
415-379-5484
www.research.calacademy.org
The Academy has an extensive library which is available to the public by appointment

Romberg Tiburon Center for Environmental Studies
415-338-6063
www.rtc.sfsu.edu
San Francisco Bay research, education, and outreach

San Francisco Estuary Institute
510-746-7334
www.sfei.org
Provides scientific interpretations to help define environmental problems, advance public debate about them through sound science, and support consensus-based solutions that improve environmental planning, management, and policy development

VOLUNTEER OPPORTUNITIES

Bay Area Ridge Trail Council
415-561-2595
www.ridgetrail.org
Trail events, construction, and maintenance

BayKeeper
415-856-0444
www.baykeeper.org/take-action/volunteer-opportunities
Invasive species removal and outreach

California Academy of Sciences
415-379-5111
www.calacademy.org/join/volunteer.php
Accepts volunteers for public services, special events, and qualified persons in research department

California Coastal Commission
1-800-262-7848
www.coastal.ca.gov
Organizes Coastweeks, an annual California coastal cleanup including the bay shoreline

California Department of Parks and Recreation
916-653-9069
www.parks.ca.gov
Docent, visitor center, public safety, and park operations volunteers

Citizens for East Shore Parks
510-524-5000
www.eastshorepark.org/volunteer.php
Shoreline cleanup events and efforts to secure an accessible shoreline

Communities for a Better Environment
510-302-0430
www.cbecal.org
Urban environmental health organization works for clean air and water, and toxics-free communities

Don Edwards San Francisco Bay National Wildlife Refuge
510-792-0222
www.fws.gov/desfbay/volunteer.html
Welcomes volunteers for a wide range of jobs, from staffing the visitor center to guiding nature walks to clearing brush

East Bay Regional Park District
888-EBPARKS, www.ebparks.org/getinvolved/volunteer
A variety of volunteer opportunities including habitat restoration, coastal cleanup, special events, trail maintenance

Golden Gate National Parks Conservancy
415-561-3000
www.parksconservancy.org/help/volunteer

A wide variety of volunteer positions, from coastal cleanup to habitat restoration

Golden Gate Raptor Observatory
415-331-0730
www.ggro.org/public/volunteer.aspx
Become a Hawkwatch volunteer during bird migration season (mid-August through early December) on Hawk Hill in the Marin Headlands

Lindsay Wildlife Museum
925-935-1978
www.wildlife-museum.org

Midpeninsula Regional Open Space District
650-691-1200
www.openspace.org/volunteer/
Invasive vegetation removal, trail maintenance, public education

San Bruno Mountain Watch
415-467-6631
www.mountainwatch.org/volunteer-information
Stewardship, habitat restoration, advocacy, and school education programs

San Francisco Bay Bird Observatory
408-946-6548
www.sfbbo.org
Field research or outreach

Save the Bay
510-463-6850
www.savesfbay.org/volunteer
Invasive weed removal, planting native species

Wildcare: Terwilliger Nature Education Center
415-456-7283
www.wildcarebayarea.org
Classes, exhibits, and nature outings for children

RESOURCES FOR TEACHING ABOUT THE BAY

California Academy of Sciences
www.calacademy.org/teachers
Workshop series, sample lessons, and other resources for teachers interested in teaching about the bay and its wildlife

Golden Gate National Recreation Area

www.nps.gov/goga/forteachers/index.htm

"Parks as Classrooms" programs in Golden Gate National Parks actively engage students in learning about and caring for national parks and their own communities

MARE (Marine Activities, Resources, and Education)

www.mare.lawrencehallofscience.org/

A whole-school, K-12, multicultural year-round ocean studies curriculum, offered by the Lawrence Hall of Science, University of California, Berkeley

Marine Science Institute

www.sfbaymsi.org

Teachers programs and resources guides for marine education

Oakland Museum of California

510-318-8400
www.museumca.org/teacher-materials

Curriculum enrichment for teachers

San Francisco Estuary Partnership

www.sfestuary.org

Brochures and booklets on many issues that affect the bay, as well as videos and podcasts about the estuary

Save the Bay

www.savesfbay.org/educators

Curriculum of over 30 experiential activities for developing an appreciation for and understanding of the San Francisco Bay watershed

RESOURCES FOR WHEELCHAIR RIDERS

The State Coastal Conservancy's *A Wheelchair Rider's Guide to San Francisco Bay and the Nearby Coast* (2006) is available from the Conservancy free of charge.
510-286-1015, www.scc.ca.gov

A Wheelchair Rider's Guide to the California Coast provides online information for accessible parks, trails, historical sites, and other points of interest.

www.wheelingcalscoast.org

East Bay Regional Park District's hiking adventures with Bob '4WheelBob' Coomber
www.ebparks.org/bobcoomber

BAY AREA REGIONAL TRAILS

Bay Area Ridge Trail

415-561-2595
www.ridgetrail.org

California Coastal Trail

707-829-6689
www.californiacoastaltrail.info

Great California Delta Trail

916-776-2290
www.delta.ca.gov

Juan Bautista de Anza National Historic Trail

510-817-1400
www.nps.gov/juba

San Francisco Bay Area Water Trail

510-286-1015
www.sfbaywatertrail.org

ADDITIONAL BAY TRAIL AND SAN FRANCISCO BAY RESOURCES

Bay Area Hiker

www.bahiker.com

Bay Nature Magazine

www.baynature.org

Quarterly magazine dedicated to the exploration of the natural places, plants, and wildlife of the San Francisco Bay Area

Natural History of San Francisco Bay, 2011

www.bayariel.com/ARO-baybook.html

San Francisco Bay Trail Cycling Guide, by Michael Cramer, Cycline, 2004

www.esterbauer.com/international.html

Written for bicycle tourists, this Bay Trail guide is divided into 26 trips around the bay that begin and end with public transportation.

San Francisco Bay: Portrait of an Estuary, 2003

www.sanfranciscobaybook.com

San Francisco Bay Trail Maps

www.baytrail.org

Saving the Bay, 2010

www.savingthebay.org

Narrated by Robert Redford, this Emmy-award winning public television series explores the history of one of America's greatest natural resources — San Francisco Bay — with four one-hour episodes tracing the Bay from its geologic origins following the last Ice Age through years of catastrophic exploitation to restoration efforts of today.

Walking San Francisco Bay

www.walkingthebay.blogspot.com

Illustration Credits

BLACK AND WHITE PHOTOGRAPHS

Bay Model Visitor Center, p. 204

California Department of Parks and Recreation, p. 166, 167

California Historical Society, FN-12610, pp. 28, 38

Center for Sacramento History, p. 166

Credit unknown, pp. 89, 105, 153

Crockett Historical Museum, p. 147

East Bay Regional Park District, p. 77

Courtesy Foster Enterprises, p. 45

Merriam C. Hart courtesy of Phoebe Hearst Museum of Anthropology, p. 118

Hercules Historical Society, p. 141

Courtesy, History San Jose, pp. 68, 69, 70

Mill Valley Public Library, p. 198

National Historic Maritime Park or Museum, p. 88

National Maritime Museum, p. 24

Naval History and Heritage Command, p. 27

Novato History Museum, p. 181

Oakland Museum, Dorothea Lange collection, pp. 101, 95

Petaluma Historical Society, p. 175

Phoebe Hearst Museum of Anthropology, pp. 118, 119

Port of Oakland, p. 104

Port of San Francisco, pp. 19, 25

Courtesy, Quinn's Lighthouse, p. 106

Richmond Museum of History Collection, pp. 125, 126, 127, 130

San Francisco History Center, San Francisco Public Library, pp. 6, 29, 33, 37

San Mateo County Historical Museum, pp. 49, 51

San Quentin State Prison Museum, p. 194

Townsend, C.H., California Department of Parks and Recreation, p. 184

U.S. Department of the Navy, p. 154

U.S. Navy Fuel Department, Point Molate Winehaven Files, p. 131

Vallejo Naval and Historic Museum, p. 152

COLOR PHOTOGRAPHS

AECOM/California Department of Parks and Recreation, p. 30 (Candlestick)

Alex Baranda, p. 57 (Ravenswood)

Baykeeper, p. 21 (Baykeeper)

Cris Benton, pp. 14, 53, 81 (Hayward shoreline), 82 (salt ponds), 121, 125 (Ford Building), 170

Bruce Beyaert, pp. 122 (trail), 124 (Richmond Marina), 125 (watching kayaker), 127 (Miller/Knox), 134 (landfill)

Tom Boss, p. 192 (tunnel)

Ann Buell, p. 7

California Department of Transportation, pp. 26, 108 (bridge pathway), 145 (bicyclist)

Cargill Incorporated, p. 82 (salt crystals)

Paul Church, p. 153 (overlook)

City of Mountain View, pp. 62 (shoreline, marsh), 63

City of Sunnyvale, p. 68 (park)

Andrew N. Cohen, CRAB, p. 156 (clams)

Richard Cohen, p. 171 (Hamilton Field)

Corinne DeBra, pp. 36 (marina), 68 (marshes), 116 (beach), 148, 152

(marina), 153 (shoreline path), 164 (fishing), 165 (poppies), 186 (painter, sheep, whimsical art, monsters, statues), 189 (cat), 198 (house)

M. C. Dobbins, p. 70 (heron)

Donald Dvorak, pp. 4-5, 199 (grebes)

East Bay Regional Park District, pp. 13 (dogs), 77 (house), 79 (freshwater marsh), 80 (hikers), 81 (bicyclist), 88 (Oyster Bay, sculpture), 90, 93 (Crown Beach, sand castle), 116 (Point Isabel), 133, 135 (Point Pinole aerial)

Will Elder, National Park Service, pp. 17 (Fort Point, promenade), 18 (Crissy Field), 128, 206

Dwight Eschliman, courtesy of Port of San Francisco, p. 22 (boats)

Golden Gate National Parks Conservancy, p. 9 (Presidio)

Scot Goodman, p. 3

Ambarish Goswami, pp. 72 (slough), 75 (loop trail)

Russell Graymer, U.S. Geological Survey, pp. 98, 132 (rock formation)

Tom Grey, pp. 39 (egret), 70 (stilt), 83 (avocets), 176 (woodpecker), 187 (Great egret), 199 (Canvasback)

Scott Haefner, p. 50

Nicole Hayward, p. 188 (storm drain)

Sam High, p. 57 (scientists)

Warren Holcomb, p. 83 (interpretive center)

Ron Horii, pp. 33 (pier), 37, 56 (bridge pathway), 59 (interpretive center, boardwalk), 60 (sculptures), 61, 64, 65 (trail over tracks), 67 (cyclists), 69, 70 (bird-watching), 71 (Coyote Creek, drawbridge), 82 (Eden Landing)

LeRoy J. Howard, p. 31

Craig Howell, pp. 23 (Alcatraz), 25 (Ferry Building), 30 (Hunters Point), 45 (Foster City aerial), 46 (bridge), 56 (Ravenswood aerial), 67 (hangars), 101, 107

Judy Irving, Pelican Media, p. 76 (mouse)

Rebecca R. Jackrel, p. 73

Alvaro Jaramillo, pp. 59 (sandpiper), 92 (Western gull)

Wilfred J. Jones, pp. 13 (fishers, BART), 16, 18 (Marina Green), 20 (Fort Mason), 21 (Aquatic Park), 22 (Pier 39), 25 (Pier 7), 29 (Islais Creek), 39 (Bayfront Park, Bayside Park, lagoon, pier), 45 (bicyclist), 46 (Island Park, Redwood Shores), 47 (bridge), 49 (Pacific Shores), 112, 113 (trail), 147 (mothball fleet), 150 (capitol building, building interior), 152 (recreation area), 154, 159, 162, 163, 182 (civic center), 184, 185 (park), 191, 192 (ferry), 193 (Bon Air Park), 195 (sailboat, Ring Mountain), 196 (downtown), 197, 200, 201, 202, 203, 204, 205

Stephen Joseph, San Francisco Estuary Invasive Spartina Project, p. 157

Stephen Joseph, Sonoma Land Trust, pp. 169, 171 (Sonoma Baylands/Sears Point), 174 (hayfields)

Greg Kareofelas, pp. 77 (butterfly), 88 (butterfly)

Patricia Koren, pp. 12 (bicyclist with map), 41 (Seal Point Park), 43, 58, 165 (bicyclist, vineyard), 167, 187 (park)

Herb Lingl/aerialarchives.com, p. 45 (Central County aerial)

Josh Maddox, p. 135 (wheelchair user)

Mike Mammoser, pp. 29 (cormorant), 51 (tern), 65 (owl), 92 (Herring gull, Glaucous-winged gull, Ring-billed gull, Mew gull), 93 (Heermann's gull, Bonaparte's gull), 103 (Caspian tern, Elegant tern), 187 (heron), 199 (Bufflehead, scaup, Ruddy duck)

Marin County Parks, p. 181 (skate park)

William K. Matthias, p. 51 (islands)

Patty McGann, p. 103 (California least tern)

Midpeninsula Regional Open Space District, p. 66

Tom Mikkelsen, pp. 78, 79 (DUST/North marsh), 80 (hills), 82 (Hayward shoreline), 85, 87, 89, 91, 94, 99, 102, 104 (farmers' market), 105, 106, 108 (park views, picnic area), 109, 111, 113 (berthing basin, launching dock, Shorebird Park playground, Adventure Playground), 114, 115, 122 (wetlands, Potrero Point), 123, 124 (Brooks Island), 126, 127 (Brickyard Cove), 129 (Point Molate), 130, 131, 132 (harbor, islands), 134 (pier), 140, 141, 142, 143

Patrick T. Miller, 2M Associates, pp. 40 (Shoreline Park), 41 (marshes), 42

Ed Nguyen, p. 59 (pheasant)

Son Nguyen, p. 187 (Snowy egret)

Liam O'Brien, p. 207 (butterfly)

Palo Alto Public Art Commission, p. 186 (Bill Bliss)

Graham Paterson, p. 40 (museum)

Richard Pavek, pp. 1, 47 (kite)

Andy Peri, p. 183

Ken Phenicie, pp. 60 (blackbird), 62 (shoveler), 92 (California gull), 103 (Forster's tern), 181 (pelican), 199 (scoter), 207 (harriers)

Pier 39, p. 23 (sea lions)

Port of Redwood City, p. 49 (port)

Port of San Francisco, p. 186 (Cupid's Span)

Mark Rauzon, p. 129 (cormorants)

Renee Reyes, p. 156 (bass)

Emmanuel Rondeau, p. 173

Pati Rouzer, p. 76 (rail)

San Bruno Mountain Watch, p. 34 (butterfly)

San Francisco Bay Trail Project, pp. 9 (San Thomas Aquino), 12

(signs), 17 (housing), 19, 20 (Wave Organ, restoration), 25 (Pier 14), 29 (India Basin), 36 (flooded trail), 40 (Coyote Point trail, playground), 72 (park), 104 (trail), 151, 179, 181 (benches), 192 (statue), 193 (Remillard Park), 195 (bicyclist)

San Mateo County Parks, pp. 33 (San Bruno Mountain), 34 (mountain)

Save the Bay, pp. 188 (coastal cleanup), 189 (replanting)

Craig Solin, pp. 28, 174 (river), 175, 176 (Deer Island), 177, 182 (preserve, wildflowers), 185 (sunrise), 196 (picnic), 198 (Richardson Bay)

Sonoma County Parks, p. 168

Lewis Stewart, Port Costa Conservation Society, pp. 137, 144, 145 (bridge aerial), 146 (shoreline, Port Costa), 147 (school, Martinez), 150 (Benicia aerial), 152 (bicyclists)

Susan Teefy, p. 47 (harrier)

Glen Tepke, pp. 47 (meadowlark), 146 (bluebird)

Terry Tracy, p. 164 (bicyclists)

U.S. Fish & Wildlife Service, p. 75 (refuge aerial, visitor center)

Larry Wade, p. 193 (pickleweed)

Art Webster, p. 71 (education center)

Don Weden, pp. 23 (sailboats), 62 (slough)

DRAWINGS AND PAINTINGS

Abrams & Stinchfield Ferris, Sanford University Press "Illustrated Flora of the Pacific States" 1960, p. 17

Lee Adair, p. 35 (strawberry, coffeeberry, willow, mugwort, daisy, checkerbloom), 38, 91, 133, 148, 149, 183, 200

California and Hawaiian Sugar Co., p. 146

Credit unknown, p. 88, 134

S.S. Gayevskaya, from "Fauna & Flora of the Northeastern Seas of the USSR" 1948, p. 157

Judy Grunwald, p. 35 (monkey, campion)

Elise Gundersen, p. 185

Courtesy, History San Jose, p. 58

Helen Muirhead, p. 196

Mimi Osborne, pp. 27, 35 (huckleberry), 48, 96, 97

Port of Oakland, p. 104

Gay Reineck, pp. 22, 58, 79, 94, 130

San Francisco Bay Conservation & Development Commission, pp. 6, 7

State Coastal Conservancy, p. 158

University of California Press, pp. 63, 76

Judy West, p. 24

CHAPTER OPENING CAPTIONS

Introduction, p. 1, White-tailed kites by Richard Pavek

San Francisco, p. 14, Heron's Head Park by Cris Benton

North San Mateo, p. 31, San Mateo Shoreline Park Bridge by LeRoy J. Howard

South San Mateo, p. 44, Redwood Shores by Patricia Koren

South Bay, p. 53, Chicago Marsh by Cris Benton

Fremont/Hayward, p. 74, Brown pelican and cormorant by Rebecca R. Jackrel

San Lorenzo/San Leandro, p. 86, Crown Memorial State Beach by Tom Mikkelsen

Oakland/Berkeley, p. 99, Windsurfer at Berkeley Marina South Basin by Tom Mikkelsen

Richmond/San Pablo, p. 120, Meeker Creek in Richmond by Cris Benton

Northeast Bay, p. 137, Eckley Pier by Lewis Stewart

Napa/Sonoma, p. 159, Kayak at Kennedy Park by Wilfred J. Jones

Petaluma/Novato, p. 172, American Avocet by Emanuel Rondeau

North Marin, p. 179, Manzanita at China Camp State Park by SF Bay Trail Project

South Marin, p. 190, Mill Valley-Sausalito path by Wilfred J. Jones

Index

DESIGNER AND COMPOSITOR   NICOLE HAYWARD

TEXT   8/10 SCALA

DISPLAY   HELVETICA NEUE

PREPRESS   EMBASSY GRAPHICS

INDEXER   THÉRÈSE SHERE

CARTOGRAPHER   REINECK & REINECK

PRINTER AND BINDER   QUALIBRE